My
HEART'S
CRY

MY HEART'S CRY

ANNE GRAHAM LOTZ

W PUBLISHING GROUP
A Division of Thomas Nelson Publishers
Since 1798

www.wpublishinggroup.com

Published by W Publishing Group, a Division of Thomas Nelson, Inc., P. O. Box 141000, Nashville, Tennessee 37214.

W books may be purchased in bulk for educational, business, fundraising, or sales promotional use. For information, please email SpecialMarkets@ThomasNelson.com.

Unless otherwise indicated, Scripture quotations used in this book are from the Holy Bible, New International Version (NIV). Copyright © 1973, 1978 International Bible Society. Used by permission of Zondervan Bible Publishers.

Other Scripture references are from the following sources:

The King James Version of the Bible (KJV).

The New King James Version (NKJV), copyright © 1982, Thomas Nelson, Inc., Publishers.

Library of Congress Cataloging-in-Publication Data

Lotz, Anne Graham, 1948–
  My heart's cry / by Anne Graham Lotz.
    p. cm.
  ISBN 0-8499-4538-0 (softcover)
  ISBN 0-8499-1741-7 (hardcover)
  1. Bible. N.T. John X-XVII–Criticism, interpretation, etc.   I. Title.
  BS2615.2 .L68 2002
  226.5'06–dc21

                                                              2002005869

Printed in the United States of America
04 05 06 07 08 PHX 5 4 3 2 1

Contents

H<small>EART</small>'S
My
C<small>RY</small>
for

CONTENTS

*Editor's Note: As you read through this volume, please take the time to check the corresponding endnotes. The information there is composed primarily of Scripture references, but there are also some amazing little gems of information and story conclusions that were too important to be deleted but too detailed to be included in the text.

Dedicated

to

those who long for more than just enough

of

JESUS

Longing for
MORE . . .

I FLEW TO MY FATHER'S SIDE straight from Belfast, Northern Ireland, where I had been speaking. I was responding to an urgent message that said my father thought he was dying and wanted me to come.

As I walked into his hospital room my heart was in my throat, tears were in my eyes, and a confused jumble of thoughts and prayers were on my mind. My father looked like a shadow of his handsome, commanding self. His body seemed unhealthily thin, his skin was drawn and gray, and his gorgeous thick hair was partially missing where it had been shaved away on one side to make way for the shunt that would alleviate his hydrocephalus. His face, softly radiant, became very emotional as he recognized me. I put my arms gently around him and just held him as I whispered how much I loved him and had come in response to his call.

As the days went on he rallied, and I left. On returning home, I received the news that he had undergone yet another emergency procedure. After consultation with several doctors, I boarded a plane and flew back to be with him. It was Father's Day 2000 when I walked once again into his hospital room. This time he was sleeping, so I dismissed the private nurse and took my place in a chair by his bed where he could see me when he opened his eyes. His head was now almost completely shaved, a little green stocking cap covering it and keeping the fresh wounds protected.

My emotions overwhelmed me, and the tears began to rush furiously down my cheeks. "God, please, oh please, I know my daddy is ready to go

'Home,' but I'm not ready to let him go. Heal him, restore him, strengthen him. I've had Daddy for fifty-two years, but it's not enough. I long for more—more time, more conversations, more hugs, more kisses, more prayers, more counsel, more walks on the mountain. Please, *just give me more of my daddy . . .*"

Because when you love someone with all of your heart, you just can't ever get enough . . .

. . . More

Than Just Enough

THE APOSTLE JOHN was living in the last days of what had been an unforgettable, life-changing experience—walking and talking with Jesus Christ during His public ministry before the Cross. None of the disciples, including John, comprehended fully the separation, crucifixion, resurrection, ascension, and resulting commission to come, but they all sensed a foreboding in their spirits as Jesus talked openly about leaving them.[1] And the more He talked, the more they not only resisted but fell into a dark, emotional abyss.[2]

For three years John, along with the other disciples, had given all he had and all he was to follow Jesus. During that time he had witnessed never-to-be-forgotten, life-changing experiences:

He had seen Him give sight to one born blind.[3]

He had watched as He opened the ears of the deaf.[4]

He had marveled when, at His word, demons fled.[5]

He had joined with Him as He fed five thousand people with five loaves and two fish.[6]

He had cried out in fright when He had walked on the surface of the lake in the midst of the storm.[7]

He had been amazed when He commanded the howling winds and crashing waves of Galilee to be still—and He was obeyed.[8]

He had been awe-struck when He proved His claim to be the resurrection and the life by raising Lazarus from the dead.[9]

But John was drawn to Jesus by more than just the thrill of seeing all the signs and wonders that accompanied His ministry. He was drawn not so much by what Jesus had done, but as by Who Jesus was. By . . .

the confident sound of His voice,
the compassionate look in His eyes,
the tender gentleness of His touch,
the powerful authority of His preaching,
the sensitive comprehension of His counseling,
the personal intimacy of His prayers,
the sacrificial example of His unselfishness,
the unbroken consistency of His character,
the unconditional nature of His love.

John had become convinced that Jesus of Nazareth was indeed the Messiah, the fulfillment of the Law and the Prophets, the Redeemer of Israel, the Son of God. Jesus had become John's life and hope and peace and reason for living. To think of giving up Jesus, of living even one moment without Him, of ever being separated from Him, was unthinkable!

John was desperate for more of Jesus—more of His time, more of His thoughts, more of His teaching, more of Him! Yet the increasingly disturbing reality was that Jesus seemed to be preparing John and the other disciples for just that—His departure.

Like John and the other disciples, I have known Jesus personally. Their knowledge was face to face while my knowledge is by faith, but mine is a personal, direct, experiential knowledge nonetheless. And it has increasingly grown, from the time I was a little girl when I confessed my sin and asked Him to be my Savior, to the time as a teenager I made the commitment to live my life for Him alone, to the time I drifted from Him in the busyness of being a young mother and returned to Him through the disciplined study of His Word, to the time I answered His call to teach a weekly Bible class, to the time I stepped out in faith to follow Him in an itinerant international ministry, to the time I picked up my pen and wrote my first word to be published, to the time when my heart's cry—under unbearable pressure and pain—has been, just give me Jesus!

Yet somehow, like John, I feel that all this time in His presence, all this devotion to His service, is just not enough. I have concluded that it will never be enough until my faith becomes sight and I know Him as fully as I am known by Him.[10] Until that day, I find that my yearning for Him is ravenous, and it has once again led me to immerse myself in the pages of His Word—in particular, the eyewitness account of His life and ministry that was recorded by the disciple with whom I most identify: John.

The majority of this book is based on the passages in John's Gospel that contain what Jesus taught His disciples at the very end of His time with them when they were trying to cling to Him. I wanted to know what He had to say to those who were desperate for more of Him.

As I have pored over the Scriptures, my heart has cried out for more than just enough . . .

to escape a fiery hell.

to be saved from God's wrath.

to call myself a Christian.

to manage my guilt.

to get a ticket to heaven.

to squeak through heaven's gate.

I long for more than just the bare minimum God has to offer.
I long for more than what the average Christian seems to settle for.
I long for everything God wants to give me.
I long for more than enough . . .

to bend my will!

to awaken my conscience!

to break my heart!

to transform my mind!

to overcome my prejudices!

to soar in my spirit!

to conform me into His glorious image!

to give me an abundant entrance into heaven!

I long to be saturated in Jesus! *So, please, dear God, just give me MORE . . .*

For this reason I kneel before the Father,

from whom his whole family in heaven and on earth derives its name.

I pray that out of his glorious riches . . .

you may be filled to the measure of all the fullness of God.

Now to him who is able to do immeasurably *MORE* . . .

—THE APOSTLE PAUL

1

MORE *of*
His Voice in My Ear

John 10:1–10

GOD TOLD ME to tell you that you are supposed to marry me." I received that astonishing bit of information on a lined sheet of notebook paper that had food stains on it when I was fourteen years of age! It was a personal letter to me from some delusional young man that had been forwarded from my father's organization. I remember writing back rather crisply, "Well, He hasn't told me!"

As amusing as that incident was, a similar attitude was conveyed to me at the beginning of my ministry that was not so humorous. Some church leaders publicly expressed disapproval of my ministry because I was willing to speak when there were men in the audience. And their stand was based on what they said God says.

A typical argument from one of these men was something like this: "God told me that you as a woman are not to speak to an audience in which there are men. God has also told me women are not to be preachers."

My initial reaction was the same as it was when I was fourteen: "Well, God hasn't told me!" But because this argument was made by those with seminary degrees and reputations for being spiritual, by godly men who held positions as shepherds in their congregations, this little sheep needed to hear her Shepherd's voice. I did not want to hear what others said He said. I wanted to hear from Him directly. I wanted to hear His voice in the ears of my spirit.

Do you have a similar dilemma in your life? Have you been confronted with those who, in essence, have said, "God told me to tell you if you only had more faith, you would be healed," or "If God really loved you, that bad thing would not have happened to you," or "It's God's will that your loved one died"? Such "words of knowledge" spoken by sincere people within our circle of Christian friends can put us in a tailspin of emotional devastation and spiritual doubt. It is especially traumatic and confusing when those words are uttered by someone in a position of religious leadership.

How can you and I know which voice speaks the truth and is therefore authentic?

The Bible tells us that God does speak to His children and that we will hear and know His voice even as sheep hear and know the voice of their shepherd.

In Western civilization, the concept of a personal shepherd is relatively meaningless. With hoof-and-mouth disease in the news, we've seen British sheep ranches flashed on the news and sheep pens in Northern Ireland pictured on the front of our morning newspapers. If you live in a rural area, you may have noticed that sheep today graze in carefully fenced-in pastures where they're guarded by specially bred dogs and identified by a number tattooed in their ears. Computers track when they are born and when they are ready for either shearing or slaughter. There is no personal shepherd. Unless the sheep are on a very small farm, even the sheep's owner can't tell one animal from another.

But the Eastern shepherd was, and in many parts of the world still is, very different. He raised his sheep from the time they were lambs and maintained responsibility for them twenty-four hours a day, seven days a week, year in and year out, for the sheep's entire lifetime. There were no dogs or fences or tattoos or computers.

The Eastern shepherd of Jesus' day raised his sheep primarily in the Judean uplands. The countryside was rocky, hilly, and creased with deep crevices and ravines. Patches of grass were sparse. So the shepherd had to establish a personal relationship with each sheep, nurturing its love and trust in him in order to lead it to where the path was the smoothest, the grass was the greenest, the water was the cleanest, and the nights were the safest. The shepherd always *led* the sheep. He knew their names, and when he called them, they recognized his voice, following him like a swarm of little chicks follows the mother hen. When he stopped, the sheep huddled closely around him, pressing against his legs. Their personal relationship with him was based on his voice, which they knew and trusted.

The Bible describes our relationship with Jesus as being similar to the relationship between the Eastern shepherd and his sheep—a relationship based on His voice. And make no mistake about it, His voice is God's Word, the Holy Bible.

THE AUTHENTIC VOICE IS BIBLICAL

God speaks primarily through the Scriptures, and at times, through other people—which is where we must be careful. One of the most familiar teachings of Jesus is one He launched into after a confrontation with the "shepherds," or religious leaders, of His day who professed to speak for God. John recorded that the confrontation had taken place after an incident involving one of the many blind beggars in the city.

Jesus had been walking through the congested streets of Jerusalem when His attention was caught by a beggar who had been born blind. Stopping, Jesus had patiently explained to His disciples and to the man that the blindness was the result of no one's fault. Instead, it was an opportunity to reveal the glory of God. The resulting display of God's glory as Jesus created sight in eyes that had never seen before should have caused everyone, including the religious authorities—especially the religious authorities!—to fall at His feet in worship. Instead, it provoked a confrontational exchange between the man and the religious leaders that resulted in the man's excommunication from the temple. Try to enter into the drama of the former blind beggar's experience:[1]

In one day, the former blind man's life had turned upside down and inside out. As he must have wandered in a daze through the narrow, crowded streets, surely he tried to comprehend all he had experienced, realizing that although he had gained his physical sight he had lost any social acceptance he would ever hope to have. Did he wage an almost superhuman battle to force his attention away from all he was seeing for the first time to all the thoughts he was thinking for the first time? And where would he go? Back to the alleyway where he had begged all of his life? Back to his home where his parents resented the disgrace he had brought on the family? Back to his "friends" who had turned him over to the authorities in the first place? Since he had received his sight, not one person had congratulated him or shaken his hand or slapped him on the back or even smiled joy and approval. Having lived in a world of darkness all of his life, surely he had never felt so alone as he did in the light.

Until he heard that familiar voice. It was coming from an ordinary-looking Man standing in front of him—

a Man Who had heard of his excommunication from the temple,

a Man Who knew what it was to be lonely in a crowd,

a Man Who understood what it felt like to be treated like a criminal because of God's presence in His life,

a Man Who would Himself experience being outcast, not just from the temple and the city, but from the human heart—

a Man Who had heard, Who understood, Who loved, and Who had searched until He found the formerly blind beggar to whom He had given sight.

Praise God! Jesus draws near to those who are afflicted and persecuted and criticized and ostracized. Jesus draws near to those who are suffering—especially when the suffering is for His sake.[2]

As the former beggar heard the voice he would never forget, did his heart leap? Did his newly focused eyes cling to the Man's face, drinking in every detail, listening to every syllable, as the Man gently inquired, "Do you believe the Son of Man?" Eagerly the man responded, "Who is he, sir? . . . Tell me so that I may believe in him."

And "Jesus said, 'You have now seen him; in fact, he is the one speaking with you.' Then the man said, 'Lord, I believe,' and he worshiped him" (9:35–38).

Jesus then gave a scathing condemnation of the Pharisees who had stood in judgment over the man and were still hounding him. He declared that the man who had been blind could now see, not only physically, but also spiritually because he recognized Jesus as the Son of God and placed his faith in Him. But the Pharisees, who claimed with all of their religious training and knowledge and experience that they could see spiritually, remained blind because they rejected the truth of Who Jesus is (9:39–41).

The haughty, superpious, elaborately dressed Pharisees who had slipped through the temple courtyard to spy on the beggar caught him in conversation with Jesus. So Jesus used what was inevitably another imminent confrontation with the religious leaders to make a point that I believe needs to resonate in the ears of Christians today. With eyes that surely flashed with righteous indignation, and with the same breath that indicted the religious leaders for their spiritual blindness, Jesus warned His followers that not all religious leaders, or "shepherds," were authentic.

The Confusion about Authenticity

This mixture of true and false shepherds can be confusing to those who have become casual in their relationship with God and their attitude toward His Word. In the Old Testament, when God's people refused to pay attention to Him or His Word, He allowed multitudes of false prophets to preach on every street corner, but none of them spoke the truth.[3] The New Testament also warns that this judgment will be repeated in the last days of human history, when once again a multitude of false prophets will permeate the religious landscape.[4]

Those of us in the church need to wake up! Just because someone . . .

pastors a church,

or uses contemporary examples,

or reads Greek and Hebrew,

or preaches with eloquence,

or moves the audience to tears,

or makes an audience laugh,

or holds degrees from a reputable seminary,

or befriends individuals with a caring and kind demeanor . . .

DOES NOT MEAN HE IS FROM GOD!

With eyes that must have narrowed fiercely on the self-righteous Pharisees who claimed to be spiritual leaders yet had sought to destroy the beggar's testimony of faith, Jesus unleashed His warning. With daring boldness He did not back down from His pompous, yet powerful, enemies—not even a little. With a voice that must have reverberated in emotional tones of outrage, He made it very clear to the Pharisees, the blind man, and the curious bystanders, as well as to His own disciples then and now, that there would be those who claim to be shepherds, leaders of His people, but they would not be authentic.

Using the very familiar setting of a winter sheepfold to drive home His point, He stated emphatically, "I tell you the truth, the man who does not enter the sheep pen by the gate, but climbs in by some other way, is a thief and a robber. The man who enters by the gate is the shepherd of his sheep. The watchman opens the gate for him, and the sheep listen to his voice" (10:1–3).[5]

The winter sheepfolds were located in the barren, rocky Judean hills. Each one was used by several shepherds who kept their flocks in the fold during the night for safety. The fold would have had high stone walls accessed by one strong, wooden door. It had no roof. One of the shepherds would act as the watchman at the door, staying inside the fold with the sheep all night, guarding against thieves, wild animals, and anything else that might harm the sheep. In the morning, the authentic shepherds of the sheep would come to the door and identify themselves. The watchman would open the door, then each shepherd would call out his own sheep by name. One by one, his particular sheep would separate from all the others in the fold and follow him out to graze the Judean hills for the day.

The Criterion for Authenticity

You and I, as God's "sheep," can determine the authenticity of the shepherds by their approach to us. The criterion for the authentic shepherd is that he or she *always approaches* through the door of God's Word, which the Watchman, the Holy Spirit, opens to us. The false shepherd approaches through a "door" that is other than God's Word. His approach may be through

a leadership position,

a denominational doctrine,

a ceremonial ritual,

a cultural prejudice,

traditional theology,

public opinion,

popular polls,

marketing strategy,

or pop psychology.

This lesson was driven home to me at the beginning of my itinerant ministry thirteen years ago. As I went into the world in answer to God's call, one of the first opportunities I accepted was to address a large convention of pastors. Eight hundred church leaders were seated around tables in a banquet-type setting that seemed to stretch as far as the eye could see. As I walked to the lectern, I was distracted by the sound of movement in the audience. I was shocked to see that many of the pastors had turned their chairs around and put their backs to me! Some of those who faced me did so with such hostile expressions of rejection that I was confused and ashamed. I managed to share the message I'd been invited to present, but by the time I concluded, I was shaking. I crawled away in my spirit.

How could godly men find what I was doing so offensive that they would stage such a demonstration, especially when their organization had invited me to speak? I was confused. Was the inaudible voice I had heard from these men—in essence saying, "Anne, you don't belong in the pulpit or on the platform when men are present"—*authentic or not?*

Rather than blindly abide by what these critics demanded or strike back in anger with a harsh exchange of words, I pleaded with God to give me His Word. I knew that many of these men were religious professionals serving in the church as "shepherds." Automatically, I considered their opinions as valuable. Yet I wanted to hear my Shepherd's voice and follow *Him*—which meant, very practically, I had to go home and open my Bible.

When I went home, I told the Lord I had never had a problem with women in ministry or with women sharing God's Word when men were present, but now I did. The problem those pastors obviously had was now my problem, too. So I humbly asked the Watchman, the Holy Spirit, to convict me if I was out of His will or to confirm His call once again.

I found myself re-reading the story of Mary Magdalene in John 20.

Following the resurrection, when Mary encountered the risen Christ, He commanded her, "Go . . . to my brothers and tell them, 'I am returning to my Father and your Father, to my God and your God.'"[6] In other words, Jesus was telling Mary, *a woman,* to go to Jerusalem and tell eleven *men* what she had seen and heard. Jesus also commanded the other women who had gone to the tomb that early Sunday morning to go and tell the disciples—not only tell them their personal testimony about their experience with the risen Christ, but His Word instructing them to go to Galilee.[7] I concluded, therefore, that Jesus Himself did not have a problem with women either sharing their own personal testimony or sharing His Word when men were in the audience.

Next, the Watchman seemed to open the door of Jeremiah, where once again I heard the Shepherd's voice say, "I have put My words in your mouth. . . . You are not responsible for the reaction of the audience. You are only responsible for your faithfulness to give out the message I have put on your heart. Prepare yourself and arise, and speak to them all that I command you. Do not be dismayed before their faces, *or their backs,* lest I dismay you before them. Anne, you are not accountable to your audience; you are accountable to Me. They will fight against you, but they will not prevail against you, for I am with you to deliver you."[8]

I felt rebuked, encouraged, and challenged as God once again confirmed His call in my life through His Word as the Holy Spirit spoke to my heart. The authentic voice of the Shepherd seemed to be breaking through all the confusing rhetoric that was competing for my thoughts. His Word was like a refreshing drink on a blisteringly hot day as one by one my questions were answered. But before putting the matter behind me once and for all, I asked Him for help in understanding 1 Timothy 2:12, where Paul forbids "a woman to teach or to have authority over a man." As I meditated prayerfully on that passage, God seemed to reveal to me that the emphasis was on the "authority over a man."

Therefore, I believe He has forbidden me to teach or preach from a *position of authority* over a man. Practically speaking, this means He has closed the door to me for ordination in ministry, or for the senior pastorate. So when I speak, I speak as a woman who is not *in authority*. Instead, I am a woman who is *under authority*—the authority of my Lord! And I speak with the authority that comes, not from any position I hold, but from the Person I know.

This lesson was reemphasized to me recently when, following an address I had given to a seminar of evangelists, I stood to greet those who came up to speak to me. For an hour I shook hands and prayed with men whose eyes were filled with tears and whose voices quivered with the emotion of having just heard God speaking clearly to them through His Word.

The last man to speak was a tall, nice-looking gentleman whose expression was in sharp contrast to that of every other man to whom I had spoken. He seemed coolly detached but prefaced his remarks by saying he was a "fan" of mine, having read my books and heard me speak prior to this seminar.

I braced my spirit for what I sensed was coming—and it did! In a rather condescending tone, he said he wanted to ask me a question about my "interpretation" of 1 Timothy 2:12. He continued by saying he believed it really meant that before women could speak or teach God's Word, they needed to be trained.

While I personally would recommend training and education for anyone going into the ministry, if it was a *requirement* for service, then I would be excluded, since I have none. And I told him so.

Not only would I be excluded, but Mary Magdalene would have been excluded also. With this evangelist's reasoning, Jesus' command to Mary would have been something like, "Mary, go tell My disciples . . . four years from now when you have a seminary degree."

Actually the disciples, themselves, would have been excluded from ministry because the Sanhedrin took note that "they were unschooled, ordinary men."[9]

In exasperation at such prejudice, I stood erect, looked my challenger in the eye, and told him this little sheep knows her Shepherd's voice. *I know* He has called me by name, commanding and commissioning me to share His Word with whomever He places before me. With all my heart, mind, soul, and strength, I am seeking to respond in faithful obedience.

THE AUTHENTIC VOICE IS PERSONAL

I have heard my Shepherd's voice speaking to me through the pages of His Word. Personally. Religious people can "fence" all day long with the "sword" of God's Word, and many do. They each produce a verse that seems to underscore the truth of their position and then jab at anyone who holds a different viewpoint. But Jesus explained that God's Word is very personal when the Shepherd "calls his own sheep by name and leads them out. When he has brought out all his own, he goes on ahead of them, and his sheep follow him because they know his voice" (10:3–4).

While my explanation for my position in ministry may not satisfy everyone, nor will all agree with it, it satisfies me. I sense within my spirit, as I have read, meditated on, and prayed through the above passages of Scripture, that I have heard my Shepherd's voice speaking to me personally. And in the end, it won't be my critics or supporters who will be held accountable by God for my service to Him; it will be me. If God has called me to this ministry, which I believe He has, and I use the criticism of others as an excuse for disobedience, then He will hold me accountable when I stand before Him. I have to follow the Shepherd as I believe He is leading me, basing my steps on His voice in my ear.

I remember standing in a circle of people that included my husband, my children, my parents, and several other dignitaries in the governor's mansion of our state. My father was speaking to the entire group, so I knew he was speaking to me because I was in the circle. But then he turned, looked straight at me, and said, "Anne, . . ." and I knew he was speaking *personally* to me. Since the Bible is God's Word, God speaks through it to everyone who has the ears to hear. But there are times when a verse or passage is illuminated or seems to leap right off the page. It's as though that specific portion of Scripture has my name on it.

His Word Is Heard Personally

The Shepherd speaks to us personally—by name. He knows us inside and out.

He knows our thoughts before they're on our minds,
    and our words before they're even formed on our tongues,

and our emotions before they're felt in our hearts,
and our actions before there is any movement.
And when He speaks, it's in the language of our own personal lives, through a verse or passage of Scripture that just seems to leap up off the page with our name on it.

Again and again God has seemed to speak to me through the pages of my Bible, giving me the secret to restoring love in my marriage when it had run out, reassuring me of my son's recovery to health *before* his cancer surgery, directing me again and again in the expansion and priorities in ministry, leading me out of one church and into another. In fact, I do not make a major decision, especially one involving others, without a specific word from my Shepherd.

So it was no exception in my life when, once again, God recently seemed to speak to me Biblically. Personally. In the language of my life. He addressed the specific issues and questions that I earnestly placed before Him. I had been bombarded by those who said they were speaking to me on God's behalf regarding my ministry, saying, "God told me to tell you . . ." Was God telling me something through them? Which voices were relaying the authentic voice of the Shepherd? Again, I had to go to my Bible and search the Scriptures, asking God to open my ears to the Shepherd's voice, and give me a Biblical word that would also be a personal word. God does speak to me at times through other people, but the test is that what others say should always be in accord with and confirmed by His Word. So, as I searched the Scriptures, I reflected on my journey in public ministry to this point.

It began twenty-five years ago when God called me to teach His Word outside of my home. I had begun reading my Bible and praying on a regular basis. One afternoon, I was led to the passage of Revelation 3:8 by my godly mother-in-law. The words almost sprang up off the page as God seemed to speak to me, calling me personally by name into service: "Anne, I know your deeds, and you haven't done much. Like all young mothers, you only have a little strength. But you have kept My word and have not denied your identification with Me. Therefore, I am placing before you an open door for service that no one can shut."[10]

I knew the open door was an opportunity to establish and teach a weekly

Bible class for women in my city. I also knew that when God sets before us an open door, He usually means for us to walk through it. Which I did. The class immediately exploded as five hundred women came to study God's Word together. As a result of the hours of disciplined study that I had to give in order to teach, my relationship with the Lord developed into the richest treasure and greatest joy of my life.

I had been teaching that weekly Bible class for twelve years when my Shepherd seemed to call to me again dramatically from Deuteronomy 1:3, 6–7: "Anne, in your fortieth year, on the first day of the eleventh month, . . . tell these people you have stayed long enough at this mountain. Break camp and advance."[11] Even though godly people at the time told me they were sure God was not calling me to walk away from the class, I knew He was telling me to leave that ministry and move out into a wider area of service. But I hesitated because the study and teaching of the Scriptures in that class had become so intertwined with my relationship with Him. And because it was also so spiritually fruitful in the lives of others, I was apprehensive about possibly misreading God's direction and succumbing instead to one of the Enemy's clever deceptions.

So to reassure the class and myself, I asked God to confirm His call. He led me to Acts 26:16–18: "Now get up and stand on your feet. I have appeared to you to appoint you as a servant and as a witness of what you have seen of me and what I will show you. . . ." I felt Him telling me, "I am sending you out . . . into an itinerant ministry that will take you around the world." And I knew if He was my Lord, I had no option but to obey.

So on the first day of the eleventh month of my fortieth year, April 1, 1988, I announced to the class I would be leaving. And at the close of that class year, I did. My obedience to that call has taken me all over the world for the past fourteen years, using our nonprofit ministry as a practical facilitator.

Our ministry is named AnGeL Ministries, not only because it's a play on my initials, but because it accurately describes my calling. Angels are messengers of God. They never go anywhere unless they are sent; when they speak, they give out God's Word, and they address whomever God places in front of them. I consider myself first of all God's servant, then a messenger sent by God, to go wherever He sends me, to speak to whomever He puts in front of me, and then, to deliver whatever Biblical passage He lays on my heart. Like a waitress who prepares the "food," I try to make it as appealing as possible then serve it to those who are hungry without messing it up.

About four years ago God began to stir my heart with the desperate need for revival in the hearts of His people. However, the doors did not open at that time for me to do anything. Instead, God began to work in my personal life to bring me to a point of desperation for a fresh touch from Him, expressed in my book *Just Give Me Jesus*. In those pages I confessed that I didn't want to *talk* about revival, I wanted to *be* revived! Only then did the Shepherd open the door and call me to follow Him into the arenas with the Just Give Me Jesus revivals, knowing I would be speaking from my own heart and personal experience. And now that work has carried me even further in my passionate pursuit for MORE of Jesus—a pursuit for richer discoveries and deeper understanding, which I share in the volume you hold in your hands, *My Heart's Cry*.

As I stepped out in faith to present the Just Give Me Jesus revivals, there was some confusion as to whether I was endeavoring to minister specifically to *women,* or to women *and* men. One primary factor that contributed to the confusion was that the revivals were open to anyone. Well-meaning religious leaders were telling me emphatically that, in essence, "God told us to tell you such an endeavor is harmful to the church. We don't want our men exposed to a woman on the platform speaking to a mixed audience." More than one pastor said something like this to me: "God told me not to lend my support, or the support of my church, or the support of even the women of my church to your revival since you allow men as well as women to attend." You better believe that had me back in God's Word, listening for my Shepherd's voice!

God had confirmed in my heart that these revivals should be free of charge so that no one would be hindered from coming for financial reasons.[12] This means we have no registration, and since the revivals are held in large public arenas, some men came. While we didn't seek this, we certainly did not turn them away.

As I prayed through this, I asked God for a personal word to confirm who He intended our primary target audience to be in the revivals. Once again, as

I met with Him early one morning for my daily quiet time, He seemed to speak to me clearly, personally, and Biblically through my devotional reading in Ezekiel 44:1–3 (NKJV):

> Then He brought me back to the outer gate of the sanctuary [I had described the arena to our production team as a "sanctuary," asking them to be mindful as they set up the platform, screens, lights, and sound that they are setting up a Most Holy Place]. . . . And the LORD said to me, "This gate shall be shut; it shall not be opened, and no man shall enter by it, because the LORD God of Israel has entered by it; therefore it shall be shut. As for the prince, because he is the prince, he may sit in it to eat bread before the LORD; he shall enter by way of the vestibule of the gateway, and go out the same way."

Almost a physical shock wave went through my system as I read those words! The Shepherd's voice was unmistakable! While I still felt called in forums other than the revivals to speak to whomever God placed in front of me, I had no doubt that He had confirmed through Ezekiel that our Just Give Me Jesus revivals were to target women—although the "prince" (select men: pastors, husbands, or anyone God chooses to draw to the arenas) was welcomed and would be fed by the Lord there.

His Word Is Heeded Personally

In the process of confirming that our revivals were primarily to be for women, God also confirmed that many of the voices I had been hearing from religious leaders challenging me on the arena audience were indeed authentic—at least He used *their* voices to get me to pay closer attention to *His!* Yet how could I ever have been able to discern the difference between the religious leaders earlier who had told me I could not speak when men were present, and the religious leaders who told me the arena revivals should be for women only? Especially when I suspected the position the leaders were coming from on both occasions was the same? I couldn't. I don't have that kind of wisdom and discernment. But I am convinced beyond any doubt that the Shepherd speaks Biblically and personally to His sheep, and His sheep know His voice and heed it! They follow Him.[13] What rich assurance that gives me!

What issues have confused you? There are some issues that are so primary, basic, and clear-cut that all Christians are in agreement on them. Issues such as these:

- We are all sinners, separated from God and on our way to hell, [14]
- God loved us even while we were in our sin. [15]
- God sent His own Son to be our Savior. [16]
- Salvation is available as a free gift through faith in Jesus alone. [17]
- God offers forgiveness of any and all sin through the blood of Jesus. [18]
- Those who receive Jesus Christ by faith are born again into the family of God.[19]
- There is no other way to be saved, or to get to heaven, except through Jesus Christ. [20]

But there are other issues that are secondary and not as clear. Issues that are related specifically to your life, such as whether or not you should marry, or take a particular job, or retire from work, or have surgery, or sell your house, or stay in a club, or embark on a ministry. Issues that can involve your lifestyle, your relationships, your business, your home, your future—the list is endless.

Who is clamoring for your attention, claiming to speak for God as he or she tells you what you should do on these issues?

A parent?

A spouse?

A pastor?

A counselor?

A friend?

A boss?

A therapist?

A doctor?

A professor?

And whose voice do you heed? How do you and I make wise choices in a world that is swirling with contradictory opinions on every subject? Even the world within the church offers conflicting viewpoints. The only way we can ever know for sure is when we hear the Shepherd's voice speaking to us through His Word.

Every day we are faced with large and small decisions for which we need a Shepherd Who will lead us in the right path.[21] Which is why Jesus promised that He would go on ahead of us, and we would follow Him because we would know His voice.

Actually, one evidence that you and I are not only being led by an authentic Shepherd but that we are genuine sheep is that His sheep "will never follow a stranger; in fact, they will run away from him because they do not recognize a stranger's voice" (10:5).

When a person claims to speak for God yet that person is false, the authentic sheep may not know specifically what is wrong, but instinctively we know it is. It's as though a warning bell goes off in our spirits. From time to time, this has happened as I have shared ministry platforms with a variety of religious leaders. On one such occasion, I was in another country when one of the other plenary speakers began preaching that God had sent Jesus to free us from all bondage and oppression and poverty. My spiritual "antennae" were alerted. As I continued to listen carefully, I heard him say things that I knew were not Biblical, but it was only later that I discovered he believed in what is called a "liberation theology" that applies politically what God wants to do for us spiritually.

So how do you and I know which speaker on the platform is authentic? The only way we can discern the true from the false is to know the Shepherd's voice—God's Word.

One of the primary reasons we need to be in a disciplined study of the Scriptures is so we can saturate ourselves in the truth. When we know the truth and we are presented with that which is false, we will instinctively recognize it. Measuring philosophies or theologies or opinions or sermons or books or doctrines or counsel by the Word of God is like exposing the crookedness of a stick by placing a straight stick beside it. The ultimate compliment an audience can pay me is to bring their Bibles and follow along as I speak so they can double-check what I say against what God says. I am authentic as a Bible teacher only in proportion to my faithfulness to God's Word.[22]

And in order to give God's Word out so that others can hear His voice in their ears, I *must*—it's not an option—*I must* . . .

read it,

study it,

understand it,

apply it,

live by it.

But that's not enough! I have to listen for my Shepherd's voice to speak *to me* through it. *Personally.* Then I must heed His voice. *Personally.* And when I do, His Word makes a lasting impact and bears eternal fruit, because it's powerful.

THE AUTHENTIC VOICE IS POWERFUL

The Scribes and Pharisees, huddling in a tight, stingy little knot of hostility, must have continued to glare at Jesus. While the curious onlookers were aware of the tense undercurrents, they "did not understand what he was telling them" (10:6) or how His words related to their situation. The disciples also must have been straining to grasp the truth of what was being said. They surely knew from experience that these words would be worth remembering and understanding. But I wonder if the beggar had eyes that glowed like living coals as he absorbed every expression, hung breathlessly on every syllable, and understood every parable that Jesus was giving. He must have known immediately when Jesus moved easily from using the winter sheepfold as an analogy to explaining the authenticity of the shepherd and then began using the summer sheepfold to explain the shepherd's life-saving role.

The Voice Has Life-Saving Power

During the summer months, the shepherd kept his sheep in the highlands without venturing into the towns at all. At night, he bedded them down within a fold that was located in the pasture itself. The fold was made very simply of walls that were basically stones gathered from the pasture and piled on top of each other. Left in the rock wall was one gap that served as the means for the sheep to go in and out. The gap had no gate or door. At night, with the sheep safely inside, the shepherd himself would lie down in the gap so that anything or anyone who came in or out would have to go through— or over—his body.

The application Jesus gave this simple pastoral scene was riveting in its meaning, offending people then and now. With eyes sweeping the gathering crowd even as He verbally and emotionally embraced the beggar, He dropped the bomb: "I tell you the truth, I am the gate for the sheep. All who ever came before me were thieves and robbers, but the sheep did not listen to them" (10:7–8). As the Pharisees must have stiffened and bristled, clearing their throats to strenuously object, Jesus repeated, "I am the gate; whoever enters through me will be saved" (10:9).

There was no mistaking His meaning. Jesus was nailing the religious leaders of His day to their sanctimonious wall, likening them to thieves who robbed the people by substituting a heavy burden of religion for a genuine relationship with God. Thieves then and now say there are other ways to God besides Jesus, that one religion is as good as another as long as the seeker is sincere, that you can work your way into God's favor by keeping all the rituals and traditions of your religion. The battle is a classic struggle between the Gospel of grace and of the law of religion. If you succumb to this struggle, you will be robbed of salvation, eternal life, peace, joy, forgiveness of sin, meaning to life, reconciliation with God, heaven when you die, and other blessings too numerous to name.

The Voice Has Life-Changing Power

Years ago I had the privilege of praying with a woman in my class as she responded to God's Word by confessing her sin, claiming the cross as her atonement for sin, and inviting Jesus into her heart and life, surrendering to Him as Savior and Lord. Her face was soaked in tears and wreathed in smiles when she got up off her knees. She was assured she belonged to the Shepherd and was safely inside the fold of a personal, permanent relationship with God.

Several days later, she asked me to accompany her as she went to tell her pastor of the decision she had made. I sat beside her on the small sofa in the pastor's elegantly appointed study as she poured out her heart. With a voice that trembled with emotion and eyes that brimmed with tears, she described the commitment she had prayerfully made earlier in the week then blurted out, "I've been born again!"

The pastor, wearing a three-piece pinstripe suit with a gold watch chain draped across the front of his vest, listened attentively as he sat in a red leather desk chair. His silver hair was immaculate, his manicured fingers were fanned out and pressed together in a thoughtful pose, and his expression was kindly patient as his deep voice resonated in the paneled chamber. With a condescending tone that might be used with a rather slow-witted child, he explained, "But my dear Susan, you weren't born again this week! Why, you were baptized when you were twelve years old! You're a member of this church. You teach Sunday school. You've been a Christian all your life."

I barely noticed the hostile dagger of a glance he threw me because I was so incredibly dumbfounded! His reaction to Susan was a totally unexpected revelation of what seemed to be a false shepherd!

She had just told him how she had confessed her sin and received God's forgiveness.

God's Word says that was so.[23]

She had just told him how she had asked God to give her eternal life.

God's Word says He had.[24]

She had just told him that she had opened her heart and invited Jesus to come in.

God's Word says He did.[25]

She had just told him she had been born again.

God's Word says she was now a child of God.[26]

She had just told him she believed Jesus had died for her and been raised for her.

> *God's Word* said that if she confessed with her mouth that Jesus is Lord, and believed in her heart that God had raised Him from the dead, she would be saved.[27]

Susan had taken God at His Word! She had heard the voice of the Shepherd, calling her by name, and she had responded by following Him in a life of faith, with the first step being her own salvation. And this professional shepherd was saying it wasn't so!

It was depressingly obvious that he was a false shepherd who had led that very prestigious church possibly without ever having entered through the Door of the fold for himself! He did not recognize or acknowledge the Shepherd's voice in Susan's life.

As astonishing as that experience still is to me today, it was devastating for us both then![28] But praise God, the Shepherd not only knows His sheep, but we know our Shepherd! Today, Susan is an active member of another church. Her ministry there has impacted the lives of literally hundreds of others as she has drawn them into God's Word as a basis for a personal relationship with Himself. Her testimony as well as her ministry underscores the authenticity of the Shepherd's powerful voice in her life.

I don't remember the exact date that I heard my Shepherd calling me to enter through the door of Himself into a personal relationship with God, but I know it was when I was a young girl. I had watched an old, black-and-white, Cecil B. DeMille film on the life of Jesus entitled *King of Kings*. It used to be shown on television every Easter. As I watched the crucifixion scene unfold on that Easter Sunday long ago, I began to weep. I knew Jesus had died for me. My wise mother recognized my tears, not as those of pity for a brutalized man, but as tears of conviction in a little girl's heart for sin that had nailed Him to the cross. And so my mother led me in prayer as I confessed my sin to God and told Him I was sorry. I thanked Jesus for dying for my sin and asked God to forgive me and cleanse me with the blood of Jesus. I told Him I believed Jesus had risen from the dead, and I invited Him to come live in my heart. I don't remember any dramatic sensation afterward. But I knew my sins had been forgiven, I knew I had been born again, and I knew I would go to heaven when I died. That prayer, which answered the Shepherd's call in my life, began a personal love relationship with Jesus that is more real and precious to me than any other. I had found life!

The Shepherd's call has echoed down through the centuries. It's a clarion call to all sheep, offering freedom and salvation to those who are willing to come out of the . . .

denominationalism,

traditionalism,

ritualism,

narcissism,

pantheism,

agnosticism

of their religion and enter into a personal relationship with God. It's an authoritative command to turn away from

doubt,

disobedience,

disregard,

defiance,

legalism and liberalism,

pride and prejudice,

fear and failure,

sin and selfishness,

and walk through the open Door of salvation into the fold of a personal, permanent, love relationship with the Creator Who became our Savior.

Just as there was one door that led into God's presence in Eden and one door that led into the safety of the ark and one door that led into the inner sanctuary of the temple, a personal relationship with God is only accessed through one Door Who is Jesus Himself.

The authentic voice of the Shepherd can be heard ringing out in

church sanctuaries and home Bible studies,

seminary classrooms and Sunday school nurseries,

radio broadcasts and television studios,

stadium crusades and arena revivals!

And how do we know if the voice is authentic? We know because

it will be Biblical—straight from God's Word.

it will be personal—in the language of our own lives.

it will be powerful—lives will be saved, and lives will be changed.

THIS CRITERION for determining the authenticity of the voice was used effectively in the first century when the Gospel was preached. For at least two thousand years the Jews had clung to their faith in the one true God as He had revealed Himself to them through the Law and the Prophets. Then Jesus of Nazareth came along, saying He was the fulfillment of the Law as well as the Messiah the prophets had foretold. The religious leaders were so outraged He was put to death. But *He is* Who He claimed to be, and on the third day He rose from the dead!

Following the resurrection and ascension of Jesus Christ, His disciples fanned out all over the known world, telling people they could now be forgiven of their sin and be reconciled with God through faith in Jesus Christ. How were the religious faithful to know if this was true? How could they discern the true Shepherd's voice?

A fascinating glimpse is given to us when the apostle Paul, who had started heated debates and even riots in practically every synagogue and city where he preached the Gospel, slipped into the little town of Berea. As was his custom, he went straight to the synagogue in order to share the wonderful good news that the Messiah had come as the Lamb of God Who had taken upon Himself the sin of the world. This time when he preached, "they received the message with great eagerness and examined the Scriptures every day to see if what Paul said was true."[29]

You and I, like the noble Bereans, would do well to listen more critically to those who stand in the pulpits of our churches and the lecterns of our Sunday schools as well as in front of our seminary and Bible-school classrooms. We will recognize our Shepherd's voice when we listen with our eyes on the pages of our Bibles as our hearts whisper the prayer,

Dear God, just give me MORE of Your voice in my ear . . .

2

MORE *of* —————
His Tears on My Face

John 12:1–8

W<small>E HAD JUST SAID GOOD-BYE</small> to a radiant young bride-to-be. She had come over to our house to tell my husband, my children, and myself some of the exciting details of the upcoming wedding. Her eyes had been flashing, her smile sparkling, her dark, glossy hair bouncing as her excitement had animatedly spilled over every word and gesture. As the door closed behind her, Rachel-Ruth, my youngest daughter, burst into tears and ran from the room! I could see my startled expression reflected in the face of Morrow, my ten-year-old, who was as astonished as I was.

We bolted after Rachel-Ruth and found her sobbing in the living room. Her hands were frantically tearing at her long braids as though she would pull them from her little head, and between choking breaths she was saying, "I hate myself! I hate my curly hair! My face is so ugly! I'm not pretty at all!"

Morrow and I stared at Rachel-Ruth aghast! Then we burst into tears, threw our arms around her, and the three of us crumpled onto the floor in a heap of despair! Over curls, instead of straight, glossy hair! Over braids, instead of a cute little bob! Over an eight-year-old body, instead of a twenty-one-year-old figure!

What ridiculous nonsense, you might say! But do you know something? When you love someone with all your heart, her pain is yours!

A few years later, Rachel-Ruth went to the big, public high school that her older brother and sister had attended. Both of her siblings had been wildly popular and had enjoyed a relatively good four years there. But Rachel-Ruth's high school experience was very different. She endured almost total rejection from those who had been her close friends for years. They turned their backs on her in the halls and refused to sit near her in the classrooms. She was invited to house parties at the beach during spring break then rudely dropped the day before she was to leave. She longed to dress up and go to the formal dances, but she was rarely asked. Every afternoon following school, I would welcome her home with a bowl of hot popcorn and a cold glass of chocolate milk—and she would recap her day, often with tears splashing down her face.

The day of Rachel-Ruth's graduation ceremony at Baylor University, I stood with her on a platform before thirty thousand women who had rallied for a Christian women's conference at the Rose Bowl Stadium in Pasadena, California. She had chosen to skip her graduation and instead had shared her testimony of God's faithfulness to her in the midst of painful rejection. When she finished the audience rose as one person to give her a standing ovation! I stood back, surrounded by the deafening sound of the applause for my daughter, and wept! Because when you love someone with all of your heart, her blessings are yours!

Then, a few Christmases ago when Rachel-Ruth came home after visiting my parents with her boyfriend, her eyes were flashing, her smile was sparkling, and her long, curly hair was bouncing as her excitement animatedly spilled over every word and gesture. The man of her dreams had asked her to be his wife! She could barely keep her hands still long enough to show me the gorgeous diamond on her finger. She was a radiant bride-to-be. And I put my arms around her and wept! Because when you love someone with all of your heart, her joy is yours, too!

As her mother, I so empathize with Rachel-Ruth that her tears are mine. And God, as our heavenly Father, so closely identifies with His children that our tears are His. This precious revelation of God's relationship to us is first glimpsed plainly when we read how God called Abraham to leave Ur of the Chaldeans and follow Him in a life of faith, encouraging him by promising, "I will bless those who bless you, and whoever curses you I will curse."[1] In other words, God would be so closely identified with Abraham that He would consider Abraham's friends and enemies His own. God not only loves His children, He identifies with them.

And in response to such loyalty and love, I, in turn, desire to so closely identify with Him—with His grief, His joy, His love, His pain, His blessings, His honor—that His tears are on my face.

TEARS OF GRIEF

Following the confrontation with Jesus that exposed the Scribes' and Pharisees' hypocrisy and falsity as shepherds, they became so enraged, they "picked up stones to stone him" (10:31). When He challenged their action, silencing their arguments with His undeniable claim to be God's Son, "again they tried to seize him, but he escaped their grasp. Then Jesus went back across the Jordan" (10:39–40).

It was while Jesus was in the Trans-Jordan that He received the urgent message that Lazarus, His beloved friend, was sick. He decided to go to Bethany, where Lazarus and his family lived, fully aware that the little village was very close to Jerusalem. He knew that He most certainly would run the risk of once again becoming the focus of public attention, arousing the passionate hatred and jealousy of His enemies.

After delaying his journey for two days, Jesus left the Trans-Jordan, walking all day on rocky roads over hills turned brown by the heat.[2] Finally, He and His disciples came to the little village of Bethany that He had come to love. As soon as He drew near, He was greeted with the tragic news—of which He was already aware—that Lazarus had died.

Word of His arrival spread quickly among all the "many Jews [who] had come to Martha and Mary to comfort them in the loss of their brother" (11:19). The sisters must have received the news together at the same time. Jesus had come! But Mary's heartrending grief coupled with her unbelief kept her at home. She did not run out to greet Him as her sister, Martha, did.

After a short time, Martha returned from speaking with Jesus, drawing Mary aside privately to tell her, "The Teacher is here . . . and is asking for you" (11:28). Mary's broken heart must have shattered even more as the "if

25

only's" flooded to the surface: *If only He had come sooner . . . If only He had been here when Lazarus became ill . . . If only He had answered my prayer the way I had asked Him to.* Without thinking of the scene or commotion she would cause, she abruptly got up from where she had collapsed in the house, and fled through the door. "When the Jews who had been with Mary in the house, comforting her, noticed how quickly she got up and went out, they followed her, supposing she was going to the tomb to mourn there" (11:31).

With almost frantic despair, as Mary ran through the narrow streets of the little village, did she stumble over the sharp stones? Did she cry afresh at the misery of her helplessness, hot tears blinding her eyes and streaming down her cheeks, disheveled hair escaping from underneath her veil and falling over her face?

Finally she "reached the place where Jesus was and [when she] saw him, she fell at his feet and said, 'Lord, if you had been here, my brother would not have died'" (11:32). She wasn't just being emotional. She was totally realistic. Her grief was coupled with a sense of total hopelessness and helplessness because death seems so final. Although Mary's attitude was worshipful and respectful as she crumbled sobbing at His feet, she had no faith to get beyond the despairing defeat of her brother's death.

That day in Bethany, as Mary wept and her friends wept with her, a tumult of grief and anger and compassion and empathy welled up within the heart of Jesus until He could no longer contain His feelings. In a voice that must have been choking with emotion, He inquired, "Where have you laid him?" When those around Him replied gently, "'Come and see, Lord.' . . . Jesus wept"(11:34–35).

Jesus, the Creator of the universe, the eternal I Am, so strong, so powerful, so wise, *so human,* stood there with tears running down His cheeks! He knew He intended to raise Lazarus from the dead, but still He wept. *Why?* Because He loved Mary and Martha and Lazarus, and their tears of grief were on His face!

When have you grieved at the grave of a loved one,
   or trembled from the shock of discovering the pregnancy of your
      unmarried daughter,
   or recoiled at the diagnosis of a doctor,

or walked through the nightmare of a precinct station to face your child's
arrest,

or felt the cold, numb shock of early dismissal from your job,

or experienced the searing pain of a spouse's betrayal?
Did you think Jesus just didn't care? That if God really loved you, He would
have intervened to prevent it? All those thoughts crowding into your mind
are like seeds sown by the Enemy. If you are not alert, those seeds will grow
up into weeds that choke out and strangle the truth—that God so loves you,
your grief is His, your nightmare is His, your shock is His, your pain is His.[3]
Your tears are on His face!

Jesus wept! Those who had gathered to support and comfort and help the
family of Lazarus observed the famous young Rabbi weeping and concluded,
"See how he loved him!" (11:36). Even though He knew the glory to come and
the heavenly Home that was being prepared and the demonstration of God's
power that was about to be displayed, Jesus wept! He wept for no other reason
than He loved this precious family, and they were weeping.[4] He was entering
into their suffering even as one day He would ask us to enter into His.

Surrounded by a crowd of friends, family, and curious onlookers, He
gazed at the scene before Him. I expect Mary and Martha followed His focus
that was fixed on the cave carved out of the hillside that served as the burial
place. A large stone sealed off the entrance to the tomb.

Martha was jolted out of any grief-filled reverie she may have felt when
she heard His familiar voice command quietly but with absolute authority,
"Take away the stone" (11:39).

Something in Martha must have been quickened. The spark of faith
was suddenly fanned into flame, and without further question or word,
she ordered the stone to be rolled away. Just because He said so. He was
all she had.

As the stone was rolled away, the sound of weeping and mourning and
whispering must have been hushed in startled amazement. Everyone was
staring at Jesus and Martha. Their conversation had been private. No one
could have heard what had been said between them, especially since they
were surrounded by the wailing and weeping of the mourners. Without any
preliminaries, the crowd was suddenly aware that the stone to the tomb was

being rolled away. Now, in the heat of the day, there was total silence. There may have been the sound of the grasshoppers whirring in the tall grass or a bird calling its mate from the tree or the rustling of a dried leaf as a breath of hot air blew it across the stones. But the silence must have been deafening.

I wonder if Martha was momentarily embarrassed when the stone was rolled away in front of all of her friends. Because even if the assembled friends had been unable to see Lazarus in the darkened depths, they would have been able to smell him. There would have been no doubt that he was dead.

With every eye fastened on Him—the red-rimmed eyes of Mary, the hope-filled eyes of Martha, the grieving eyes of the friends, the hostile eyes of the unbelievers, the astonished eyes of the casual observers—Jesus boldly, loudly lifted His voice for all to hear as He prayed, "Father, I thank you that you have heard me. I knew that you always hear me, but I said this for the benefit of the people standing here, that they may believe that you sent me" (11:41–42). Jesus was letting everyone know that if Lazarus was raised, the power to raise him came from God.

Then, in the same voice that had brought the worlds into being, the same voice that had called Abraham from Ur, the same voice that had reverberated from Mount Sinai—*the same voice* thundered, "Lazarus, come out!"(11:43).[5]

In the heavy silence that followed, the sound of His voice must have echoed from the stone walls and wafted on the gusting breeze while every eye must have strained toward the cave, peering into the black hole where the stone had been. Then, out of the shadows appeared a mummy-like figure "wrapped with strips of linen, and a cloth around his face"(11:44). Was there a collective gasp? Did some of the mourners swoon in a faint to the ground? Was everyone frozen into place, temporarily paralyzed by the shock of seeing something that *just couldn't be?* Dead men don't come back to life! But Lazarus did! At the command of the One Who is the resurrection and the life, he walked out of the tomb![6]

In the stunned silence, with Lazarus standing bound in the tomb's entrance, Jesus could be heard once again giving Martha instructions: "Take off the grave clothes and let him go" (11:44). And she did!

I wonder if Mary joined her sister Martha, at first gingerly plucking at the graveclothes that bound her brother then tearing at them with eager fingers as she felt the life underneath those clothes. Her brother was alive! Jesus had raised him from the dead! Her prayers had been answered even more abundantly than she could have thought to ask![7]

When the graveclothes dropped away, did she gaze in wonder at the pink, healthy flesh of her brother? Did she place her hands on Lazarus's shoulders and run her fingers over the features of his face? Did her sobs of grief give way to tearful shouts of joy that reverberated throughout the stunned silence of that courtyard?

I wonder if Jesus stepped back into the shadows, His eyes glistening with tears and His heart swelling with emotion as He rejoiced with those He loved over Lazarus's new life. Surely it's the same joy He shares when a person who has been spiritually dead is raised to spiritual life!

TEARS OF JOY

His tears of joy were on my face one night as I witnessed firsthand a "resurrection from the dead" in the back room of a sports arena. I was with Robert, a young man who was part of our technical crew, assisting us in our Just Give Me Jesus revivals.[8] He began his involvement with us with the attitude that we were just another part of his job as a stagehand. Over a year's time, his attitude progressed from viewing us as the strangest, weirdest "gig" he had ever worked on to being intrigued, then finally drawn to the Jesus we sought to exalt in the arenas. During our last revival of 2000, as I said good-bye to him, I spontaneously blurted out, "Robert, do you know Jesus?"

He looked at me a little timidly as he said he was trying to. I replied, "Robert, have you ever invited Jesus Christ into your life?"

This time his eyes locked into mine as he shook his head no. When I asked him if he would like to, he said yes. Because I had another commitment at the time and he had to immediately begin breaking down the equipment in the arena, I asked him if he would give me time to talk to him later. He agreed.

Finally, at 8:30 that evening, with both of us exhausted from a very long, grueling day, we were able to meet in a back room. In response to my questions, he told me he had never read the Bible, never been to church, never heard anything close to what he had been hearing in the arena during our revivals. As he continued to tell me something of his background, I knew he was as spiritually dead in his relationship with God as Lazarus had been physically dead in the tomb.[9]

When Robert finished briefly sharing his story with me, I had the opportunity of explaining the Gospel to him, showing him in my Bible the gifts of forgiveness, salvation, and eternal life that God promises when we place our faith in His Son as our Savior. In response to my gentle query, he said he would like to pray to invite Jesus to be his Savior. We both bowed our heads. The seconds turned into minutes as the silence was broken only by his labored breathing. Finally I prayed for his strength and courage to overcome any barrier the Enemy might be placing before him. I offered to lead him in prayer in order to help him articulate the decision he wanted to make. He refused my offer, saying he was struggling with some major issues.

I silently prayed for the power of God to raise this "dead man" to new life. As we continued to wait with heads bowed, his breathing turned into sobs as he finally told God he was a sinner, he was sorry, he wanted to turn from his sin, and he was asking for forgiveness and eternal life. I knew, based on God's Word, that God had answered that simple prayer of faith!

When I looked up, I knew also I was looking at a young man who had been raised from spiritual deadness to spiritual life in Christ! Robert had been born again into God's family! I put my arms around him, and he laid his head on my shoulder and we both cried like babies. Tears of release! Tears of joy!

And I am confident, if I could have seen the visible face of Jesus at that moment, I would have seen tears of joy on His face, too! Because He had told His disciples there is "more rejoicing in heaven over one sinner who repents than over ninety-nine righteous persons who do not need to repent."[10] Every time someone like Robert is raised into new life in Christ the tears we shed are His tears of joy on our faces!

When have you wept for joy over the salvation of a friend or loved one? Last year I attended one of my father's evangelistic crusades. When the invitation was given to the audience members to come to the platform in order to receive Jesus Christ as Savior and Lord, thousands of people responded by pouring down from the stadium seats onto the football field. Within a few moments the entire field was jammed with people who were spiritually being raised from the dead as they placed their faith in Christ. When I leaned over to comment on the scene to my husband, who was sitting with me, I saw tears streaming down his cheeks! And as I focused on others around me, beside and behind me, I saw one friend after another with tears running down his or her face—tears of sheer joy for those who were walking from darkness into the light and passing from death to life!

In the case of Lazarus, we are not told what happened during the remainder of that momentous day, except that very quickly word was relayed to the enemies of Jesus, who redoubled their efforts to arrest and kill Him. Once again, the climate was so dangerous that He quietly withdrew to "a region near the desert" until "six days before the Passover, [when] Jesus arrived at Bethany, where Lazarus lived, whom Jesus had raised from the dead" (11:54, 12:1).

When Jesus returned to Bethany for the first time since raising Lazarus from the dead, we can be sure that the welcome He received was an ecstatic outpouring of love and joy! As He entered the dusty little village, followed by His faithful handful of disciples, did a child spot him first? With the energy that comes with youth and the thrill of being the bearer of glad tidings, did the child yell to a friend as he raced down back alleyways, darted through the legs of braying donkeys, ducked past freshly washed clothes drying in the noonday sun, ignored the curious stares and shouts of the villagers, until he stood at the gate leading into the courtyard of Lazarus's home? Did he bang furiously until Martha, wiping her hands on her apron, appeared at the doorway to see what all the commotion was about? When the little boy blurted out the news— Jesus was coming! . . . He was even now entering the village! He would be at the house in a few moments!—did Martha spring into action, racing into the kitchen to see what there was to set before Him? With the intuition of a gracious hostess, she knew Jesus would be thirsty and hungry and tired after His journey, and she must have quickly assessed how she could serve Him.

And I wonder if Mary overheard the little messenger's outburst of good news. Did her hands go first to her heart that suddenly began to beat too fast, then to her face as tears rushed to her eyes, then to her hair as she smoothed it back? Jesus was coming! She was going to see Jesus again!

And was Lazarus in the midst of a business transaction, going over a contract with one of his merchants, when he heard the child's excited words? Surely his handsome head jerked up, his dark eyes flashed with instant excitement, and his lips parted in a wide grin as he rolled up his scrolls, pushed back from the desk, told the merchant that would be all for the day, and strode swiftly to the courtyard to greet his beloved and honored Guest.

Regardless of where Mary, Martha, and Lazarus were when they received the news that Jesus was coming, I have no doubt they were all three at the front gate to throw their arms around Him as He arrived! With tears of joy they must have welcomed Him once again into their home.

The celebration dinner that night in the home of Simon the Leper was one that would long be remembered.[11] In the flickering light of candles on the table and torches along the walls, the dinner would have been lavish in the abundance and variety of the food, luxuriously comfortable in its setting, delightful to the eye, and meaningful in the fellowship of those invited to honor this One Who had made such a difference in the lives of those in Bethany.

The table was probably long and low. Instead of the guests being seated upright in chairs, they would have reclined around it on cushions. Their feet would have been stretched out behind them, their bodies propped up on their left arms, freeing their right hands to partake of the food and drink.

It would have been obvious from the seating pattern as well as the attention lavished on Him that although everyone rejoiced over Lazarus's new life, this "dinner was given in Jesus' honor. Martha served, while Lazarus was among those reclining at the table with him" (12:2).

As capable as Martha was in the kitchen, she had learned to serve humbly.[12] While she moved quickly and efficiently around the table, her heart must have basked in the sheer pleasure of serving her Lord. And as she drew near to refill glasses and replenish plates, she must have hung on every word that was spoken as she took full advantage of the opportunity to listen to the conversation. *His* conversation. Her service was indeed an act of heartfelt worship.

In the course of serving the dinner, I wonder if Martha's hand deliberately brushed her brother's shoulder as though to reassure herself that he was actually alive. And as Lazarus relished every bite of precious food, grateful for his appetite that was such evidence of health and life, did he have a difficult time taking his eyes off the face of his Friend? Perhaps Jesus Himself struggled to keep His own eyes from misting over with tears of joy as He relaxed in the company of those that He loved.

TEARS OF LOVE

The warm spring air may have carried the delicious aromas of roasting meat and baking bread from the kitchen into the banquet hall as the meal progressed to the tune of happy voices, easy laughter, and the muffled clatter of utensils. It was into this intimate setting that Mary slipped like a shadow. Had she hung back in shame from the festivities because she was so acutely aware of her lack of faith that had been revealed the last time she had seen Jesus? Was she filled with remorse over her attitude that was so quick to blame Jesus for not answering her prayer the way she had asked when Lazarus had become ill? Had she verbally flogged herself again and again because *she*, Mary, the one who had sat at Jesus' feet and listened to His Word, had collapsed in unbelief when Lazarus had died?[13]

In some way, Mary must have felt personally compelled to let Jesus know how grateful she was for His grace that had raised her brother to life in spite of her seeming unbelief. And she loved Him.

And so she entered the banquet hall, carrying an alabaster jar of expensive perfumed oil. The oil would have been exceedingly precious to Mary. Its estimated value was equivalent to the average working man's yearly salary—possibly equal to Mary's life savings.[14] Today people invest in fine art, antiques, or jewelry as a way to increase the value of their holdings. But Mary, as was the custom in her day, collected perfumed ointment, adding to her cache as her savings would allow. The ointment never spoiled and actually increased in value as time passed. It may even have served as Mary's dowry, collected not only by herself but also contributed to by family members in order to ensure a secure future for her. Without question, the alabaster jar of perfumed ointment was Mary's most precious possession.

As Mary clutched her alabaster jar, her eyes may have swept around the room, taking in the identity of the various guests who were present. In addition to Jesus, Lazarus, and Simon, the host, it was attended by Jesus' twelve disciples, plus other special guests. All men. It was obvious that the only other woman in the room was Martha, who darted in and out of the kitchen as she served.

And so it was with gentle courage and resolute determination that Mary glided quietly through the room to where Jesus was reclining at the table. I doubt that anyone noticed her at first—except Jesus. Surely He had watched her enter, fully aware of her intentions. He must have ceased eating, the expression on His face softening into one of total acceptance and love. Feeling His eyes on her, she must have glanced at His face and seen the welcome that was there. "Then Mary took about a pint of pure nard, an expensive perfume; she poured it on Jesus' feet and wiped his feet with her hair" (12:3).

Without any hesitation or embarrassment, Mary took the gleaming alabaster jar containing a veritable fortune of perfumed ointment, broke the seal, and extravagantly poured the contents on Jesus' head and feet.[15] As she poured it all out, the tears must have begun to fall—tears of overwhelming love for this Man Who had loved her and her sister and her brother and had made such a difference in their lives. Without any self-consciousness or pretense, she reached up and gracefully unwound her hair, humbly using it to wipe His feet, her tears mingling with the perfume.

In this simple, profound act of loving devotion, Mary gave Jesus *every-thing*—her future, her hope for a future, her financial security, her status in society, her reputation, her pride, her self. By breaking her alabaster jar, she withheld nothing from Him and expected nothing in return. "And the house was filled with the fragrance of the perfume"(12:3). The entire home and many others were blessed because of her sacrificial act of worship.

What is your alabaster jar—your most precious possession? Is it . . .

> your children?
> your spouse?
> your desire for a child?
> your desire for a spouse?
> your career?
> your desire for a career?

your plans for the future?
your financial portfolio?
your time
your reputation?

Would you be willing to break it, pouring it out at His feet?

Pour out your pride and be the first to say you are sorry?

Pour out your spouse, releasing him or her for full-time Christian service?

Pour out your child, supporting his or her call to the foreign mission field?

Pour out your reputation and take a public stand for your faith in Christ?

Pour out your future as you surrender your goals and dreams to Him?

When have you filled your home with the fragrance of your love for Jesus—a love that is costly and demands that you give Him everything, without reservation? Or is your home filled with the scent of your own selfishness? Do you carefully calculate what you will—and you won't—give to Him? Do you deliberately determine how much time or effort or money you can give to Him without having to give up time or effort or money you want for yourself? Do you give to Him painlessly because you don't give until it hurts or until it costs you any real sacrifice?

Years ago, when I first studied this passage, I was struck by the fact that I myself was my husband's alabaster jar. My husband had "broken" me on the altar of service, releasing me to answer God's call in my life. He gave up time with me, he gave up my undivided attention, he gave up my moment-by-moment availability as a deliberate act of his worship and love for Jesus. The most wonderful result is that our entire home has been filled with the fragrance of his sacrifice. Our children grew up loving Jesus, and they have each committed their lives to serving Him, breaking their own alabaster jars at His feet.

Again and again, as I have shared God's Word around the world, people have come up to me and said, "Anne, please thank your husband . . ." And I inwardly praise God that the fragrance of my husband's sacrifice has crept outside of our home, permeated our community, blessed people across our state, and even swept beyond to our nation and various parts of the world. Only eternity will reveal the extent of the fragrance that has resulted from one man's loving devotion to Jesus that has prompted him to break his alabaster jar within our home.

With the first sound of cracking alabaster, Simon and his guests must have stiffened, quickly scanning the dining room until their eyes fell on the form of Lazarus's sister. The clatter of utensils must have ceased and the food remained untouched and the goblets poised in midair as everyone stared incredulously at the scene before them. In stunned silence they watched Mary as she knelt beside Jesus, bathing Him with her priceless ointment, her soft sobs and swishing hair the only sounds in the stillness.

The silence was finally shattered and the very tender, poignant, and beautiful moment of unrestrained love marred when "one of his disciples, Judas Iscariot, who was later to betray him, objected, 'Why wasn't this perfume sold and the money given to the poor? It was worth a year's wages'" (12:4–5). Like someone grinding a beautiful rose under his heel, Judas revealed his disdain for such love lavished on Jesus. In essence, he was curling his lip and sneering, "Don't you know, Mary, that Jesus *isn't worth* such sacrifice? You're *wasting* your ointment on Him."

Judas! Judas was one of Jesus' twelve closest friends! Judas was a disciple! Judas was supposed to be a spiritual leader! How could Judas be so out of sync that he would mock something that was exceedingly precious to Jesus? How could he be so piously concerned about the "poor" while being so totally unconcerned with Mary's feelings?

Who has sneered at your love for Jesus? What "disciple" has advised, "You're wasting your time" or "You're wasting your money" or "You're wasting your energy" or "You're wasting your gifts" or "You're wasting your education" or "You're wasting your mind" because you have sacrificed lavishly for Him?

Who has made fun of your faith or criticized your commitment or faulted your service? Who has observed your precious, intimate sacrifice of love for Jesus and verbally lashed you for it? What Judas—what so-called "disciple" or Christian leader—has flatly told you that Jesus is not worth:

> giving up tennis
> —in order to go to Bible study?

going without sleep
    —in order to make time for prayer?
quitting your job
    —in order to raise your children?
staying in your marriage
    —when the love has run out?
forgiving someone
    —before he or she asks for it?
forfeiting a luxury
    —in order to support a missionary?
refusing to get drunk
    —when everyone else is drinking?
remaining sexually pure
    —and never having a date?

It's painful, isn't it?

God recently seemed to reveal to me a precious insight into His Word that also contained specific instructions concerning an action He wanted me to take. I knew obedience to those instructions would require an almost humiliating sacrifice on my part that would be observed, and perhaps misunderstood, by others. But I obeyed. As I was explaining my obedience to a friend who is also a pastor, he turned on me and said vehemently, "The verse means nothing like you say." He then verbally assaulted my sacrifice, making me feel shame for even having made it. And the tears on my face were tears of pain.

TEARS OF PAIN

With the sound of Judas's biting criticism still hanging in the air, Mary must have frozen in place, her face going white with shock then deep red with humiliation and shame. What she had intended as an act of worship had been trashed and misunderstood. But before she could slink away, Jesus intervened.

I hope I never see Jesus looking at me the way I am sure He looked at Judas—and perhaps is looking at my pastor friend. His look must have been withering as His eyes flickered with the fire of righteous indignation and narrowed in focus on the one He knew would betray Him—the one He knew cared nothing for the poor but had a hidden motive of greed. *Jesus knew* Judas "did not say this because he cared about the poor but because he was a thief; as keeper of the money bag, he used to help himself to what was put into it" (12:6).

Attacks on your sacrifice for Jesus—and mine—may also be based on a hidden motive. The motive could be deep conviction because our sacrifice reveals the lack of love for Jesus in the accuser's life. It could be jealousy because our relationship with Jesus is intimate and the other person's is distant. It could be that in some way the person feels threatened by the reality of our relationship with Christ and the impact our sacrifice makes on others. It could be resentment over the attention we receive as a result of the fragrant blessing that our sacrifice brings into the lives of others.

Whatever the motive might be, Jesus sees right through it today, just as He did then. He silenced the criticism with a scathing rebuke: "Leave her alone" (12:7). His rebuke is one that echoes down through the centuries and needs to be heeded today.

Whenever a mother is told by her husband that she cannot read the Bible to her children nor take them to church . . .

leave her alone.

Whenever a woman is told by her pastor that she cannot obey God's call in her life as she understands it . . .

leave her alone.

Whenever a woman is told by her employer that she cannot name the name of Jesus in the workplace . . .

leave her alone.

Jesus then revealed the most amazing thing about Mary's motive as He continued, "It was meant that she should save this perfume for the day of my burial. You will always have the poor among you, but you will not always have me"(12:7–8).

Had Mary, with a woman's keen intuition and sensitivity, *sensed that Jesus was going to the cross?*[16] Had she heard Him speak of it?[17] Had something inside of her quivered with horror as she somehow *just knew* that although

He had raised her brother from the dead, He Himself was going to die? And did she in a tender, womanly way want to communicate to Him that she was willing to share in the fellowship of His suffering?[18] The tears that flowed, mingling with the ointment as she anointed His head and feet—were they His tears of pain that streamed down her face?

When have you shared His cross? When have you ever entered into the fellowship of His suffering? Just because you love Jesus, when have *His tears* of pain and rejection been on your face?

His tears are on my face . . .

whenever I share the Gospel with someone and am rejected . . .[19]
whenever family members try to talk me out of costly service . . .[20]
whenever promoters try to push me into the public eye . . .[21]
whenever religious leaders question my motives in ministry . . .[22]
whenever someone tries to use my ministry or reputation to their advantage . . .[23]
whenever my neighbors question the credibility of my witness . . .[24]
whenever my relationship with God is mocked or ridiculed . . .[25]
whenever I am insulted or threatened for doing good . . .[26]
whenever I am told I am refusing to submit to the authority of Scripture even as I am obeying it . . .[27]

My tears—and yours—are precious to Him![28] How He loves those who love Him enough to shed His tears as they share His cross!

With her face still wet from tears, surely Mary felt embarrassed to have caused such a scene. She must have hung her head, wishing she had never entered the room and wondering how she could escape.

And then Jesus turned His full attention to her. Did He reach over and gently cup her chin in His hand as He turned her face toward Him so she would look Him in the eye? Did she feel the warmth of His compassionate understanding and His tender appreciation for what she had done? Did she see His own eyes brimming with her tears?

Mary had had no words to express her utter abandonment in worshiping Him. She hadn't needed them. Her actions had been more eloquent than a thousand words. And in response to such devotion, in a voice loud enough to be heard throughout the room by every ear that had just heard Judas, yet soft enough to convey the heartfelt praise that was just for her, Jesus commended her action: "I tell you the truth, wherever the gospel is preached throughout the world, what she has done will also be told, in memory of her."[29]

Did her tears begin to fall once again? If so, this time they were surely tears of blessing!

TEARS OF BLESSING

As Mary received her Lord's commendation, her shame and embarrassment must have melted away. Regardless of anyone else's opinion, every drop of her precious ointment—*all of it*—had been worth pouring out on Him ten times over! What did it matter if others were critical, or skeptical, or hostile, or judgmental as long as He was pleased?

By His commendation, Jesus valued her loving act of worship so highly that He gave it eternal value. What Mary did may have seemed like a small, womanly gesture, but it was highly significant to Him because He knew it came from the depths of her heart. So He decreed that every time His story is told—the big events like the miracles, the cross, the resurrection, and the ascension—her beautifully tender act of devotion is also to be told.

There is no reward for service or sacrifice that even comes close to the reward of His pleasure![30] His "well done" more than balances any pain or sacrifice we have experienced because of our relationship to Him. And sometimes, He communicates His commendation to us through others.

In the course of leading our Just Give Me Jesus revivals, I have encountered stiff opposition and criticism from some religious leaders who do not feel a woman's place is on the platform—any platform—*especially* a platform where men might join the audience. So it was with some apprehension that I agreed to talk with the pastors of several dozen large metropolitan churches in a city where we had been invited to hold a revival. As I visited informally with several of the pastors before the luncheon, I was put at ease by their friendliness and warmth. During the luncheon itself, the pastor sitting to my right, who led the largest congregation in the world in his particular denomination, leaned over and said, "Anne, we love your father. But we are here to show you our total support for your ministry. We believe in what you are doing." His comments were so unexpected and so genuine that I was deeply moved to tears! Tears of blessing!

Not too long after that pastors meeting, following a particularly difficult assault by another group of religious leaders who were seeking to block my ministry, I was invited to give the commencement address and receive an honorary doctorate of divinity from a prestigious theological seminary. Before the service, I was again at a luncheon that was held in my honor. The president of the seminary as well as others on the board of directors who were oblivious to my personal battles stood up and affirmed again and again my obedience to God's call in my life as I understand it. And again tears welled up within my eyes. Tears of blessing! I knew God was using these dear people to let me know He was pleased.

When have you done something you would never have done for anyone else—but as an act of worship, you did it for Jesus? On both of the above occasions, God gave me the undeniable, distinct impression that He had noticed my labor of love, that He had accepted it as an expression of devotion to Him from the depths of my heart, that He was personally pleased and blessed by it, and that He would never forget it.

As Mary's head touched the pillow on her bed that night, I'm sure she must have reflected on the evening's events. Even in the shadowy darkness of her room, she could see that the place on her table where her alabaster jar had previously rested was now empty. As she sighed deeply, she must have inhaled the scent of the perfumed ointment that had permeated her hands and hair, reminding her of her sacrifice. She was going to bed this night knowing she now possessed no dowry and therefore had no hopes for a good marriage or a secure future. She now had no independent financial security. She had even lost her sterling reputation as her story would surely be twisted in the retelling by town gossips. For a moment she must have questioned her own action. And then she remembered the expression on His face—and His words in her ear. Once again, did the tears slip down her cheeks and dampen her pillow?

Because when you love Someone with all of your heart, His grief is yours . . .

His joy is yours . . .

His love is yours . . .

His pain is yours . . .

His blessing is yours . . .

His tears are on your face!

⚜

IN THE EARLY LIGHT of creation's dawn, the Father held His Alabaster Jar.[31] It gleamed with the beauty of the Morning Star and was scented with the fragrance of the Rose of Sharon.[32] It was His most precious possession. As His omniscient eyes looked down the years that stretched out before Him into generations and centuries and ages and millennia, *He knew* . . .[33]

The Father slipped into the darkness of the world He had made and loved.[34] The hands that held the Jar with such tender, eternal love, relaxed and opened as He placed the Jar ever so gently on the small manger bed of hay. During the years that followed, the beauty and the glory of the Jar were shared and admired by those who had eyes to see.[35]

And then, with hands that were trembling yet certain, the Father once again picked up His Alabaster Jar. And on a hill so far away from His celestial home—a hill that was cold, barren, and bleak, swarming with an angry mob that was unruly and obscene—the Father smashed His Alabaster Jar on a rugged, wooden cross. As the contents of flesh and blood were poured out and the fragrance of His love permeated human history forever, our tears were on His face . . .

3

MORE *of*
His Praise on My Lips

John 12:12–19

*I*N THE PAST THREE YEARS, my spirit has often been overwhelmed. At times,

> the emotional pain has run so deep,
> > the challenges have been so great,
> > > the opportunities have been so numerous,
> > > > the burdens have been so heavy,
> > > > > the pressure has been so intense,
> > > > > > the pace has been so hectic,
> > > > > > > the attacks have been so fierce,
> > > > > > > > and the details have been so
> > > > > > > > confusing,

that the tears on my face have been dried by weariness and weakness, discouragement and depression. Are you surprised? Surprised that Bible teachers and Christian leaders have problems like you do? Actually, for the majority of people, including Christian leaders and teachers, life is just not fair! It's hard and often unlike what we expect.[1]

However, like Isaiah, I have glimpsed something of God's purpose in allowing the skies to blacken in my life. I am confident that God has been strengthening my faith, weaning me away from my feelings as a basis for any part of my walk with Him. I believe He wants to give me the beauty of His will for my life in place of the ashes of my dreams. He wants to give me the oil of sheer joy in Himself in place of my happiness that depends on circumstances. He wants to give me "the garment of praise for the spirit of heaviness," that I might become a tree "of righteousness, the planting of the Lord, that he might be glorified."[2]

When I was growing up in the mountains of North Carolina, every Sunday afternoon, weather permitting, my parents, my siblings, and I would go hiking. Inevitably, our climbs would take us to the ridge where the trees were so enormous we could all hold hands and still not be able to encircle the trunks. When I asked my mother why the trees were so much larger on the ridge than anywhere else, she replied that it was because the winds were the strongest and the storms were the fiercest on the ridge. With nothing to shelter the trees from the full brunt of nature's wrath, they either broke and fell, or they became incredibly strong and resilient.

God plants you and me in our faith as tender saplings then grows us up into "trees of righteousness," using the elements of adversity to make us strong. And He leads us to endure, not just somehow, but victoriously as we choose to praise Him, regardless of the storms swirling within us or the winds howling outside of us.

King David knew that the secret of victory over adversity was a conscious choice to praise God. Again and again, as he cries out to God in prayer, we hear his *choice* to praise: "How long must I wrestle with my thoughts and every day have sorrow in my heart? . . . Look on me and answer, O Lord my God. . . . *But I will* trust in your unfailing love; my heart rejoices in your salvation. *I will* sing to the Lord, for he has been good to me."[3] David, hounded by Saul and living as a fugitive for years in a nation where he was the national hero as well as the anointed king, exercised his will to praise God even when he just didn't feel like it.[4]

Jeremiah knew the secret of victory when he lamented, "I have been deprived of peace; I have forgotten what prosperity is. . . . I remember my affliction and my wandering, the bitterness and the gall. I well remember them, and my soul is downcast within me. *Yet this I call to mind* and therefore I have hope. Because of the Lord's great love we are not consumed, for his compassions never fail. They are new every morning; great is your faithfulness."[5] Jeremiah had learned to praise God even though he had preached faithfully for sixty-five years without ever having a positive response to his message and instead had been scorned and imprisoned, and faced being stoned to death.

The apostle Paul knew the secret of victory when he and Silas were thrown into the inner cell of a prison, their feet fastened in stocks, because they had preached the Gospel of Jesus Christ. "About midnight Paul and Silas were praying and *singing hymns* to God."[6] As a result of their praise, an earthquake collapsed the prison, the jailor was converted, and they were set free! Paul maintained that spirit of praise until the end of his life when he once again found himself in chains in a Roman prison yet emphatically declared, "*I will* continue to rejoice."[7]

I doubt if, during either of those imprisonments, Paul *felt* like praising. But he had learned to walk by faith, not by his feelings. And today he commands you and me to exercise our will, making the deliberate, conscious choice to "rejoice in the Lord always. I will say it again: Rejoice!"[8]

Paul knew from personal experience the same secret of victory that King David and the prophet Jeremiah knew. It's a secret that's illustrated by the modern convenience of electricity. Even when it's dark outside, I can flip a switch and turn the light on. Praise is the switch that turns on the light of joy in our lives even when it's "dark" outside. And the resulting "light" causes others to see the glory of God in our lives. As my life gets more complicated and my problems and pressures seem to have become permanent fixtures, I want to turn on the "light." *So please, dear God, just give me MORE of Your praise on my lips!*

PRAISE HIM FOR WHO HE IS

The fragrance of Mary's sacrifice would still have been lingering in the air when the celebration dinner concluded that night in Bethany. The dinner guests inside must have increasingly become aware of a rising swell of noise that began to penetrate their conversation, a sound they could no longer ignore. The source of the noise was quickly and easily identified as coming from a throng of people who had gathered outside the door. A large crowd of people had "found out that Jesus was there and came, not only because of him but also to see Lazarus, whom he had raised from the dead" (12:9). Feeling the same curiosity that causes people to flock to a burning building or slow down to rubberneck at a traffic accident, everyone wanted to see! Overnight, Lazarus had become a tourist attraction!

Perhaps to relieve and protect Lazarus, and also because He had a very important appointment with prophetic destiny, Jesus left Bethany the day after the dinner in His honor. Followed by the large throng of curiosity seekers, He began walking the short distance to Jerusalem. Having followed His instructions, the disciples met Him on the way, leading a donkey and her foal.[9] The disciples placed their coats on the back of the young foal, and Jesus rode the colt the rest of the way into Jerusalem.

As Jesus neared the city, "the great crowd that had come for the Feast heard that Jesus was on his way to Jerusalem" (12:12). Historians estimate that the "great crowd" was drawn from what could have been up to two million people jamming Jerusalem that year for Passover.

The great crowd that was already in Jerusalem for Passover converged with the crowd that had followed Jesus from Bethany, forming a human sea of people who "took palm branches and went out to meet him, shouting, 'Hosanna!' 'Blessed is he who comes in the name of the Lord!' 'Blessed is the King of Israel!'" (12:13).

Like the thunderous roar of a stadium crowd acknowledging the winning touchdown of the home team, the acclamation of the crowd approaching Jerusalem must have been deafening. Very likely the sky was blue, the sun was shining, and the winds were calm on that Sunday in spring, but the excitement of anticipation was electrifying! The religious population of Jerusalem knew the Old Testament Scriptures backward and forward. As the entire city seemed to rock in praise of Jesus Christ that reverberated off the old stone walls and through the narrow city streets, it was plainly apparent that this was no pious wish. This was deliberate, conscious worship of Jesus of Nazareth as the Messiah who was fulfilling prophecy before their very eyes![10] And Jesus accepted their praise as homage due to Himself as their King!

When have you praised Jesus for no other reason than the fact that He deserves your homage, simply because of Who He is? When your spirit is heavy,

when your heart is broken,

when your future is bleak,

when your dreams are shattered,

when your memories are haunting,

when your burdens are unbearable . . . *praise him!*

If He never answers your prayer,
If He never heals your disease,
If He never solves your financial crisis,
If He never reconciles your relationship,
If He never lifts your burden,
If He never erases your memories,
just exert your will and praise Him for Who He is! Why? Because He deserves it! And because praise is the switch that turns on the light in the darkness of your life.

At a time of mounting pressure and problems, I wrote the following descriptions of Jesus as I deliberately exercised my will to praise Him just for Who He is. This description was inspired by a homemade cassette tape someone handed me with the handwritten title "My King Is . . ." From what I could gather, a man named S. M. Lockridge had been called to the platform during a church service and asked to tell the congregation Who his King was. The tape was a recording of his eloquent answer. In a rich voice that resonated with passion and increased in volume and tempo as he warmed to his subject, he thundered his description of his King, Jesus—in three minutes!

When the tape clicked off, I rewound it and replayed it. This unknown brother in Christ had absolutely thrilled my soul with his description of *my* King, Jesus! I have taken Dr. Lockridge's idea, and at times, some of his very phrases, and written a description of Who Jesus is that I pray will get you started in your own litany of praise . . .[11]

He is enduringly strong.
He is entirely sincere.
He is eternally steadfast.
He is immortally gracious.
He is imperially powerful.
He is impartially merciful.
He is the greatest phenomenon that has ever crossed the horizons of the globe.
He is God's Son.
He is the sinner's Savior.

He is the captive's ransom.
    He is the breath of life.
He is the centerpiece of civilization.
    He stands in the solitude of Himself.

He is august and He is unique.
    He is unparalleled and He is unprecedented.
He is undisputed and He is undefiled.
    He is unsurpassed and He is unshakeable.

He is the lofty idea in philosophy.
    He is the highest personality in psychology.
He is the supreme subject in literature.
    He is the unavoidable problem in higher criticism.
He is the fundamental doctrine of theology.
    He is the cornerstone, the capstone, and the stumbling stone of all
        religion.
He is the miracle of the ages.

Keep on praising Him for Who He is . . .

He is the key to knowledge.
    He is the wellspring of wisdom.
He is the foundation of faith.
    He is the doorway of deliverance.
He is the pathway to peace.
    He is the roadway of righteousness.
He is the gateway to glory.
    He is the highway to happiness.

Just keep on praising Him . . .

His office is manifold
    and His promise is sure.

His life is matchless
    and His goodness is limitless.
His mercy is enough
    and His grace is sufficient.
His reign is righteous,
    His yoke is easy,
    and His burden is light.

                    He is indestructible.
                He is indescribable.
            He is incomprehensible.
         He is inescapable.
       He is invincible.
     He is irresistible
   He is irrefutable.

I can't get Him out of my mind . . .
    And I can't get Him out of my heart.
I can't outlive Him . . .
    And I can't live without Him.

The Pharisees couldn't stand Him
    but found they couldn't stop Him.
Satan tried to tempt Him
    but found he couldn't trip Him.
Pilate placed Him on trial
    but found no fault in Him.
The Romans crucified Him
    but couldn't take His life.
Death couldn't handle Him
    and the grave couldn't hold Him.

And keep on praising Him . . .

He's the Lion and He's the Lamb.
    He is God and He is Man.

He's the seven-way King:
>> He is the King of the Jews . . .
>> That's a racial King.

>> He is the King of Israel . . .
>> That's a national King.

>> He is the King of righteousness . . .
>> That's a moral King.

>> He is the King of the ages . . .
>> That's an eternal King.

>> He is the King of heaven . . .
>> That's a universal King.

>> He is the King of glory . . .
>> That's a celestial King.

He is THE KING OF KINGS AND THE LORD OF LORDS!

Would you just keep on praising Him for Who He is *for the rest of your life?* Use the list I've shared here for inspiration and then make up your own list. Take the time to meditate on each descriptive phrase. You will discover not only that you have activated the "switch" that will totally transform your attitude as it revolutionizes your perspective, but you will also discover that praising Jesus is contagious!

The apostle John gives us a thrilling glimpse into a universal celebration that one day we are going to participate in. He describes four living creatures who surround the throne on which Jesus reigns supreme over the universe. These living creatures "day and night . . . never stop saying: 'Holy, holy, holy is the Lord God Almighty, who was, and is, and is to come.' Whenever the living creatures give glory, honor and thanks to him who sits on the throne and who lives for ever and ever, the twenty-four elders fall down before him who sits on the throne, and worship him who lives for ever and ever." And as the elders praise the person of Jesus Christ, millions of angels join in the chorus, singing in a loud voice, "Worthy is the Lamb, who was slain, to receive power and wealth and wisdom and strength and honor and glory and praise!" Then John describes the entire universe beginning to rock and roar in the continuous, contagious acclamation of Christ as "every creature in heaven and on earth and under the earth and on the sea, and all that is in them [sings]: 'To him who sits on the throne and to the Lamb be praise and honor and glory and power for ever and ever!'"[12]

What an awe-inspiring, spine-tingling worship experience that is going to be! And it begins as four living creatures praise Jesus.

Who is praising Jesus because you are? If your praise—and mine—is interrupted by . . .

> our circumstances or our complaints,
>> our selfishness or our suffering,
>>> our desires or our depression,
>>>> our indifference or our insistence,
>>>>> or by anything at all . . .

the light will grow dim in our lives as we sink into the mire of self, and instead of causing others to praise Him, we will drag them down into the darkness with us.

So would you praise Him? And keep on praising Him! Praise Him for _____. You fill in the blank with an attribute of Christ.

On that first Palm Sunday, praise of Christ became contagious as people began running from every part of the city to see what the commotion was all about. The crowd swelled until it became almost frightening to the disciples in its size and intensity. They knew that this entrance by Jesus into Jerusalem had to be an historical event of mammoth importance. There was no doubt about the momentous implication when they recalled the Old Testament messianic prophecy written four hundred years earlier by the prophet Zechariah:[13] "Do not be afraid . . . ; see, your king is coming, seated on a donkey's colt" (12:15). Even though "at first his disciples did not understand all this" (12:16), the scene was stunning as the mass of humanity rolled like a human tidal wave toward the city gates.

When the people on the periphery began to comprehend that Jesus was coming into Jerusalem, they "continued to spread the word" that He had called Lazarus from the tomb, raising him from the dead (12:17). The news that flashed throughout the city was not only praise of Who Jesus is, but praise for what He had done!

PRAISE HIM FOR WHAT HE HAS DONE

What has Jesus done for you? What things have your family, friends, neighbors, co-workers, classmates, teammates, employers, employees, professors, doctors, lawyer, counselor, pastor, and anyone else heard about that Jesus has done for you? John testified that, "Many people, because they had heard that he had given this miraculous sign, went out to meet him" (12:18). Who is seeking to meet Jesus because of what He has done for you?

When have you told someone about how He raised you from spiritual death?

When have you told someone about how He forgave your sin and removed your guilt?

When have you told someone about the disease He healed,

or the prayer He answered,

or the blessing He gave,

or the promise He fulfilled?

One of the most tragic scenes to me in all of Scripture is one that took place later that week in Jesus' life. He was arrested at midnight on Thursday, and during the early hours of Friday morning, He was placed on trial. Not one person stepped up to testify to what Jesus had done for him or her. He faced many accusers who blamed Him for treason, treachery, and tax evasion, but where was the blind man who was given sight? Where was the leper who had been cleansed? Where was the adulterous woman who had been forgiven? Where was the demoniac who had been set free? Where was Jairus's daughter who had been raised from the dead, or Peter's mother-in-law who had been relieved of a fever? Where was the paraplegic who now walked? Where were those whose lives had been touched and transformed by the power and love of Jesus? *Where were they?* They weren't there!

Maybe it was too early in the morning.
Maybe it wasn't convenient for them to come.
Maybe they were just too tired to make the effort.
Maybe they were afraid of what others would say.
Surely they hadn't forgotten!

Whatever the reason was, they remained silent when they should have spoken out. They missed the opportunity of a lifetime—even if it would have made no difference whatsoever in the official outcome of the trials—to praise Jesus for what He had done as He went to the cross for them. Don't be silent. Not one more minute. Praise Him for what He has done for you. What *has* He done for you? Meditate on the following phrases:

No means of measure can define His limitless love . . .

No farseeing telescope can bring into visibility the coastline of His shoreless supply . . .

No barrier can hinder Him from pouring out His blessings . . .

He forgives and He forgets.
He creates and He cleanses.
He restores and He rebuilds.
He heals and He helps.
He reconciles and He redeems.
He comforts and He carries.
He lifts and He loves.

He is the God of the second chance,
the fat chance,
the slim chance,
the no chance . . .

Keep on praising Him . . .
He discharges debtors,
He delivers the captives,
He defends the feeble,
He blesses the young,

53

He serves the unfortunate,
He regards the aged,
He rewards the diligent,
He beautifies the meek.

And keep on praising Him . . .

He guards the young.
He seeks the stray.
He finds the lost.
He guides the faithful.
He rights the wronged.
He avenges the abused.
He defends the weak.
He comforts the oppressed.
He welcomes the prodigal.
He heals the sick.
He cleanses the dirty.
He beautifies the barren.
He restores the failure.
He mends the broken.
He blesses the poor.
He fills the empty.
He clothes the naked.
He satisfies the hungry.
He elevates the humble.
He forgives the sinner.
He raises the dead!

Just keep on praising Him . . .

He supplies strength to the weary.
He increases power to the faint.
He offers escape to the tempted.

He sympathizes with the hurting.
He saves the hopeless.
He shields the helpless.
He sustains the homeless.

He gives purpose to the aimless,
reason to the meaningless,
fulfillment to the emptiness,
light in the darkness,
comfort in the loneliness,
fruit in the barrenness,
future to the hopeless,
life to the lifeless!

Just keep on praising Jesus *for the rest of your life!* Praise Him for
_____. Fill in the blank with your own list of the things He has done
for you. Meditate on it during the day. Add to it each night before you go to
bed. Cultivate the habit of continuous praise. It will not only be the switch
that turns on the light in the darkness of your life, it is one of the secrets to
overcoming your enemies.

The enemies of Jesus had determined that the only way to contain the
threat He had become to them was to kill Him, and they had actually begun
to plot and plan His arrest and execution.[14] These falsely pious religious
leaders had gone so far as to hire Judas to betray Him at the first opportunity.[15] But now, as Jerusalem exploded in an outburst of adulation and praise
of Jesus, His enemies watched in total consternation, exclaiming in vengeful
rage, "Look how the whole world has gone after him!" (12:19).

One way to drive Satan to distraction, and to overcome him, is through
praise of Jesus. Regardless of whether the enemy is a visible foe in front of us
like the Scribes and Pharisees or an invisible foe outside of us like the devil
himself or an invisible foe inside of us like depression, praise drives the
enemy away. In the very prophecy that describes Jesus' inmost thoughts and
feelings as He hung on the cross, tortured, bleeding, and dying, the psalmist
declared, "But You are holy, enthroned in the praises . . ." of Your people. In

other words, He is enthroned—He rules in power, authority, and supremacy—through our praise.

Whenever I have control of a meeting where I will be speaking, I arrange to have hymns and choruses of praise precede the message as a means of cleansing the invisible, spiritual atmosphere, giving Him absolute authority over the proceedings.

In some supernatural way, praise ushers the authority of God into any given situation. The psalmist continued, "Our fathers trusted in You; they trusted, and You delivered them. They cried to You, and were delivered; they trusted in You, and were not ashamed."[16] Just as surely as Jesus claimed and even quoted the words of this psalm while He hung on the cross, He also claimed the victory that was His through sheer faith expressed in praise. The upper hand the Enemy seemed to have over Jesus at the cross on Friday was just temporary, because Sunday came, and the Enemy was totally, permanently defeated.

Using praise as a practical weapon of spiritual warfare was dramatized to the children of Israel when they advanced through the Jordan River to enter the Promised Land. Blocking their continued progress was the enemy fortress of Jericho. God instructed Joshua to lead the people to march around Jericho silently once a day for six days. On the seventh day, they were to march around the city seven times; then on command they were to give a loud, unified shout of praise to God. They did as God commanded. On the seventh day, following their seventh lap around the city, they gave a shout of praise and victory, and the walls of the fortress came tumbling down![17]

It was almost as dramatic when God gave Isaiah a glimpse of the glory of the preincarnate Jesus Christ "seated on a throne, high and exalted." Spellbound, Isaiah described the angels praising Him as they "were calling to one another: 'Holy, holy, holy is the LORD Almighty; the whole earth is full of his glory.' At the sound of their voices the doorposts and thresholds shook and the temple was full of smoke."[18] It was obvious to Isaiah that praise of Jesus Christ could even move the church! And the smoke that filled the temple was not wood smoke but the visible glory of God! What a difference it would make in our world today if the church, God's people, rocked in praise that was rooted in faith—not feelings—to the extent that God's glory was revealed to those who are watching!

The highest form of genuine praise is not necessarily a sentimental feeling with tears streaming down your cheeks, hands raised, body moving to the rhythm of some musical band on Sunday night. Genuine praise is the gut-wrenching affirmation of faith uttered in the darkness of desperation as you cling to Him alone.

One practical way to maintain your praise is, every time you pray, to begin your prayer with praise. First praise Him for Who He is. Then praise Him for something He has done for you. Only when your prayer is properly focused on Him through praise do you then bring before Him your needs. And as your needs become overwhelming, your prayer, like mine, becomes,

Please, dear God, just give me MORE of Your praise on my lips!

WHEN I ANSWERED THE KNOCK at the door, I found the pest-control man standing on the doorstep. I recognized him as Brad,[19] the son of the company's owner, whom I had not seen for almost a year. I knew he was battling cancer, so I greeted him with genuine pleasure at his obvious return to a measure of good health.

As I looked at him more carefully without seeming to be too intrusive, I couldn't help but notice that his skin looked a little sallow and there were dark circles under his eyes. But a wide grin stretched across his face when I inquired as to how he was doing. He told me about his reoccurrence of the disease and of his bouts with radiation and chemotherapy. Then, standing in the middle of my kitchen with the pesticide can dangling from his hand, he said, "But, Miz Lotz, let me tell you what God has done for me. He's been so faithful to me. He's brought me through to the point where I can work again. He's put my cancer in remission. He's helped me gain weight. Why, Miz Lotz, He's even giving me my next breath!"

When Brad left the house, the fragrance that filled it was not from the pesticide but from the praise that put a song in my heart.

Dear God,

How I praise You for Your goodness and Your faithfulness to Brad and to all Your children. I even praise You for the blackness of disease and death, of depression and discouragement, of pain and problems, of stress and suffering, because it makes the brilliance of Your glory more visible in our lives. Thank You for not leaving us alone, but giving us Yourself to comfort and strengthen us for the task of just living day by day.

I praise You as my Comforter in sorrow, my Healer in suffering, my Deliverer from bondage, my Strength in weakness, my Hope for tomorrow, my Shepherd for today. Thank You that my faith does not rest in my feelings or in my circumstances but solely in Your character as revealed in Your Word. Thank You for Your Word, which gives me a place to stand when all else in my life is unraveling.

And I ask that You continue to restore Brad's health that he might live to the praise of Your glory. Help him to maintain his focus on You.

I pray this in the name of the One Who understands the feelings of our infirmities; the One Who set His face like a flint, unmoved from Your will by His feelings and unwavering in His commitment to bring You glory through His life—and through His death. In Jesus' name. Amen.

4

MORE *of* ———————————— *His Death in My Life*

OXYMORONS ARE WORDS or terms that are contradictory in meaning yet are often used together without the speaker's realizing the irony of what is being said. They can be fun to collect. Some of my favorites are:

• Airline food • act naturally • alone together • Amtrak schedule • bittersweet • clearly confused • constant variable • deafening silence • deliberately thoughtless

• Hospital food • even odds • exact estimate • extinct life • family vacation • fish farm • found missing • freezer burn • friendly fire • genuine imitation

• School food • good grief • government organization • hell's angels • holy war • ill health • jumbo shrimp • larger half • least favorite • minor crisis • paid volunteer • plastic glasses • pretty ugly • rolling stop • same difference

• Cafeteria food • second best • small crowd • soft rock • taped live • tragic comedy • unbiased opinion • United Nations • working vacation

The Bible has its own "oxymorons"—phrases that seem contradictory but are profoundly true. For instance . . .

Those who humble themselves will be exalted.[1]

Those who lose their lives will find them.[2]

Those who are poor are rich.[3]

Those who are weak are strong.[4]

Those who are hungry are filled.[5]

Those who are persecuted are glad.[6]

But perhaps the most astounding of all the seemingly contradictory principles is *the crucified life.*[7] Jesus considered the truth contained in this principle to be so pivotal, so critical, so essential, so crucial to His disciples that in the midst of the climax of His life and ministry on earth, He made the time to teach them what it meant.

DEATH PRODUCES POWER

Jesus was at the height of His popularity. The raising of Lazarus from the dead was the climax of His meteoric rise in fame over a brief three-year period. Hundreds of thousands of holiday seekers had proclaimed Him with wild enthusiasm to be the Messiah, the King of Israel, as He entered Jerusalem. His worst enemies seemed to be powerless to interfere in the surging swell of the ranks of His followers. And now the Greeks, representing the world outside of Israel, "came to Philip . . . with a request. 'Sir,' they said, 'we would like to see Jesus.' Philip went to tell Andrew; Andrew and Philip in turn told Jesus" (12:21–22).

The disciples must have been ecstatic! It was obvious to them that with the entire city of Jerusalem at the feet of Jesus, with His enemies apparently helpless, with even the outside world clamoring for His attention, this was the moment they had all been waiting for!

The disciples must have exchanged knowing looks and found it difficult to restrain the jubilation they felt. Their minds may have even begun to fantasize about what it would be like to be a disciple of Someone Who was going to rule the world. Visions of leadership positions and authority for themselves in the new kingdom must have danced in their heads. They had already been rebuked for discussing such ambitions, so none of them dared to bring it up again, but their thoughts must have been tumbling with a dozen different possibilities.[8]

Jesus' emphatic response to the inquiry of the Greeks seemed to confirm what the disciples were thinking when He replied, "The hour has come for the Son of Man to be glorified" (12:23). Everything seemed to be falling perfectly into place. His hour had come! After all the teaching and walking and talking and debating and performing of miracles, finally Jesus was going to seize the moment and rule Israel! And then from Israel, rule the world!

Jesus must have gazed at the eager faces and sparkling eyes of His disciples with a measure of sadness. They just didn't get it! He knew exactly what they were thinking. He interrupted their daydreams by jerking them back to reality with emphasis: "I tell you the truth, unless a kernel of wheat falls to the ground and dies, it remains only a single seed. But if it dies, it produces many seeds" (12:24). Dies! Who said anything about death? The disciples were thinking about the power and privilege with which they would rule the world!

As you have grown in your knowledge of Jesus, what have been your fantasies? As you have become increasingly convinced that He is the Son of God, have you been equally convinced there is nothing beyond His ability? You know you belong to Him, He loves you, and He cares about the details of your life. All true. Then the fantasies begin: *With that kind of Friend in high places, He can get me that job I've been dreaming about. And He can certainly heal me of that disease that has been diagnosed and documented as being terminal. And it would be a small matter for Him to erase my financial troubles, or place me in an elected office, or get me accepted by that club, or acquire that beautiful home for my family. Hasn't this been confirmed by the popular little book that has challenged me to pray for more of His blessing in my life every day?*

Like the disciples so long ago, you and I and the entire church today once again need the object lesson Jesus gave His disciples. We need to understand the principle that death produces power that results in more blessing.

I wonder if Jesus had entered Jerusalem mobbed by the wildly adoring crowd that now thinned out because the narrow city streets could only accommodate a handful of people at a time. As He walked through the city, surrounded by His disciples, did He pass a vendor with large baskets of grain for sale? Seizing the opportunity to give the object lesson, did He scoop up a handful of grain, letting the seeds flow through His fingers until only one was left? Holding up that one seed, perhaps He then explained that if it remained as it was, without being planted, it would always be just one seed. It would never fulfill the potential it had to sprout with life and cover an entire field with wheat. But if it was planted, the ground would press down upon it, rain would fall and soften it, and the shell or the chaff would break. The seed would then be released to press upward, sprout, and grow into a stalk of wheat with hundreds of seeds of grain in its head.

The lesson was clear. For one grain to produce more grain, it had to be broken. It had to die. But the result of the brokenness or death was the power to reproduce an enormous multiplication of grain.

How clear is His lesson to you? From our perspective on this side of the cross, we can look back and see the truth of this principle worked out in Jesus' own life. It was not on the throne of world rulership that Jesus came into power, as the disciples had imagined, but it was on the cross where He was broken. Like the grain of wheat, He had to die in order to be raised up with the power to reproduce His life hundreds of thousands of times over—in the lives of you and me and believers all through the centuries.

Every time we take Holy Communion in our churches, isn't this one of the reasons we remember His death with such gratitude? As we eat the bread, are we not thanking God for His body that was broken? As we drink the cup, are we not thanking God for His life that was not only poured out but raised up to give us eternal life?[9] The only reason you and I are spiritually alive is because He died!

While Jesus was trying to communicate this principle, not just as it related to Himself, but as it related to His disciples—and to you and me—I imagine that the disciples were staring at Him. With brows furrowed in concentration, did their minds scramble to understand how in the world the object lesson they had just been given related to what they believed was unfolding in their lives? What did death have to do with the kind of power and authority they were envisioning as they ruled the world with Jesus? And what does death have to do with the kind of power you and I need as we not only claim more of His blessings but conquer the world in Jesus' name?

Without allowing His disciples much time to ponder what He was teaching them, Jesus explained, "The man who loves his life will lose it, while the man who hates his life in this world will keep it for eternal life" (12:25). Did the disciples inwardly recoil while outwardly frowning their resistance to the implication that they would be called on to hate their lives—*to die?!*[10]

What is your reaction to such an implication? Jesus is the One Who died *for you and me!* Surely He's not saying you and I *must die for Him!* Death is a pretty big stretch from your daily prayer, "God, bless me indeed," isn't it? And it's not nearly as full of wonder and excitement, and if we're honest, personal profit. Which is why, perhaps, Jesus prefaced His remark by reminding you and me that He was speaking the truth. God wants to bless you and me even more than we could think to ask, but the power that produces the blessing comes through brokenness and death. And not just any death, but death by crucifixion.

I will tell you honestly from experience that crucifixion is a slow, painful death to your *self*. It is impossible for victims to crucify themselves. Crucifixion is the result of our decision to yield ourselves to God as He allows various pressures and problems and pain into our lives. These things are often a part of our lives anyway, but in the lives of God's children, they are not wasted. They are used to put us to death that we might be raised to an abundant . . . victorious . . . blessed . . . fruitful . . . powerful . . . Christlike . . . Spirit-filled life.

God has used pressures and pain and problems in my life as the nails that have pinned me to the cross. By submitting to Him in those things, I have entered into an experience of death to myself. Some of the "nails" He has used include losing a baby, being dismissed from a church, experiencing a robbery in our home, watching a fire that destroyed my husband's dental office, witnessing the execution of my friend in prison, stepping out in faith to establish AnGeL Ministries, traveling the world, speaking in a broad variety of settings to an even broader variety of people, enduring—and learning to enjoy—an empty nest, caring for my son through his struggle with cancer, marrying off all three children within eight months of each other, receiving criticism and rejection in ministry . . . The list could go on, but the apostle Paul articulated it best when he personally testified, "I have been crucified with Christ and I no longer live, but Christ lives in me. The life I live in the body, I live by faith in the Son of God, who loved me and gave himself for me."[11]

The apostle John had a similar experience when he glimpsed the vision of the glory of Jesus and fell at His feet as though dead.[12] As a "dead" man, he was silent—no longer was he arguing with God's plan for his life, or making excuses for his sin, or telling God what he wanted Him to do, or rationalizing

63

his behavior, or insisting on his way. And as a "dead" man he was still—no longer wrestling against God's will for his life, or going off in his own direction when God was going in a different direction, or impatiently running ahead of God. John was describing his "crucifixion."

Just as I can look back over my life and see the tremendous increase of God's blessing, I can also look back over my life and see the corresponding brokenness. God has blessed me with three fabulous children, but I can remember the deliberate choice I made to die to my desire to even have one child. God has blessed me with a wonderful marriage that of this writing is thirty-six years old, but I can remember the deliberate choice I made years ago to die to my expectations of my husband. God has blessed me abundantly in so many ways, but I can trace each blessing's multiplication to my own "death."

Most recently, as I have traveled all over the country to share God's Word, I have increasingly seen the desperate need there is for revival in the hearts of God's children. I believe God wants to wake up His people to their relationship with Himself. And so I began to pray that God would bless me with opportunities that He would use to revive His people. As I stepped out in faith and expectancy, the door of opportunity slammed in my face. Then came three years of personal death, even while I was engaged in public ministry.

During those three years, God allowed the pressure of my empty nest, the erratic health of my parents, the incineration of my husband's office, the destruction of our property by hurricanes and other storms, and the intensity of my speaking and writing schedule to break my "chaff"—my expectations, my plans, my dreams, my desires—until, on a deeper level than I have previously known, I just died to myself.

And then He raised me up! He opened the door of opportunity once again, increasing the power until tens of thousands of lives are being transformed through our ministry of Just Give Me Jesus Revivals, and *we* are blessed indeed.

The power in your life and mine that results in blessing is in direct proportion to the extent that you are willing to "hate your life"—to die to . . .

your own will,

your own goals,

your own dreams,

your own desires,

your own wants,

your own plans,

your own rights,

your own reputation.

It's what Jesus meant when He challenged His disciples, "If anyone would come after me, he must deny himself and take up his cross and follow me."[13] However, before you get too hung up on the cross,[14] don't forget—after the cross comes the resurrection and the power and the glory and the crown! The writer to the Hebrews reveals that Jesus kept His focus on the joy of abundant blessing as He "endured the cross, scorning its shame, and sat down at the right hand of the throne of God."[15] Because Jesus was willing to die, He was blessed by God with a position of power and authority at His right hand.

DEATH PRODUCES BLESSING

As Jesus explained these things to His disciples, did their hearts sink and their hopes of earthly glory and material blessings fade? Did their faces reflect the bursting of their emotional bubble as they looked at Jesus with crestfallen countenances, resigned to what they foresaw as the misery and drudgery and poverty of discipleship?

Sensing that their keen disappointment might have brought them to such despair they would leave Him at this critical time, Jesus reiterated, "Whoever serves me must follow me" . . . and He was going to the cross (12:26). He didn't back down or water down or trim down even a shred of the truth He had just spoken. But included in their "following" Him was a threefold promise of blessing.

The Blessing of His Purpose

As I go through life, sometimes my eyes involuntarily dart to people in front of me—on the TV screen I am watching, or on the pages of the newspaper or magazine I am reading, or in an audience to which I am speaking. And just for a moment, as I contemplate the accomplishments of someone else, I

65

wonder, *What if . . . ?* Almost immediately I am reminded that I have a unique purpose in life that God has given me. I could spend a lifetime trying to make His purpose for someone else fit me, but I would wear myself out, and in the end it would be a waste of time.

Recently I was invited to address a group of professional women golfers the night before the U.S. Women's Open. I was struck by the intensity of their focus as they pursued their goal of competing in and winning the golf tournament. Their entire lives, including diet, schedules, activities, friendships, and material resources, revolved around their one purpose—of being the best golfers they could be. I told them I also had a similar sense of purpose that dictated where I went, how I spent my time and money, what I said and did, and who I interacted with. For approximately the past twenty-five years, I have nailed down what I believe to be God's purpose for my life, and I have sought to achieve it. Simply stated, it is to increasingly grow in my personal knowledge of God as I follow Him in a life of faith.

I want to know God today better than I knew Him yesterday. I want to know Him better next year than I do this year. I want to know Him until one day, like Abraham, God refers to me as His friend! To work out that purpose requires hours spent in reading and studying His Word as well as in meditating on how it applies to me. I then have to work out on the anvil of my own experience what His Word has said, which involves obedience, service, and sacrifice. I don't obey Him, or serve Him, or sacrifice for Him because I have to, but because I want to know Him, and that's the avenue He's laid out before me. With all my heart, I am just following Jesus. As a result, I am blessed with a deep sense of fulfillment and satisfaction and eternal significance, as well as with His presence in my life.

The Blessing of His Presence

Jesus added a brilliant silver lining to the dark cloud of His principle about death. He encouraged His disciples by promising, "where I am, my servant also will be" (12:26). There is nothing in this world that I desire more than the presence of Jesus in my life.

Nothing . . .

> not houses or honors or health,
> not cars or careers or children,
> not vacations or victories or vitality,
> not money or marriage or ministry,
> not fame or family or freedom,
> not promotion or pleasures or position,
> not strength or success,
> not gifts or gold,
> not ability or achievement,
> not even love or life itself.

Nothing!

What would it be like not to have Christ in your life? I think that it would be hell—literally. Praise God that you and I can be where Jesus is—now, and for all eternity—because He lives within us and has promised that He will never leave us nor forsake us![16]

When your parents forsake you through death or abandonment, or your spouse forsakes you through divorce, you have His presence.[17]

When the fire of adversity increases in intensity, you have His presence.[18]

When even other church members criticize your personal testimony, you have His presence.[19]

When you are overwhelmed by burdens or depression, you have His presence.[20]

When you are isolated from those you love and cut off from people, you have His presence.[21]

When you and I follow Jesus, He promises that we will be where He is. And there is not one place in the entire universe, visible or invisible, where He is not! What a blessing!

The Blessing of His Pleasure

How the heavenly Father must shake His head and smile ruefully at His children! We hold so tightly to things we can see and hear and taste and feel and smell right here and now, when all along, He is planning to give us things that "no eye has seen, no ear has heard, no mind has conceived what God has prepared for those who love him."[22] His blessings for us are going to be way beyond our wildest imaginations.

One of the pictures in John Bunyan's *Pilgrim's Progress* is of a man bending double from his waist, sorting through a can of garbage, carefully extracting the little bits of tinsel he finds there. Behind him is standing an angel who is offering him a solid gold crown studded with precious jewels, but the man is so engrossed in the garbage he never notices the angel.

Perhaps the blessing I live for the most is simply the blessing of knowing that my heavenly Father is pleased with me. Jesus added the final "jewel" to the crown He was offering His disciples when He promised, "Whoever serves me must follow me; and where I am, my servant also will be. My Father will honor the one who serves me" (12:26). When Jesus says we will be with Him where He is, *where will He be?* He will be in heaven, at the Father's right hand! The disciples had been disappointed that they would not rule with Jesus in an earthly kingdom, yet here He was promising them a place of honor in a universal kingdom![23]

If for no other reason, because of our love for His Son,[24]

our obedience to His Son,[25]

our faith in His Son,[26]

and our service to His Son,[27]

the Father loves us, accepts us, takes pleasure in us, and will one day honor us.

When we get to heaven, will you and I be ashamed of our preoccupation with "garbage" in this life—garbage that prevented us from dying to our desire for it, turning around, leaving it all behind, and reaching out for what God wanted to give us?[28] Why is it that we seem to cling so tightly to what we want, and in the process lose what God wants us to have? God wants us to have power and blessing and glory. But you don't obtain it by *adding* Jesus to your life—He has to *be* your life!

DEATH PRODUCES GLORY

Jesus gave His disciples a rare glimpse into His own personal, agonizing struggle and the anguish of His own soul as He anticipated the cross. By encouraging His disciples with the promise of blessings that would be theirs through dying to self, He was not implying death would be easy. On the contrary, He revealed, "Now my heart is troubled, and what shall I say? 'Father, save me from this hour'? No, it was for this very reason I came to this hour. Father, glorify your name!'" (12:27–28).

The Hebrew word He used for "trouble" is a strong one and implies horror. The thought of the pain and humiliation and separation from His Father that was coming was one that caused Him later in Gethsemane to so wrestle with God's will that He sweat as though it were great drops of blood. The struggle alone brought Him to a near-death experience. God had to send an angel to restore a measure of His strength so that He could make it through the final hours of trial and crucifixion.[29] Jesus fully understands the dread of dying! Yet He focused beyond His death to the glory that was to come.

When you are horrified by the thought of risking your reputation,

or denying your dreams,
or sacrificing your success,
or giving up your goals,
or changing your commitments,
or letting go,
or laying down,
or leaving behind

. . . *anything you want* in order to embrace what *He wants*, remember the glory to come!

The *glory* of His power and blessing and honor and wisdom and strength—fully![30]

The *glory* of a character that reflects His—perfectly![31]

The *glory* of other people's lives transformed by the Gospel—totally![32]

The *glory* of His commendation—personally![33]

The *glory* of a heavenly Home—literally![34]

The *glory* of reigning with Him—eternally![35]

Almost in the same breath with which Jesus questioned whether or not He should ask the Father to save Him from the cross, He answered Himself by declaring He had been born to die! Instead of shrinking from the cross, He embraced it as He exulted, "Father, glorify your name!" (12:28).

The disciples as well as others had jammed around Jesus to listen to what

He had to say. All around them Jerusalem was teeming with pilgrims who had come for Passover, bringing with them crying children, braying donkeys, shouting vendors, and the myriad sounds that accompany any holiday crowd. Suddenly the rumbling, resonating, thunderous sound of a single Voice drowned out every other sound in the city! It was as though a giant megaphone or the high-tech speakers to some rock star's sound equipment were turned up to full volume, as Someone immediately answered Jesus' prayer: "I have glorified it, and will glorify it again" (12:28).

Chills must have run up and down the spines of the bystanders as they crouched in fear, looking around and above them for the source of the Voice. Some people rationalized that it was thunder. Some were bold enough to guess it was an angel. But Jesus knew! It was His Father's Voice! The eternal God Himself had leaned out of heaven to commend and encourage His only Son.[36] What unspeakable joy must have swept through His entire being, not only because of the audible sound of the beloved Voice, but because of the tangible expression of pleasure in Who He was and all He was doing and what He was about to accomplish!

Just as Jesus had sought to encourage His own disciples who had recoiled from the thought of His dying, so His Father caused His own spirit to soar in the midst of the encroaching horror of the cross. And what a resounding affirmation His Father's Voice must have been to all those who had ears to hear! It gave confirmation to the disciples and the surrounding crowd of the victory that would be won through His death.

DEATH PRODUCES VICTORY

Has the Devil got you down? Are you feeling depressed by the way he has twisted the truth today and exchanged it for a lie so that . . .

Abomination is applauded as an alternate lifestyle?
Murder is claimed as our right to choose?
Ridicule of truth is tolerated as moral pluralism?
Worship of other gods is called multiculturalism?
Exploitation of the poor is called the lottery?
Children are spoiled in the name of self-esteem?

Abuse of power is called political savvy?

Profanity and obscenity are protected as freedoms of expression?

Pornography is honored as art?[37]

How can the devil be overcome? Do you think that the way to overcome him is to get more involved in politics?[38] Or has he convinced you he is so powerfully entrenched in our society that he cannot be overcome? That he has won the victory over righteousness and truthfulness and goodness and holiness?

Are you feeling defeated personally . . .

      by temptation he dangles in front of your eyes?

        by doubts he sows in your mind?

          by division he drives between you and others?

        by dead ends he paints over your future?

      by memories he haunts you with in the night?

    by depression he blackens you with in the morning?

by death or by drugs or by disease or by discouragement or disappointment?

How have you sought to overcome him? Are you trying to gain the victory through pills, alcohol, therapy, or by just pretending he doesn't exist? Are you rationalizing evidence of his activity in your life by calling it something else? Are you simply resigned to living in defeat?

Then there is resounding good news for you! Jesus, speaking of His death on the cross, gave not only the shout of victory but the secret to victory when He proclaimed, "Now is the time for judgment on this world; now the prince of this world will be driven out. But I, when I am lifted up from the earth, will draw all men to myself" (12:31–32).

The key to victory over the "prince of this world," the devil, is the cross!

As the prince of this world seems to exercise total authority over our culture and our society, I am convinced victory lies in the Gospel of Jesus Christ. The devil will be defeated when men and women come into a right relationship with God through faith in Jesus Christ and His atoning work at the cross. Once they are in a right relationship with God, their relationships with others will begin to be set right, even as they themselves experience their own character being conformed to His image.

This victory, not only in our own lives, but through us in the lives of others, is illustrated by one of my favorite stories:[39]

An old Gypsy woman who was wandering through Eastern Europe happened to pass by an open doorway to an ordinary-looking building in a little village. From within the building came the sound of people singing. Out of curiosity, the old woman stepped inside the doorway and into a church service that was in progress. Drawn by the sound of the music, she stayed and heard the Gospel message of God's love and forgiveness extended to all through His Son, Jesus. The old woman's heart was touched, and she responded at the end of the service by slipping up to the front of the crowded room in order to speak with the pastor. Sensing her need, he prayed with her and led her to a personal relationship with God through faith in Jesus Christ as her own Savior and Lord.

The old Gypsy, who had been a member of a rejected minority in society, was so thrilled by God's love and acceptance of her that she immediately went out into the street and told everyone, "God loves you." She told those who passed her by, "God loves you." She told the shopkeepers in the stores, "God loves you."

One day soon after her experience with God, she walked passed the train station where two drunken men were lounging. Their shoulders slumped, cigarettes dangled from their lips, and their entire expression was of such dejected hopelessness that the old woman walked over and repeated what she had been tirelessly telling everyone else, "God loves you." One of the drunks responded by slapping her across the face. As the woman recovered from the emotional shock as well as the physical pain, she blurted out, "God loves you, and I forgive you." The drunk slapped her again. Again her response was, "God loves you, and I forgive you." The drunk slapped her again. *Again* her response was, "God loves you, and I forgive you." This scene was repeated until in the end, the woman lay bloodied and senseless on the ground, and the two drunken men ambled off.

Christians in the town heard what had happened to the old woman, and they took her in. For three months she was nursed and fed and cared for until finally her health and strength were restored. She moved into a little room in a dilapidated building. Once again she was on her own, telling everyone of God's love. A year went by, and everyone forgot the ugly incident at the train station.

One day, the old woman heard a knock on her door. When she opened the door, she saw a man standing on the narrow sidewalk. He asked her if she remembered him.

She shook her head—no.

"Do you remember a year ago when you told two drunks at the train station that God loves them?"

"Yes," she replied.

"Well," the man continued, "I am the drunk who slapped you and left you for dead. But for weeks and months afterward, what you said to me haunted me. I could not get out of my mind your words that God loved me and you forgave me. So I found someone who could tell me about God. And I told God I was sorry and He forgave me. I have become a Christian because of what you said. And I've been looking for you ever since, because I want to say I'm sorry and ask you to forgive me, too."

Because they lived in a repressive society, the old woman was alarmed, thinking perhaps this man was a spy for the secret police. So to prove the truth of his claim, she demanded that he kneel down on the public sidewalk and pray, knowing that no KGB agent would ever do such a thing. The man immediately dropped to his knees and prayed, thanking God for His love and mercy and grace. When he got up from his knees, he and the old woman embraced!

Dying to her own feelings of anger, dying to her own desire for retaliation, dying to herself simply because she had been to the cross where Jesus had died for her, this old woman was victorious!

Are you willing to pay the price for real victory? And power? And blessing? And glory? Then would you pray simply, *Dear God, please give me MORE of Your death in my life?*

IN THE SPRING OF 1986, I began planning for a July trip to a conference in Amsterdam, the Netherlands. I worked to coordinate my schedule with that of a friend and her family so that following the conference we could spend four days together touring Germany. Since two of my children, accompanied by a friend of theirs, would be working as volunteers in the conference, I had also planned to take them on a sightseeing excursion through the Black Forest.

My children and their friend left for Amsterdam three weeks before I did because they had preparatory work to do on the conference. Before they left, my husband gave them each some spending money along with instructions to save it for the time in Germany following the conference when we would have time to relax and have fun.

The conference was everything the organizers and participants had hoped for—and more. I was thoroughly blessed by the variety of sessions and the interaction with people from every part of the globe. From time to time I would see my children and their friend happily busy in their various roles. I would give them a quick hug or wave, telling myself there would be time later as we relaxed in Germany to hear all about their experience.

The day before we were to leave for Germany, on the last day of the conference, I was in my hotel room preparing for the closing service while my daughter Morrow took a nap. When the phone rang, I answered it and heard my friend's voice say, "Anne, my husband, his parents, our friends, and I have decided to take off for Switzerland. We will meet you at the airport here in Amsterdam when we go back to New York on Thursday. I'm sorry this is different than what we planned, but I may never get another opportunity to go to Switzerland." Then she hung up.

I was stunned! It took a few minutes for what she had said to sink in! When it finally did, I was hurt and angry! I wanted to call her back and say she couldn't do this; she had made a commitment, and I was going to hold her to it!

But I didn't pick up the phone. Instead, I got down on my knees and cried. I knew she loved Switzerland, and I was genuinely glad for her to be able to go. It was obvious I wasn't included in the new plans and couldn't have afforded Switzerland even if it had been offered. But I didn't feel confident enough to drive through Germany with three kids by myself either. So I was stuck in Amsterdam with three teenagers for four days—three young people to whom I had promised a very special trip! With tears splashing down my face, I poured it all out before the Lord, words and fears gushing out in a torrent of emotion: "I have been serving You, and I get left like this? What am I going to do? The conference ends tonight—everyone is leaving—our hotel reservations end in the morning—this is peak tourist season with no rooms available in any respectable hotel—I can't change the plane tickets back to the States or I'll be penalized more than I can pay—I can't even get around in Amsterdam with all the bicycles on the road—I don't speak the language—this is the drug capital of Europe—it's not safe for vulnerable people like me. What am I going to do? I am helpless! Stranded in Amsterdam! With three children! God, all I have is You!" At that moment, I consciously let go and chose to die to my anger, my desires, my fears, my hurt, and just submit it all to God.

Exhausted and emotionally spent, I finally stopped praying. I remained kneeling on the floor, quietly sniffling in my despair, my head resting on the edge of the bed where Morrow continued to sleep. In the stillness of the room, inaudibly but unmistakably these words formed clearly in my mind, "Anne, I am going to do for you more abundantly than you can even think to ask."[40] Everything in me froze. I listened intently. Morrow's regular breathing let me know she still slept, the windows and door were shut, no one else was around, the TV and radio were off, yet I knew I had "heard" a voice. God had spoken. I knew it as surely as if He had been visibly sitting there in the room. Instead of bowing my head in wonder and awe, I had the audacity to respond, respectfully, but skeptically, "Well . . . let's just see!"

I was determined not to tell anyone about our situation. If I had heard God's voice, and He was going to do something wonderful, He didn't need anyone's help.

When Morrow woke up, I told her about my friend's call because it meant we would not be going to Germany. When she burst into angry tears, I put my arms around her and wept all over again. I confided in her the verse that I believed God had given me. I encouraged her to trust Him with me to do more abundantly than we could even think to ask, but in my heart I was saying, "Lord, how can You stand to have her hurt like this? I'm counting on You to come through."

We went to the meeting that night, saying nothing about our abrupt change in plans. After the service, I broke the news to my son, Jonathan, and his friend. I will never forget his friend standing there, hands blackened from working the television cables, tired, sweaty, tears filling his eyes, saying, "Mrs. Lotz, that's all right. There's plenty of work around here to do. I will just get a job."

For four days? I wanted to scream! But at the same time, I was so proud of both guys who I knew were extremely disappointed yet were so manly and mature in their responses. Again, in my heart, I was crying, "Lord, do You see that? Even if I don't deserve Your help, how can You resist helping them?"

My responsibilities in the conference center were not completed until 11:30 P.M. that evening. Since my ride had long gone, Morrow and I had to walk back to the hotel in the rain. We were famished as we hadn't had a chance to eat supper, so we went into the dining room. Seated at a long table were my friend and her husband, along with others, including a stranger I had met briefly the day before. They motioned for us to join them. We sat down at the table, hungry, tired, depressed, and feeling more and more helpless and hopeless as time was running out.

As we conversed over dinner, the stranger turned to me and asked, "Anne, when are you going to New York?" Almost choking at the reminder of my uncertain immediate future, I replied tersely, "Thursday."

"What are you going to do between now and then?" Hoping that he did not notice that I was fighting back tears, I answered, "I'm not sure. My plans have suddenly changed." Then I quickly switched the subject and continued with the conversation at the table.

The stranger interrupted the conversation. "Anne, why don't you come to London?" Refusing to even contemplate something so ludicrous, I responded, "There are many reasons why I cannot go to London." But the stranger persisted, "Anne, why don't you come to London? We're having a wedding! Prince Andrew is marrying Lady Sarah! Come on. You'll have a good time."

In my heart, I was starting to feel very resentful and hurt. In my spirit, I started complaining, "Lord, I can't go to Germany, I can't go to Switzerland, and now I can't go to London. I want to know what I can do. And by the way, it's past midnight. You're running out of time. If You're going to do something, You better do it quickly. Check-out time is 11:00 A.M.! Then I'm going to be on the street with three kids!" Outwardly I answered in what I hoped

76

was a frosty, you-are-beginning-to-irritate-me tone of voice, "I'm sorry, but I just can't go to London."

Would you believe it! The stranger wasn't put off in the least! "Anne, tell me exactly why you can't go to London."

I was tired, stressed, and beginning to get angry. So in a voice that was meant to put an end to the subject, I looked him square in the eye, lifted my chin, and replied firmly, "I will give you three good reasons I am not going to London: Number one, I do not have the money. I am responsible for three children, and I cannot possibly afford the round-trip plane fares, hotels, and meals. Number two, as a woman traveling with three children, I would not feel comfortable roaming about in a strange country even if I had the money." With eyes flashing, I saved the most logical reason for last: "Number three, I am too tired to even think about it." Then I deliberately turned away from him and forced myself into the conversation at the other end of the table.

A few minutes later, the stranger boldly confronted me once again. "Anne, I will take care of the first two reasons if you take care of the third." Not comprehending in the least what he was saying, I just looked as aloof as possible and said, *"What?"*

He answered, "I will have four prepaid plane tickets at the airport for you in the morning. You will fly to London. I will have my chauffeur-driven private car meet you at the airport. You will stay in my club, two blocks from Buckingham Palace. It's a club . . . you do not belong . . . so you cannot pay for anything. I will give you and your children all the spending money you need."

As I stared at him, what he was saying began to sink in! I was incredulous! My irritation began to melt, and my heart was genuinely touched by his obvious sensitivity and generous offer. So in a softer, gentler voice, I explained I could never accept such a gift from a stranger.

To this day, I get chills when I think of what he said next. I would not have been any more shocked if he had suddenly sprouted wings! This stranger looked me clearly in the eye and said, *"Anne, the Lord is wanting to do for you more abundantly than you could even think to ask!"*

Praise God! We went to London! . . . And I learned a never-to-be-forgotten lesson—that *power* and *blessing* and *glory* and *victory* and *life come from death!*

5

MORE of
His Dirt on My Hands

John 13:1–17

LITTLE HOPE LAUREN GUTHRIE was ushered into the world on Monday, November 23, 1998, cushioned in the loving prayers and happy plans of her father and mother and brother. Having been eagerly anticipated, she was tenderly embraced as a treasured blessing from God. Within moments of her birth, however, the doctor expressed concern over several physical problems he detected, including clubfeet and an inability to suck. His medical alarm was confirmed when a battery of tests determined that Baby Hope had Zellweger syndrome, an extremely unique metabolic disorder. Zellweger syndrome is rare, and it is also relentless; it rarely allows its victims to live more than twelve months.

On June 9, 1999, Hope Lauren Guthrie was once again tenderly embraced, this time by the One Who had created her as He welcomed her to her heavenly Home. For those of us who were privileged to observe her brief breath of life on earth, we were left with tears in our eyes and pain in our hearts and questions on our minds.

Even though the tears have dried and time will ease the pain, many of the questions will not be totally resolved until we get to heaven. So the aftermath has been a time to just trust Jesus.

Shattering the delicate balance of faith and feelings during this trusting time was the news that Hope's parents, Nancy and David Guthrie, were expecting another baby! In spite of medical procedures that were taken in order to ensure Nancy would never again become pregnant, she was! Just as when God gave Hannah many sons and daughters to make up for the loss of Samuel, many friends felt the new baby was a gift from God to David and Nancy to make up for the pain of losing little Hope[1]—until the news came that the new baby also had Zellweger syndrome![2]

I talked with Nancy the week before her baby was due to be born. Her weary voice still expressed an unshakeable faith in a loving God, but the horror of what she was about to face had descended upon her. Almost unbearable was the fear of just how badly the baby would be disabled, the dread of the twenty-four-hour care for a newborn who could not suck or function normally, and the hopelessness of knowing that in the end their baby would die and be laid to rest in the tiny little cemetery plot next to Hope.

Yet in the midst of that suffocating nightmare, Nancy and David were focused on being able to minister to their family during the coming weeks. With all her heart, Nancy desired that in every word and deed and thought and detail, God would be glorified! So she asked me to pray for her loving patience and thoughtful sensitivity within the home. She was asking me to pray for more of His dirt on her hands!

And just what is His dirt on our hands? It's . . .

serving others when we need to be served,

praying for others when we need to be prayed for,

helping others when we need help,

ministering to others when we need to be ministered to,

giving to others when we feel like keeping,

hurting with others when our own hurt can't be spoken,

and doing it all willingly, humbly, obediently, and gladly . . . for Him!

When you are overwhelmed with problems and pain and pressures, when you're facing the most terrifying challenge of your life, do you look for opportunities to get involved in the needs of others? *No?* What do you do? Do you throw a pity party and invite others to come? And do you have a lot of well-meaning "partygoers" who give you cheap sympathy and, in the process, increase your pain and prolong your suffering and deepen your despair, because the focus remains on you and your needs? Then it's time for you to stop it. Call off the party, thank the revelers for caring as you show them the door, then drop to your knees and cry out to God, *Please, just give me MORE of Your dirt on my hands!*

Deliberately changing our focus from ourselves to Him and to others is a wonderfully effective way to overcome the private battle we are in. Getting our hands "dirty" is poignantly illustrated by Jesus' own example on the night He was betrayed. His teaching had increasingly polarized the general public into three main groups—those who adamantly refused to believe His claim to be the Son of God in spite of their firsthand knowledge of His miracles, those who believed in Him but kept their faith hidden out of fear of what others would think, and those who were so eaten up with jealousy and hate they were actively plotting His death.[3] And in the midst of this tremendous stress and tension, on the Thursday evening before His crucifixion on Friday, Jesus took His disciples and retreated into an upstairs room somewhere in Jerusalem where *He served them.*[4] Their dirt was on His hands . . .

IN SERVICE OFFERED WILLINGLY

It was springtime, "just before the Passover Feast" (13:1). The evening air would have been pleasantly balmy as the disciples noisily climbed the outside steps that led to the rooftop porch and upper room of the nondescript, inner-city building. The early spring rains would have turned the dust of Palestine into miry mud several inches deep on the roads of the countryside and even on the streets of Jerusalem. The dust and mud from the disciples' journey easily penetrated their open sandals and caked their feet with grime, so it was necessary to have their feet washed before entering for dinner because again, their dinner setting would be typical of the East. Instead of sitting upright on chairs around a table with their feet on the floor as is customary today in the West, these men would be reclining around the table. Their head and shoulders would lean in toward the table with their legs and feet stretched out behind or beside them. Since all would sit at floor level, it was possible for someone's feet to be very close to the face of the person sitting next to him.

As the disciples reached the small porch of the upper room, they must have looked around for the customary slave with a basin of water and a towel who would wash their filthy feet before they went inside. They easily spotted the basin of water and the clean towel, but there was no slave present to do the washing. They would have been well aware of the regulations of their day, which stipulated that the disciples of a rabbi were permitted to perform any task for their master except one—they were not to loosen his sandals or wash his feet as it was considered too degrading.

Without a slave to carry out this very menial but necessary task, the disciples must have begun to argue as to who would do it. With each one looking expectantly at the person next to him, did they one by one reject the humiliation of taking on the servant's role?

"Bartholomew, you do it."

"Are you kidding? That's not my job!"

"Peter, what about you?"

"Never! I'm the leader of this group!"

"Hey! Don't even look at me! I'm Peter's brother!"

"Don't push me, buddy! Remember! I'm the son of thunder!"

Perhaps Judas just curled his lip at the others and haughtily walked inside, tracking mud all the way to his place at the table.

The sound of their voices would have carried easily on the evening air as their bantering became belligerent and their conversational tone became forceful. Even a casual listener could have detected that a serious argument was in full swing. The tension that so permeated the atmosphere surrounding Jesus in public on the streets now permeated this very private, intimate setting where He had planned to confide His heartfelt last words to His disciples. With the discerning wisdom that comes from being totally in tune with God, "Jesus knew that the time had come for him to leave this world and go to the Father" (13:1).

No one can ever fathom the unprecedented pressure and emotional stress that Jesus was under that Thursday night. He knew His time had come—time to be betrayed, time to be arrested, time to be tried, tortured, mocked, blasphemed, and finally, time to be crucified. Time to offer Himself as the sacrificial Lamb for the sin of the world. Time to die. Time to be buried. Time to rise from the dead and ascend back to His Father in heaven. Time to be glorified as not only the Son of Man in His humanity but as the Son of God in His deity. Time to take up again His rightful place on the throne at the center of the universe. It was *time,* and Jesus was fully aware of the nightmare that would begin unfolding within hours—and the glory that would ultimately be His.

It's hard to imagine a worse time to think of serving others. How could He even consider getting involved in the needs of others when His own needs were so enormous and immediate?

What enormous needs do you have? What crisis are you facing? As a result, have you withdrawn from Christian activities? Have you even ceased going to church? Are you ignorant of the needs of those around you—even those within your own home—because you are so focused on your own needs? Isn't it amazing how pain and pressure and problems can so totally preoccupy our attention that they make even the best of us completely self-centered? If someone suggested to you that you help another person in need, would you respond harshly with a scowling face, "I couldn't possibly. You have no idea what I'm going through myself." Like me, you may need reminding that serving Jesus by serving others when it's not convenient to do so is one secret to overcoming the pain and pressures and problems in our own lives.

When It's Not Convenient

There could not have been a more inconvenient time for Jesus to get involved in serving others, but He did. In what way are you involved in meeting the needs of others? You're not involved? Why? Are you waiting for a more convenient time? When do you think that will be?

When you have more money?

more free time?

more energy?

When you have better health?

a better paying job?

a better church?

When you are happier?

thinner?

stronger?

When you get out of school?

83

When you get married?

When you start a family?

When your children go off to school?

When your children get married and leave home?

When your spouse retires?

From experience, I know that there will never be a convenient time to serve the Lord. We have to make the decision to just do it—now. That's what His dirt is—service offered willingly when it's not convenient.

If ever there was a time when

Jesus should have had His personal needs met,

If ever there was a time when

Jesus should have been tenderly comforted and lovingly cared for,

If ever there was a time when

Jesus should have had the sympathetic ear of His friends,

If ever there was a time when

Jesus should have been prayed for,

If ever there was a time when

Jesus should have been served,

If ever there was a time when

His dirt should have been on the hands of His disciples,

it was at *this time!*

If Jesus had crawled off to be by Himself saying He had a headache . . .

If Jesus had curled up into a fetal position, whimpering pitifully . . .

If Jesus had sat alone, staring off into space, withdrawn in preoccupied silence . . .

If Jesus had wept uncontrollably as He poured out His fears in an emotional flood . . .

we would all have understood! The gut-wrenching sorrow of leaving His disciples and the encroaching horror of the cross must have descended on Him like a heavy, clinging, smothering, loathsome wet blanket.

Little Hope Guthrie's mother and father have had a personal glimpse of that same oppressive emotional blackness. In a minuscule shadow of what they have experienced, I have felt that same sense of being sucked into a swirling black abyss on the night before one of our Just Give Me Jesus revivals, or the night before I leave home for a multi-week international trip, or the night before surgery. My stomach becomes so nauseated I can't eat, and my chest feels so heavy I feel that I can't breathe. The dread of the spiritual battle, the dread of the separation from loved ones, the dread of the physical suffering can be so overpowering that I almost lose the ability to function. So not in my wildest imagination can I understand how Jesus was not only able to function on the night before the cross but was able to willingly serve His disciples.

In serving them when He "knew that the time had come," Jesus taught His disciples a timeless principle that is a secret to overcoming emotional pain. The principle is to get more of His dirt on your hands. It sounds incredible, doesn't it? A directive to extend tender, loving care to others just when you and I need it ourselves doesn't seem fair. Doesn't seem right. Doesn't seem even plausible. And yet, "having loved his own who were in the world, he now showed them the full extent of his love" by serving them when it wasn't convenient! (13:1).

While sitting at my computer writing this very chapter, I received a telephone call from a woman whose past year had been filled with one tragedy and crisis after another. She has lived with haunting memories and heartache and emotional pain all of her life, but problems and pressures have greatly intensified in recent months. She currently is wrestling with a physical disorder that at times erases her memory so completely she has total amnesia. She is therefore forbidden to drive a car and is required to take daily medication that makes her nauseated and dizzy. There could not be a more inconvenient time in her life to serve others. Yet that's exactly what she is doing!

She was calling to share with me the fact that she had opened her lovely home for a Bible study, using our video series *The Vision of His Glory*. I could hear the joyous lilt in her voice as she described the excitement of the women who had come for the first time and were learning how to read God's Word in order to hear His voice speak to them personally through the pages of their Bibles. She related how her home had been filled with the sound of their chatter as they discussed the Scripture passage and what it meant to them. At the conclusion of the study, when the ladies departed for the night, she praised God for the blessing of having His dirt on her hands!

My friend's service mirrored our Lord's on the same night He was betrayed. It was something that the young disciple John never forgot. Looking back on that night, John must have recalled the tender tone of His voice, the loving look on His face, the gentle grace of His gestures, the piercing passion in His eyes, the princely posture of His person, and been awe-struck that Jesus had expressed His love for His disciples to the utmost degree of which He was capable—*through serving them!*—at a time when His own needs were overwhelming and through service that was not appreciated by all.

When It's Not Commended

As John recalled that night, he distinctly remembered that "the evening meal was being served, and the devil had already prompted Judas Iscariot, son of Simon, to betray Jesus" (13:2). Judas was present! Judas was in the midst of those who had withdrawn to this quiet place to be alone with Jesus the night before He was crucified!

Do you remember Judas? He had been handpicked by Jesus to be one of His disciples. He had been given the special responsibility of looking after the disciples' financial affairs. He had been in the boat when Jesus walked on the water. He had helped to serve five loaves and two fish to five thousand people, constantly passing the baskets until everyone was filled. He had seen the lepers cleansed, the blind given sight, the deaf hear, the lame walk. He had witnessed the resurrection of Lazarus!

But increasingly Judas had comprehended, regardless of Who He said He was and what He had done to validate His claim, that Jesus was not going to seize power and rule the world—not this time. Instead of lording it over people to impress them with His superiority and asserting His power to make them cringe in submission and flashing miracles to dazzle them with His greatness, Jesus served others-and helped others-and taught others-and thought of others-and cared for others. Judas seemed to despise the humility and meekness in Jesus that was a hallmark of His greatness. So Judas was deeply disillusioned. Jesus just wasn't what he had expected or wanted.

To serve those you love and who love you while you're in the midst of personal problems and pain and pressures is certainly a labor of love. But the full extent of our Lord's love was demonstrated when—facing the unparalleled horror of the cross—He served even the one who despised Him and sneered contemptuously at Him and quietly plotted with His enemies to kill Him.

Is that one reason you're all wrapped up in your own problems and pain? Because you know that those in your home or neighborhood or church or school wouldn't appreciate your service anyway, so why bother? They are too young, too elderly, too poor, too hardened, too lost to really care. Maybe there's even the good possibility that your efforts to get involved in meeting the needs of someone else, instead of being commended, would provoke criticism or ostracism or sarcasm. It just seems to be safer and more comfortable to withdraw into your own world of woe.

With the late afternoon sun dipping down below the western hills, the gloom of the upstairs room would have been relieved by smoking torches fixed in brackets on the stone walls of the room. The room itself had been prepared for the evening meal with a long, low table that had been set with food, including wine and freshly baked bread.

As the disciples gathered around the table, John sat next to Jesus. Peter was nearby.

Judas had positioned himself closely enough to Jesus to privately exchange words with Him. But like a rattlesnake poised for the perfect opportunity to strike, Judas was ready at a moment's notice to betray Him.

It was at this very moment, in the shadow of the cross, that Jesus not only knew Judas and His other disciples inside and out, He was also fully aware of Who He truly was. Without any doubt, He "knew that the Father had put all things under his power, and that he had come from God and was returning to God" (13:3). It was with the full knowledge of His own exalted position and power and glory and greatness and authority that He served His disciples. Such service didn't seem compatible with One Who is the Son of God, the Messiah, the King of Kings and the Lord of Lords! Yet Jesus demonstrated the full extent of His love by serving His disciples willingly when it was not convenient, when it was not commended, and when it was not compatible with His true position.

When It's Not Compatible

What position do you hold? Are you the president of the company?

the chairman of the board?

the pastor of the church?

the parent of the family?

the manager of the office?

the officer of the bank?

the winner of the pageant?

the star of the show?

the champion of the game?

the senior partner in the firm?

the chief surgeon in the hospital?

the best-selling author of the book?

What opinion do you have of yourself? Because of the lofty position you hold, at least in your own eyes, what service do you think is degrading and "beneath" you?

Washing dishes?

Cleaning toilets?

Changing diapers?

Mowing grass?

Emptying trash?

Making coffee?

Fixing breakfast?

Baby-sitting children?

Visiting prisoners?

The apostle Paul, writing from a Roman prison cell, exhorted you and me to have the same attitude of Jesus, "Who, being in very nature God, did not consider equality with God something to be grasped, but made himself nothing, taking the very nature of a servant, being made in human likeness. And being found in appearance as a man, he humbled himself and became obedient to death—even death on a cross! Therefore God exalted him to the highest place."[5] How repulsive and prideful to think anything—any job, any person, any position, any service, any task, any place—is beneath you and me when Jesus, Lord of glory, Creator of the universe, left heaven's throne and took upon Himself the form of a servant! The way up is down! *Please!* Just give me more of His dirt on My hands through service that's offered willingly . . . *and humbly!*

IN SERVICE OFFERED HUMBLY

As the dinner progressed, so did the argument that the disciples had been engaged in since arriving in the upstairs room.[6] Instead of the pleasant clatter of cutlery and the soft murmur of beloved voices and the comfortable laughter of good friends, the atmosphere of our Lord's last supper with His disciples was tense and angry. He had been eagerly anticipating the joy of sharing this particular meal with them. It would be the last time the Passover was celebrated from the Old Testament side of the cross.[7] But, like someone slashing a priceless painting with a knife, the disciples were unwittingly slashing with their tongues the high and holy moment that should have been exceedingly treasured. They verbally jockeyed for position, each asserting he was greater than the others and therefore deserved a more prominent position in the world kingdom they believed Jesus was on the verge of establishing. "So [Jesus] got up from the meal, took off his outer clothing, and wrapped a towel around his waist. After that, he poured water into a basin and began to wash his disciples' feet, drying them with the towel that was wrapped around him" (13:4–5). Jesus humbled Himself by taking on a task that was so menial no one else would touch it! He washed the disciples' dirty feet! *He got their dirt on His hands!*

Humbled Literally by Serving

Jesus—the Messiah, the fulfillment of Old Testament prophecy, the Redeemer of Israel, the Creator of the universe, the Savior of the world, the King of Kings, the Son of God—*Jesus* quietly rose from the table, slipped off His cloak, picked up the basin and towel not one of His disciples had been willing to touch, and began washing the smelly, filthy feet of His disciples!

The discordant din of the table talk must have been suddenly silenced as all eyes were on Him. With food and drink suddenly forgotten, and harsh, prideful words frozen on angry lips, the disciples surely stared at Jesus in disbelief! When the realization of what He was doing finally hit them, their faces must have burned crimson in shame. Without one word of rebuke from Him, their hearts were stabbed with grief and remorse! What they had considered too humiliating, too degrading, too menial for men of their great self-importance to do, Jesus did! Willingly! Humbly! On the night He was betrayed!

What have you refused to do because it's just too humiliating for someone of your "position" and "importance"? Too degrading. Too menial. Have you arrogantly waited for the need to grow to such overwhelming proportions that somebody else, *anybody else,* would be pressured into doing it? Besides, it's such a dirty job and no one has *asked you* to do it.

During high school, our daughter Morrow went on a missions trip to Jamaica with a church youth group. When she returned, one of the adult leaders took me aside and told me about their arrival at the camp where the group was to be housed while they helped build a school for the deaf. Instead of the individual cottages they were expecting to stay in, he described one large room with two outhouses in the back. He was horrified to realize this was where his group would be living for ten days! As he surveyed the place, it was obvious that the expanse of concrete floor in the main room needed to be swept and scrubbed before they could unroll their sleeping bags. But he said he was at a total loss as to what to do about the outhouses in the backyard! Without even investigating, he knew they were filthy because the stench coming from them was overpowering!

The leader looked at me intently as he reflected on what then transpired. He said he was surrounded by three dozen pairs of incredulous teenage eyes all focused directly on him. For the first time since embarking on the trip, every mouth was silent, every face attentive as the young volunteers waited to see what he would do. He cleared his throat then asked feebly if anyone would volunteer to clean the outhouses. The young people remained frozen in place as though what he had said had not even registered on their conscious minds. As he opened his mouth to repeat his request more forcefully, Morrow's hand went up. "I will," she offered.

The youth missions leader then looked at me with grudging admiration as he told me how shocked he had been. Having met Morrow for the first time the day the youth group gathered at the airport to leave for Jamaica, he had formed the opinion that she was spoiled and selfish. His opinion had been based on nothing more than an assumption that she would be that way because she came from a high-profile home, was physically beautiful and wildly popular at the public school she attended. With a sheepish apology, he confessed how wrong he had been and said that for the rest of the trip, Morrow was the one who had worked the hardest, stayed up the longest, and been willing to do the dirtiest jobs.

Even now, as I reflect on Morrow's service, I seem to hear the scrape of the water basin across the stone floor in the upper room, the sound of water being splashed on dirty feet, and the soft swish of the towel. His dirt was on her hands in service that was offered willingly and humbly.

Humbled Personally by Being Served

As Jesus approached Peter with the obvious intention of washing his feet, Peter pulled back, asking, "'Lord, are you going to wash my feet?' Jesus replied, 'You do not realize now what I am doing, but later you will understand'" (13:6–7). As Jesus bent down to pour the water over Peter's grimy feet, Peter protested proudly, "No, . . . you shall never wash my feet"(13:8).

"Never wash my feet"? Peter was not only displaying an unwillingness to trust Jesus with something he didn't understand, but he was also revealing an attitude so typical of you and me today—pridefulness. It can be a serious wound to our pride, not only to serve, but *to be served.*

For twelve years I taught a weekly Bible class of five hundred women and approximately 150 children on Wednesday mornings in my hometown. In order to better facilitate the study, I met on Monday mornings with sixty-five women who were each responsible for discipling a small group of either women or children. Because I not only taught and supervised the running of the class but also maintained my own home and family of 3 small children, I was continually overwhelmed with more to do than I seemed to have time for. So the sixty-five women quietly organized themselves into pairs who, each week, were responsible for providing an entire dinner for my family on the weeknight that seemed most stressful.

As much as I needed the help of these wonderful ladies and as deeply moved as I was by their beautiful, generous expression of loving support, the first few times the dinner was delivered I felt embarrassed. The dinner seemed to represent my failure to provide for my family myself. It called attention to the fact that I wasn't as invincible and self-sufficient as the image I wanted to portray. It clearly pointed to the fact that I was needy. With shame, I realized that my resistance was rooted in pride. From then on, each night my family sat at the table to partake of someone else's provision for us, I offered a silent prayer of praise to God and thanksgiving for the women who had sacrificed their time and effort to serve me.

But even after twelve years, it was never easy to receive that weekly offering. I never took it for granted nor accepted it casually or as something that they "owed" me for the time I invested in the class. Every week I had to consciously nail my pride to the cross and humbly acknowledge my need for their help.

Whose offer of help are you refusing for the same prideful reasons? Are you refusing to even admit that you need any help at all? God clearly commands you and me: "humble yourselves."[8] One way to obey that command is to willingly serve in menial, practical, physical ways. But obedience to that command is also expressed in a willingness to be personally served by others. Jesus took this simple truth and gave it a spiritual application.

Humbled Spiritually through Submission

As Peter defiantly resisted our Lord's service, drawing his feet up under him, Jesus patiently but firmly responded, "Unless I wash you, you have no part with me" (13:8). It was only later, after the cross, that Peter understood what Jesus meant by the spiritual symbolism of what He had done during dinner on that unforgettable Thursday evening. Jesus had given His disciples a glimpse of the humility required of Him as He had left His rightful position, not at the head of the table in the upper room, but at the right hand of the Father in heaven. He willingly stripped off, not just His outer cloak, but His robe of righteousness and was nailed to the cross in order to take up the "basin" of His own blood to wash away our sins.

What is your attitude toward the blood of Jesus shed at the cross? Like Peter, are you proudly resistant, protesting,

> *Jesus will never wash away my sin! If there is any washing that needs to be done, I'll do it myself, thank you! I'll wash my sin away with my good works. Or my church activities. Or my religion. Or the money I give to the poor. Besides, I don't think that I'm all that dirty. Everyone worries, tells white lies, and gossips. I'm not so bad. And God is loving. He understands I'm not perfect.*

God understands, all right. He understands that your pride is keeping you from humbling yourself, admitting your need, and coming to the cross for cleansing. Be still. Do you feel the penetration of Jesus' eyes on you? Listen. Do you hear Him saying lovingly but firmly, "Unless I wash you, you have no part with me!"?

Instantly, the impulsive Peter, who desperately wanted a part with Jesus, must have stuck out his feet and thrust out his hands and leaned over his head as he hastened to capitulate: "Then, Lord . . . not just my feet but my hands and my head as well!" (13:9). Instead of smiling in amusement at Peter's immediate and enthusiastic submission, Jesus must have gazed at him thoughtfully. Squatting barelegged beside the water basin with His tunic twisted about His waist, His muscular, tanned shoulders hunched over His task, the now damp towel gripped in His strong, unscarred hand, Jesus spoke quietly, but seriously: "A person who has had a bath needs only to wash his feet; his whole body is clean. And you are clean, though not every one of you" (13:10).

It was customary in Jesus' day for the people to go to common baths, similar to a public swimming pool, where they would bathe all over. However, as soon as they left the bath and walked along the streets, their feet would get dirty again. So when they arrived at their homes, it was unnecessary to have another complete bath. They only needed their feet washed of the dust and dirt they had picked up along the way. They would therefore be greeted at the outside door by a slave holding a basin of water and a towel in order to wash their feet before entering.

Jesus was explaining to Peter that once you and I have been to the cross for our complete "bath," we are clean. All of our sin—past, present, future, small, medium, large—is washed away by the blood of Jesus and we are totally, completely, permanently forgiven![9] Praise God! *But* we still sin! Our feet get dirty again! So every day we come back to the cross, not for forgiveness since we are already forgiven, but to confess our sin and be cleansed that we might maintain a right fellowship with God and with others and with ourselves.[10]

Even as Jesus explained this to Peter, I wonder if He looked straight at Judas when He qualified His statement: "You are clean, though not every one of you" (13:10). We are told He was thinking of Judas, "who was going to betray him" (13:11). Jesus knew that Judas refused to "take a bath." He refused to acknowledge his sin, humbly ask for forgiveness, and receive cleansing.

Could it be that Jesus is looking over my shoulder at you right now and saying, "You, Anne, are clean. Some of those who will read this book are not." If Jesus says you are not clean, *you are not clean,* and there's nothing you can do to cleanse yourself.

Judas was the ultimate hypocrite. He had deceived John and Peter and Andrew and Matthew and everyone. Everyone except Jesus. Yet Jesus chose Judas to be a disciple. Have you ever wondered why? Why did Jesus eat with Judas? Talk to Judas? Live with Judas? Pray with Judas? *For three years?* Maybe Jesus wanted to show you and me that Judas was what he was by his own choice. Maybe Jesus wanted to show you and me that in spite of Judas's hypocrisy and treachery, he was given chance after chance after chance. Maybe Jesus wanted to show you and me the full extent of His love—even to the end.

Are you praying for a "Judas"? If you're not, I encourage you to do so. Jesus loved Judas! And Jesus worked in his life until the end, seeking to draw him to Himself. You can be assured that Jesus loves your "Judas," too, and in answer to your prayers of faith, He will work in that person's life to draw him or her to Himself. But never forget. It's that person's free choice as to whether he or she chooses to respond.

If I had been Judas and had overheard Peter and Jesus talking, I would have been jerked upright on the inside, thinking, *If Peter needs washing, what do I need?* Like ice water hitting me in the face when Jesus said not all were clean, I would have silently exclaimed, *He knows!* Surely I would have burst out, "Lord, I'm the one who is not clean! Bathe me! Cleanse me! Wash me! I've done a dreadful thing! I've betrayed You to Your enemies! I'm so sorry! What can I do to make it right?" But Judas closed his heart to the beautiful appeal of Jesus and sat there *as Jesus washed his feet,* smugly pretending he had "bathed"!

The solemn thing about Judas was that he sat next to Peter and John and James. He looked and acted and talked just like any other genuine disciple. He was so slick no one was able to tell the difference. But Jesus knew the difference. He looked on Judas's heart and saw that although he would regret his actions, he would never repent of his sin.[11] Jesus said it would have been better if Judas had never been born.[12] *Please! Don't be a Judas!*

Are you sure you have had your "bath"? When? Can you remember that point in time when you humbly confessed to God that you are a sinner? That you are sorry and willing to repent of your sin? Did you ask Him to wash you clean with the blood of Jesus? Then you're clean! Just enjoy it! But having had a bath, are you going around with dirty feet? When was the last time you came to the cross, confessed your specific sins of the day by name, and asked for cleansing? Could it be that you have come to the Lord's table, using this book to help you eat the Bread of life, without washing your feet?

Later, as John meditated on the dialogue between Jesus and Peter, he specified that if you say you are not dirty, that you have no need for a once and for all "bath" or for daily cleansing of sin, you are deceiving yourself and the truth is not in you.[13] So right now, bow your head and ask God to bathe you if you are not sure you are completely clean. Then every day confess your sin by name, asking God to "wash your feet." John encourages us, "If we confess our sins, he is faithful and just and will forgive us our sins and purify us from all unrighteousness."[14]

It's worth noting that the Hebrew word John used for "confess" does not mean a glib acknowledgement of wrongdoing. It means to say the same thing about our sin that Jesus does. In our day, we have become professionally slick about the way we switch the labels we give sin to make sin seem less serious.

We call lying, exaggeration.

We call unbelief, worry.

We call stealing another person's reputation, gossip.

We call murder, the right to choose.

We call fornication, safe sex.

We call homosexuality, gay.

We call greed, ambition.

We call lust, adult entertainment.

We call profanity, obscenity, blasphemy, and pornography, freedom of expression.

Don't switch the labels, or you won't be cleansed. Just call sin by its rightful name and thank God for the blood of Jesus that still has the power to remove any and all stains in the wash! The entire church today needs a good foot washing![15] Don't wait one more minute! Wash your feet! It's a command that you and I are to obey.[16]

IN SERVICE OFFERED OBEDIENTLY

One by one, Jesus had circled the table and washed the feet of His disciples. Gently. Thoroughly. The deafening silence in the room was broken only by the sound of the sloshing water and the swishing towel and the strained breathing of the disciples. After Peter's outburst, no one had dared to speak. The silence was finally broken as He returned the basin to its proper place, hung up the towel, and re-dressed. "When he had finished washing their feet, he put on his clothes and returned to his place. 'Do you understand what I have done for you?'" (13:12).

Do *you* understand? Looking out at the dumbfounded expressions on the faces of His disciples, Jesus made sure they understood what He had done by giving them a good reason for following His example, explaining, "You call me 'Teacher' and 'Lord,' and rightly so, for that is what I am" (13:13).

Because of Who He Is

The first and most profound reason Jesus gave His disciples for getting His dirt on their hands through willing, humble, and obedient service was because of Who He is.

And Who is He? He is our Savior Who, after He had finished washing away our sin by His own blood on the cross, put back on His glory clothes and returned to His rightful place on the throne at the center of the universe as our risen Lord and reigning King! You and I are to serve Him by getting involved in meeting the needs of others simply because He says so! He is Lord! And while we should never forget Who He is, we should also never forget who we are!

You and I are . . .

> sinners saved,[17]
> filth cleansed,[18]
> blood bought,[19]
> captives ransomed,[20]
> prisoners freed,[21]
> spirit certified,[22]
> glory bound.[23]

We are not our own.

We belong to Him.[24]

Our lives no longer are to be lived according to what *we want* but according to what *He says*. We are His faithful servants. Jesus asked, *"Do you understand?"* Then He emphasized the importance of what He had just said by driving it home: "I tell you the truth, no servant is greater than his master, nor is a messenger greater than the one who sent him" (13:16).

How could you and I ever think of walking into the presence of Jesus with clean hands when His are dirty? Who do we think we are? Why do we think we are exempt from the dirty work when *He wasn't exempt?* And what *is* "the dirty work"? It's showing others—and Him—the full extent of our love when we are experiencing unbearable pain, unspeakable problems, and unbelievable pressures by serving them willingly, humbly, and obediently. For no other reason than because His hands are dirty, too!

The Prayer of Jabez has recently become a literary phenomenon beyond anything anyone could have foreseen.[25] It was originally uttered over three thousand years ago by a man who knew pain and pressures and problems firsthand from his earliest days. For Jabez, "the time had come" the day he was born. His heart's cry was expressed simply, "Oh, that you would bless me and enlarge my territory! Let your hand be with me, and keep me from harm so that I will be free from pain."[26] Along with that prayer was an obvious willingness to serve God in humility and obedience. "And God granted his request."[27]

Today, the prayer of Jabez is uttered by literally millions of people, many of whom recite it as a formula in order to provoke more of God's blessing. No one can dispute that God not only answered this ancient Judahite's prayer during his own lifetime but is still answering his prayer today. In his wildest dreams, Jabez could never have conceived that three thousand years after he cried out to God his prayer would be number one on the *New York Times* bestseller list! What a dramatic testimony to the truth in our cynical, skeptical age that indeed God does answer prayer! While I'm thrilled to see such widespread response in the secular world to a Biblical idea, perhaps as we celebrate this extraordinary attention we need to keep our prayers for increased blessing in proper perspective.

As Jesus and His disciples concluded their evening meal, He looked around at their solemn faces and their clean feet. With simplicity that rivals that of Jabez, Jesus put the exclamation point on His teaching: "Now that you know these things, you will be *blessed* if you *do* them" (13:17).[28] Jesus emphasized that the blessing of God in our lives is in direct proportion to our knowledge of "these things" and our willingness to humbly apply and obey them.

The blessing God wants to pour out on your life and mine is not necessarily increased wealth or problem-free health or material prosperity. And it is not obtainable by prayerfully reciting a formula as though you are rubbing Aladdin's lamp, waiting for the Divine Genie to pop out and grant your request. The fullness of the blessing God wants to give you and me can be summed up in one word—*Jesus!* [29] And if we want more blessing, then what we are really asking for is *more* of Jesus. And in order to get more of Jesus, you must—it's not an option—*you must* have His dirt on your hands!

6

MORE *of*
His Hope in My Grief

John 14:1–11

*D*OES HEAVEN TRULY EXIST? If there is such a place, how do we get there? And before I start counting on it, how can I be sure? A national poll was conducted not too long ago with some of those same questions posed to a sampling of Americans. Eighty-one percent of the respondents said they believed in heaven as a place where people live forever with God when they die. Fifty-seven percent believed the way to get there was through a mixture of faith in God and doing good things. Applying what they believed to people they knew, 79 percent of the respondents said they believed Mother Teresa is in heaven, 66 percent believed Oprah Winfrey will one day be there, 61 percent believed Princess Diana is there, 19 percent believed O. J. Simpson will go there one day, and 87 percent believed they themselves were on their way to heaven.[1] But unless a pollster asks us to answer questions about heaven, I don't think the average American ever gives it a second thought. Until someone they love *dies* . . .

One of the things that impressed me most about my husband, Danny, when I first met him was his family. His father was the pastor of a small church in the Bronx who worked weekdays at the New York Telephone Company because the church couldn't afford to pay him a salary. His mother was a dental hygienist for a dentist on Fifth Avenue in Manhattan. And he had three brothers—two older, one younger. His oldest brother, Sam, who conscientiously kept scrapbooks on Danny's athletic career, was an astute businessman who worked for Dow Chemical Company. His youngest brother, Denton, after graduating from Harvard Divinity School, went on to get his doctorate from Hamburg University in Germany and now serves as the general secretary of the Baptist World Alliance. Simply because when I first met Danny he and his older brother, John, were rooming together, I always felt I knew John best. He coached basketball and became the assistant athletic director at the University of North Carolina at Chapel Hill.

For the past thirty-six years of my marriage to Danny, John and his family have lived nearby. His daughters are similar in age to ours, and his wife has become a beloved sister to me. Through the years, because of the close proximity, we have seen him more frequently than we have seen either Sam or Denton, regularly spending holidays and vacation time together.

In October 2000 the entire family gathered in Birmingham, Alabama, for the wedding of Denton's oldest son. John, who has been a much sought after motivational speaker, seemed unusually quiet. He privately complained of not feeling well and of having trouble with his digestion. When he and his family returned to Chapel Hill, his visit to the doctor began a maze of treatment as his physical condition rapidly declined. Neither the University of North Carolina Medical Center nor the doctors at Duke University Medical Center had any answers that could halt his downward spiral. Within weeks, he had difficulty walking and talking. On May 5, 2001, surrounded by his family, John died.[2]

As I sat at John's magnificent memorial service, I felt my husband's loneliness even more than my own grief. His brother Sam died twenty years ago of complications from diabetes. His mother died ten years ago as a result of a car accident. His father's death at eighty-two years of age was also hastened by diabetic complications. And now John was gone. Out of a vibrant, loving, energetic, loyal family, only Denton and Danny remain. As I sat in the church, listening to the thrilling, moving, and often humorous eulogies by friends and family, I quietly prayed, *Please, dear God, give me MORE of Your hope in my grief!* And He has! He has given Danny and Denton and John's family and me the promise of heaven!

THE PROMISE OF HEAVEN

Like most modern-day people, the disciples may not have given any previous thought to heaven, either. Then, after Jesus had washed their feet, He once again reclined at the long, low table. The night was descending, and Jesus knew the clock of His Father's will was ticking, drawing Him closer and closer to the hour of His death. In the soft darkness that followed the rosy glow of the sunset, the flickering torchlight would have cast moving shadows over the now serious, attentive faces of this band of men who seemed so incapable of forever changing the world—as He knew they would. He gazed around the table, looking into the skeptical face of Thomas, the quizzical face of Philip, the fiercely loyal face of Peter, the sensitive face of John, the thoughtful face of James, and the brooding, hypocritical face of Judas.

It was on this last face that the eyes of Jesus must have lingered. Knowing full well what Judas was thinking and plotting even at that very moment, Jesus became deeply "troubled in spirit," horrified, and heartsick (13:21). It was obvious that the beautiful, tender gesture of service as Jesus had washed Judas's feet had not moved Judas in the least. If anything, his heart was even harder and his mind even more focused on betraying Jesus. As Jesus' eyes locked with those of Judas, what did He see? Eyes that were smoldering in hate? Mocking? Contemptuous? Cocky? And what did Judas see? Eyes that held full comprehension? Compassion? Submission to the Father's will?

With a voice that must have resonated with emotion, Jesus made one more effort to call Judas to repentance by openly speaking of the imminent betrayal. Surely the verbal evidence of his Lord's knowledge was a warning to Judas. But in his evil arrogance, Judas ignored the warning and must have quickly looked around to see if any of the other disciples had caught on. He didn't need to be concerned. They hadn't.

As Jesus no longer hid the horrifying dread that had descended upon Him but began to speak openly of the betrayal that would take place in a few short hours, a ripple of consternation swept around the table. Peter nudged John, signaling him to ask Jesus, "Lord, who is it?"(13:25). And in Jesus' last, loving effort to keep His disciple from a deed that would condemn him for all eternity, He fingered Judas as the betrayer. But Jesus signaled Judas in such a subtle way that the disciples did not understand the significance of His action. Because Jesus singled out Judas as *the honored guest* of the dinner: "Dipping the piece of bread,[3] he gave it to Judas Iscariot, son of Simon"[4] (13:26). *How could Judas have resisted such love?*

The height of His love reached right up to the heart of God . . .

The depth of His love reached right down to a conniving, contemptuous sinner . . .

The length of His love would go all the way to the cross . . .

The breadth of His love extended to every single person around that table—*including Judas*—as well as to everyone in the entire world . . . regardless of when they lived or who they were or what they had done![5]

All of His love was poured out on one who trashed it!

In what ways has God extended His love to you—again and again? Like Judas, do you resent the fact that Jesus is different from what you expected and wanted Him to be? Are you so offended that He hasn't answered your prayer the way you asked, or He hasn't blessed you the way He has seemed to bless someone else, or He has allowed some terrible thing into your life, that you have turned away from Him? Every time you refuse to respond to the gentle wooing of His love, your heart grows harder and harder until you may reach the point, as Judas did, that you are unable to respond.

Finally, Jesus dismissed Judas, who, with a heart of stone, had hypocritically accepted his Lord's gracious honor, and "as soon as Judas had taken the bread, he went out. And it was night" (13:30). In all of history, there was no blacker night than the night Judas was dismissed from the presence of God. "It was night" in Judas's life as he walked away from the Light of God's love into the eternal abyss of God's wrath and judgment. *Please, don't do the same!* Regardless of what you have done, God loves you and even now, through the pages of this book, is extending His love to you once again. Would you quietly, deeply, earnestly, respond to Him in prayer:

> *Thank You, dear God, for loving me. There is so much about You that I don't understand, but I accept Your love. Help me to know You as You truly are, not as I have imagined or want You to be. Keep me in the Light of Your love and truth and mercy and grace. Amen.*

As the door clicked shut behind Judas, Jesus must have been filled with sorrow . . . *and relief!* The atmosphere of oppression, rejection, hate, and evil that had surely presided in the upstairs room through the presence of Judas was now gone. The freedom and release Jesus must have felt in Judas's absence can be heard in the exultation that came next: "When he was gone, Jesus said, 'Now is the Son of Man glorified and God is glorified in him'" (13:31). Yet almost immediately, the heartbreak of imminent separation from these men who were closer to Him than any sons to their father rose up to engulf Him as He began to say good-bye. Did His voice drop and become husky with emotion as He addressed them, saying, "My children, I will be with you only a little while longer. . . . Where I am going you cannot come"(13:33)?

In the tanned, rugged faces of the young men who belonged to Him, Jesus must have seen shock, grief, confusion, and a thousand unspoken questions. Their manly faces must have given evidence of the vulnerability of their love for Him and their loyalty to Him and their resistance to His words as Peter blurted out, "Lord, where are you going?" (13:36).

Jesus repeated, "Where I am going, you cannot follow now, but you will follow later" (13:36). With typical rash boldness, Peter's eyes must have flashed and his chin come up and his shoulders squared back as he argued, "Lord, why can't I follow you now? I will lay down my life for you"(13:37). The other disciples must have nodded their agreement, glancing at each other in silent affirmation of their allegiance.

I wonder if Jesus was silent for a moment. What could He say, and how could He say what He needed to in order to prepare these disciples for the total collapse of their world that would begin within a few short hours? Jerking them all into reality, Jesus looked squarely into the eyes of the one who was the leader of the rest and predicted, "Will you really lay down your life for me? I tell you the truth, before the rooster crows, you will disown me three times!" (13:38).

Peter's face must have turned crimson then blanched white as all the blood drained from it. *Disown Him!* How could that ever be?

As the other disciples stared at Peter, they must have been terrified, thinking, *If Peter is our leader and he disowns Jesus, what are we capable of doing?* Their faces must have registered revulsion and even horror at the unseen menace that apparently would transform them from loyal friends to backstabbing enemies. And after giving up everything to follow Him, in the end was their impending disloyalty going to separate them from Him forever? Was He telling them that their blind ignorance and bumbling failures had caused them to be disqualified as disciples? That they just hadn't made the grade? Otherwise, why would He now leave them, refusing to allow them to accompany Him to wherever it was He was going? They must have felt as though they had suddenly fallen into a swirling vortex of events that would suck them away from the One Who had become their life, their hope, their purpose, their whole reason for living.

The emotional pain that was intensified by their lack of understanding must have caused them to squirm, push back from the table, and shake their heads in disbelief. But before they could protest or question or turn away, Jesus spoke to them once again. In timeless words that have calmed the overwhelming fears of His children down through the centuries—fears that have threatened to . . .

> silence their voices,
>> paralyze their feet,
>>> erase their minds,
>>>> break their hearts,
>>>>> and destroy their faith,

Jesus said with quiet authority, "Do not let your hearts be troubled"(14:1).

The Promise of Heaven Calms My Fears

"Do not let your hearts be troubled" is a *command* the disciples and you and I are to obey! Deliberately calming ourselves is a choice we are to make in the face of shocking setbacks,

> catastrophic circumstances,
>> abrupt accidents,
>>> irritating interruptions,
>>>> devastating dissension,
>>>>> agonizing addiction,
>>>>>> frequent failures,

all of which cause us to be terrified of the consequences and repercussions. In the midst of the swirling, cloying fog of fear, Jesus commands, "Stop it!"

Stop letting your imagination run wild.

Stop analyzing every detail over and over again.

Stop flogging yourself with the "if only's" and "what if's."

Stop being afraid!

How in the world is it possible to obey a command that involves so much of our emotional feelings? Our obedience begins with a choice to stop being afraid, followed by a decision to start trusting God.

It has been stated that "peace is not the absence of danger but the presence of God." Jesus commanded His disciples who were on the brink of emotional disintegration, if not at that moment, then surely within a few hours, to "trust in God; trust also in me"(14:1).

The antidote to fear is faith.

When I toss and turn in the middle of the night, worried and fearful over something that is impending in my life or the life of someone I love, I am comforted and calmed as I meditate on Who God is. It helps me plant my faith in Someone Who is bigger than my fears, because He is

Able . . . [6]

Benevolent . . . [7]

Compassionate . . . [8]

Dependable . . . [9]

Eternal . . . [10]

Faithful . . . [11]

Good . . . [12]

Holy . . . [13]

Immortal . . . [14]

Just . . . [15]

Kind . . . [16]

Loving . . . [17]

Merciful . . . [18]

Near . . . [19]

Omniscient . . . [20]

Powerful . . . [21]

Quick . . . [22]

Right . . . [23]

Sufficient . . .[24]

Truthful . . .[25]

Unique . . .[26]

Victorious . . .[27]

Wise . . .[28]

XYZalted![29]

Praise God! When I tend to be afraid, I just fall back on Who God is and rest in Him. He cannot be less than Himself! And my God *is God!* He is the God of gods Who has made Himself visible and knowable and approachable through Jesus Christ[30]—which is why Jesus commanded us to "trust also" in Him.

Several years ago I had a dear young friend who began experiencing dreadful panic attacks. On the advice of some friends, she began seeing a psychiatrist who walked her through a simple exercise of listing everything she was afraid of. When she finished her list, her fears so dominated her thinking that she could no longer even function.

While it can be helpful to pinpoint the source of our worries and fears, to dwell on those things will plunge us into a downward spiral. Next time you feel afraid, make up your own list—not of your fears but of the characteristics of God. Find a Scripture verse or passage to substantiate each one as you reconsider your situation in light of Who God is. Then, if you feel it would be helpful to list your fears, make sure beside each one you write down the attribute of God that applies. The secret to peace lies in your focus.

The Promise of Heaven Sharpens My Focus

What do you think heaven is like? Do you think it's like the Emerald City in the *Wizard of Oz*? Do you think it's like the palace of Cinderella's Prince Charming? Do you think it's just lots of fluffy clouds where we lounge around forever? Jesus described heaven very simply as "my Father's house" as He sought to encourage His disciples to get their eyes off of their immediate, *but temporary,* grief and instead, focus on the big picture: "In my Father's house are many rooms; if it were not so, I would have told you. I am going there to prepare a place for you" (14:2).

The disciples must have started to perk up, thinking perhaps they had jumped too hastily to the conclusion that they had been disqualified from service! Maybe there was hope after all! Jesus was just going home! Going home to get things ready for them! The very fact that His Father's house had many rooms implied that there would be room enough for them!

How often I have dashed home from church to get things ready for guests I have invited to lunch! I want to get the ice in the glasses, take the roast out of the oven while I pop the rolls in, make the gravy, steam the broccoli, and generally get things organized so that when my guests walk through the door everything is prepared for their enjoyment. I want them to know by the delicious aromas coming from the kitchen, and the elegant setting of the table, and the sideboard laden with dishes brimming with steaming food that they are expected and they are welcome.

Jesus was telling His disciples that He was going to dash home to get things ready for them so when they walked through the door they would know they were expected, they were welcome, and His home was theirs to enjoy! Surely . . .

> the grief-filled expressions of the disciples became tentatively hopeful,
> and the tear-filled eyes began to expectantly sparkle,
> and the fear-filled hearts stopped racing,

as the words of Jesus compelled them to *look forward!*

After living with Jesus for three years, they knew that *He knew* exactly what they liked and enjoyed. If He was going to personally prepare a place for them, they could get excited about going there! It would be wonderful—filled with all the things, large and small, that would give them comfort and happiness.

As a mother, I know something about preparing a place for my children. While my two daughters have returned with their husbands to live in our hometown, my son, Jonathan, as of this writing, is living in California. But Jonathan is coming home for a visit in two weeks! I know he loves a homemade apple pie and barbecued spareribs and time to play tennis with his dad. And so as I prepare for his visit, I am not only vacuuming and dusting his room, I will be baking and grilling and arranging his dad's schedule to make sure that when Jonathan walks through the door he will know he is expected, he is welcome, and this is his home!

If I know how to make my son feel welcome and at home, I can only imagine what Jesus is doing to prepare for my arrival in heaven. He knows the colors I love and the scenery I enjoy and the people I long to see and the music that causes my heart to soar! When I walk through those gates of pearl, I will know, as a result of His thoughtful, personal, meticulous preparation, that I am expected and I am welcome, because I have come home!

Regardless of your present
circumstances or crisis,
pressures or pain,
suffering or sorrow,
failures or frustrations,
danger or disease,
memories or misery,
temptations or trials,
problems or persecutions,
burdens or brokenness,
your situation is temporary compared to eternity. And eternity is going to be spent with Jesus in His Father's house that has been lovingly prepared just for you! That's the truth![31] Your future has been confirmed!

The Promise of Heaven Confirms My Future

The tense atmosphere in the upper room must have eased slightly as the disciples contemplated their future home. The horror of the present seemed to be greatly diminished by the hope of living one day in His Father's house. Observing His disciples' attentiveness and eagerness to understand, Jesus continued, "And if I go and prepare a place for you, I will come back and take you to be with me that you also may be where I am"(14:3).

Receiving His personal guarantee that He would not leave them to grope and stumble and guess their way to His Father's house but would personally return to take them there must have caused the disciples to finally take a deep breath and relax considerably. Maybe they even took a moment to chew a forgotten bite of food or sip their drinks as they thought through what He had just said. Whatever was menacing their immediate future, in the end everything would be all right because Jesus would be coming back to get them and take them to live with Him forever in His Father's house. Now *that* was a promise to live by! And die by!

One by one, our Lord's disciples did die by this promise. One of the first to give his life for Christ was a young evangelist in the early church whose preaching was so compelling and convincing none could withstand it. He made a powerful impact in Jerusalem for the Gospel. The authorities became so enraged and jealous they dragged him out of the city and stoned him to death. But before he died, his face reflected the light of glory as he looked up and exclaimed, "Look, . . . I see heaven open and the Son of Man standing at the right hand of God."[32] Yet the Bible distinctly tells us that when Jesus rose from the dead and ascended into heaven, He was *seated* at the right hand of God.[33] How, then, could this young martyr have seen Him standing? Could it be that Jesus was standing to personally honor and welcome to His Father's house one who had not loved his life "so much as to shrink from death"?[34] Had the bold, courageous disciple seen Jesus poised to fulfill His promise—ready to come for His own and take him safely home?

Miss Audrey Wetherell Johnson lived and died by that promise. She was the very godly woman who taught me how to teach the Scriptures, and in the process she taught me much about the Scriptures.[35] She was the founder of Bible Study Fellowship, directing that powerfully challenging ministry for thirty some years and authoring the commentary notes that have been life-changing for so many.[36] While she was intellectually keen to the point of brilliance, she did not teach from her head, but from her heart. And she lived out a life of such vibrant faith in God's Word, it was contagious.

On many occasions, I heard Miss Johnson (as she was respectfully and lovingly called) say that she was confident when she closed her eyes to this life she would be opening them to the face of Jesus.[37] As she struggled with a recurrence of cancer, many of us prayed that her eyes would be opened to His face even before that moment of death, to give comfort to herself and those of us who loved her. For the last few weeks of her life, she had been immobile and unable to speak. But on the morning of the day she went to our Father's house, she sat straight up in bed, joy radiating from her eyes and a thrilling smile on her lips as she exclaimed, "I see Jesus! He has come for me!" Then she fell back on her pillow . . . *and was gone!*

When my husband's mother walked into a room, it was as though the lights came on. She had such a vivacious, happy, energetic disposition that the sun still seemed to shine in her presence even on a gloomy day. Mother-in-law jokes have never been really funny to me because I can't seem to relate to the negative perspective they are rooted in. Gramma, as we affectionately called her, not only raised four strapping sons who adored her, she was also the "first lady" of the churches pastored by her husband. She sang in the choir, supervised the church suppers, led women's Bible studies, visited the sick and infirm, and cared for the helpless. And until she was seventy-five years old, she worked as a dental hygienist on Fifth Avenue in New York City. Yet she never did learn to drive a car!

When she retired, one of her small, favorite pastimes was to ride to McDonald's with her husband—"Grampa," as we knew him—for a cup of coffee and a biscuit. One morning when she was eighty-one years of age, she and Grampa were on their usual outing when Grampa ran off the road and hit a telephone pole. Although he was just shaken up, Gramma was critically injured. Six weeks later it seemed as though she would make a full recovery and be able to come home from the hospital.

At six o'clock in the morning on the day before she was to go home, she called my husband. She vividly described what she said had been a dream in which she had walked along a beach. The cloudless sky was crystal blue, and the sand had been soft beneath her feet, and the waves had rolled gently into shore, and Jesus had been walking with her, holding her hand! She hung up the phone, and an hour later we received the call that she had gone to His Father's house!

Often at death a person is drugged, or unconscious, or strapped down, or connected to so many tubes and wires and machines he or she is unable to move or speak. But once in a while, through those who have ears to hear and eyes to see, we are given a glimpse of the fulfillment of our Lord's promise that confirms our future. At the moment of death, Jesus comes personally to take His children to His Father's house!

Many years ago, God gave to King David a promise that has been claimed by God's children down through the ages, especially during times of grief. It may be the most frequently quoted Bible passage at funerals and memorial services the world over. God's children can almost see His outstretched hand and feel the strong, divine grip when they read, "Even though I walk through the valley of the shadow of death, I will fear no evil, *for you are with me.*"[38]

Throughout the history of the church, believers have been filled with a gentle peace and confident hope as they have claimed Jesus' comforting promise to return for them personally at death and take them home to His Father's house. However, there is another meaning to Jesus' promise that has been an equal source of comfort since His words were first uttered that Thursday night so long ago in the upper room. This comfort is drawn from applying His promise of return to His second coming.

Did you know that Jesus is personally, physically coming back? *Here?* To planet earth? Approximately one out of every twenty verses in the New Testament refer to His return, including John 14:3, the verse we're focusing on in this discussion. The promise was reinforced to His disciples immediately following His ascension. They were standing on the Mount of Olives, gazing up into the cloudy sky where they had just seen Him disappear, when two men dressed in white suddenly stood beside them. These men echoed Jesus' words spoken forty days earlier following His last meal with them: "This same Jesus, who has been taken from you into heaven, *will come back* in the same way you have seen him go into heaven."[39] What promise could be more pregnant with hope or more thrilling than that?

The apostle Paul gave tantalizing details concerning this historical event to the new believers in Thessalonica. He explained to these baby Christians that he did not want them "to be ignorant about those who fall asleep"[40]— those who have placed their faith in Jesus Christ as their Savior and Lord and who have died, like Danny's brother John. While Paul acknowledged the unavoidable presence of human grief at the death of a loved one, he pointed out that their grief is not "like the rest of men, who have no hope."

The reason we as believers do not grieve at the passing of a loved one like the rest of the world grieves is because we believe that the same Jesus Who died on the cross to offer us forgiveness of sin, and Who was raised from the dead to give us eternal life, is the same Jesus Who one day will come again!

And when He comes, "God will bring with Jesus those who have fallen asleep in him." When Jesus comes, He will bring Danny's brother with Him! In response to Paul's teaching, the Thessalonians, like you, must have worn a skeptical expression. So his next statement is like an exclamation point that emphasizes this is "the Lord's own word," not his wishful thinking or over-active imagination!

Paul went on to say that those believers who are alive on earth when Jesus returns will not hinder those believers who have already died. "For the Lord himself will come down from heaven, with a loud command, with the voice of the archangel and with the trumpet call of God, and the dead in Christ [that includes John] will rise first."

When Danny's brother John died, everything he really was—his mind, emotions, will, personality—all of him that resided inside the "tent" of his body, went to be with Jesus.[41] His body was buried in a lovely cemetery in Chapel Hill, North Carolina. But at any moment, the trumpet may sound, and his body will be raised up from the ground, with certain chemical and physical changes to make it like Jesus' glorious body.[42] John will then be "clothed" so that when I see him (if I am alive on earth at this thrilling event), he will be residing in his new body, coming back from the Father's house with Jesus! "After that, we who are still alive and are left will be caught up together with them [Jesus and John] in the clouds to meet the Lord in the air. . . . Therefore, encourage each other with these words."[43]

What will it be like on that day when we hear the clarion call of the archangel's trumpet? Quicker than you or I can blink an eye, believers will feel their feet lifting up off the ground, we will be aware of certain changes taking place in our bodies that will enable us to physically live in eternity, and we will look up—into the face of Jesus! We will be swept into the clouds of His glory![44] And if we can drag our eyes away from His beautiful face, we will see that Jesus is surrounded by our loved ones who had trusted Him by faith and who had been raised from the dead![45]

Jesus Christ is coming! He is coming! On any day, at any moment, "in the twinkling of an eye . . . at an hour when you do not expect him . . . he who is coming will come and will not delay."[46] The Bible says so! Now that's a promise that gives me much MORE of His hope in my grief!

THE PATH TO HEAVEN

On hearing Jesus say He was leaving and would return, I wonder if the disciples began to fidget nervously. They knew what Jesus was saying was vitally important. They could tell by the intensity of His eyes and the way He measured His words that this was something that was imperative for them to understand. But they didn't.

Did they begin to toy with the food still on their plates? Did they give exaggerated attention to removing the crumbs at their place? Did they glance sideways at each other to determine if anybody else was confused? They didn't have to wait long, because Thomas spoke up for all of them.

It's not surprising that all of this brought questions to Thomas's mind, as it may have brought to yours. And it's not surprising that Thomas spoke up while the others remained silent. The only surprising thing is that Thomas just voiced one of his questions out loud! In response to Jesus' reassuring words, "You know the way to the place where I am going" (14:4), Thomas argued, "Lord, we don't know where you are going, so how can we know the way?" (14:5).

The ever practical, realistic, bottom-line Thomas would have been much more at home reading the sports or business section of the newspaper than the arts and culture section. He liked things spelled out in black-and-white facts. Jesus' talk of "my Father's house" must have been too subtle and poetic to make any logical sense to him. I'm so thankful to Thomas for asking the question, because Jesus' answer to him has become one of the stones in the bedrock of our faith.

Jesus very patiently, but very pointedly, must have nailed Thomas with His eyes as He gave directions that were crystal clear: "I am the way and the truth and the life. No one comes to the Father except through me"(14:6).

Like Thomas, are you confused about how to get to heaven? Then listen carefully to what Jesus was saying: "Thomas, My Father's house is heaven. Just think of it as the literal presence of God. And the only way you will ever get into the presence of God is if you place your faith in Me. I am the way that you get there. My words give you the true directions, and My life will empower you. Thomas, if you miss Me, you miss everything."

Does that offend you? Do you react by saying that's unfair? Exclusive? Intolerant? Politically incorrect? What about all the good, moral, religious people out there? What about all the Jews and Jehovah's Witnesses,

Holy Rollers and Hindus,

Muslims and Methodists,

Buddhists and Baptists,

Pentecostals and Presbyterians,

Anglicans and animists,

Catholics and charismatics,

who *don't* place their faith in Jesus but are sincere in what they believe? Does that mean they are *not going to go to heaven?* I didn't say that. *Jesus* did! That's exactly what He said. He did not say that He *knew* the way to heaven; He said that He Himself *is* the only Way to get there!

During the Vietnam War, a story was reported about a paratrooper who had been air-dropped into the jungle and couldn't find his way out. A native guide had to be sent into the jungle to find the lost man then lead him safely to his base. The guide became the man's way to safety—his "way home." In the same manner, Jesus is "God's Guide," heaven-dropped into the world to lead lost sinners safely "Home." It stands to reason that if you refuse to acknowledge that you are "lost," then you will not accept God's Way home. But for those of us who know we have been lost, our overwhelming gratitude for the Guide is enough to compel us to tell others about Him—about the truth of their lost condition and the truth about the Way out.

Last summer, I was invited to address the 125th anniversary convention of Keswick, the world's premier Bible conference, which is held every summer in the Lake District of England. For years, I had heard about the legendary beauty of the area and decided not to miss the opportunity to enjoy it. So I rented a car. Along with the rental papers, I made sure I had a map of the country. I knew there were roads that would lead me to Keswick, but unless I had a map to give me accurate directions, I would never get there. Again, in the same way, Jesus is not only the Way out of the jungle of sin into the presence of God in heaven, His Word is our "map" that gives accurate directions about how to get there.

And Jesus is also the "Gasoline," the Life that empowers us along the way.

The first time I stopped for gas in England, I received a shock! Instead of the usual $1.50 per gallon that we pay in America, British petrol was closer to $4 a liter! But I had to have gas, or even though I had directions, I would never have arrived in Keswick.

Likewise, even though we have acknowledged that we are lost and Jesus is our Way to heaven, and even though we have the truth of His Word to give us directions, we must have the indwelling life of His Spirit to enable us to make the journey safely and surely. How simple! How basic! How absolutely necessary in our journey to heaven that we have God's Guide, God's Guidebook, and God's Gasoline! Everything necessary to get us to heaven is summed up in the person of Jesus Christ. He Himself is our hope in grief.

THE PROOF OF HEAVEN

I wonder if Philip was drumming his fingers on the table as Jesus was talking. He was the analytical disciple, the one who sized things up, organized everybody's thoughts as expressed in a discussion and then summarized them.[47] Philip evidently felt he needed more information before he could process what he was hearing. He essentially said he could figure all of this out if, "Lord, [You] show us the Father and that will be enough for us" (14:8). In other words, "Jesus, please give us proof that Your promise of heaven is true and Your path to heaven is the right one. This is way too important to mess up. When You're talking about how we are going to be able to see You again and where we are going to spend eternity, we don't want to leave any room for a mistake, or even for a doubt. This is major."

Helloooo! Philip, wake up! Where have you been? Jesus had just told Thomas, "If you really knew me, you would know my Father as well. From now on, you do know him and have seen him" (14:7). Jesus' patience with Philip, Thomas, Peter, and His other disciples was truly remarkable. And He is still patient today.

Are you afraid to ask Jesus questions? Afraid that He may blame you for not knowing the answers? Afraid He may think you're stupid? Afraid that if you ask questions you may reveal to Him that you *are* stupid? Afraid perhaps of getting an answer you don't want to hear? He knows you and me inside out. He knows what we're thinking even if we don't voice it. His disciples have given all of us the encouragement to go ahead and ask. Jesus welcomes honest, sincere questions respectfully asked. In fact, it's not until we ask our questions that we begin to get the answers on which we can not only build our faith but build our relationship with Him.[48]

In a voice that gently rebuked Philip, not for asking the question, but for the obvious shallowness of his relationship with Jesus after three years of discipleship, Jesus inquired, "Don't you know me, Philip, even after I have been among you such a long time? Anyone who has seen me has seen the Father. How can you say, 'Show us the Father'? Don't you believe that I am in the Father, and that the Father is in me?" (14:9–10).

Once again, the upper room must have been frozen still in stunned silence! *What was that He said?* "Look at Me, Philip. Look at My eyes, My face, My life. Look at everything you know about Me. Look at Me now, Philip. *You're looking at God!*"

Eleven pairs of eyes must have been glued to the face of Jesus as though seeing Him for the first time! *God? Here at this table? In this room? With us? Now?* It was almost unbelievable. Before they could blurt out any more questions or doubts, Jesus gave them a twofold proof of His assertion.

The Proof of His Words

God's infallible Word is the outward expression of all that God is, which is why Jesus explained, "The words I say to you are not just my own. Rather, it is the Father, living in me, who is doing his work" (14:10). There is no other God besides the God of creation. He is the God of Abraham, Isaac, and Jacob. He is the Father of Jesus of Nazareth. He is Jesus, in homespun and sandals, Who walked the shore of Galilee and the streets of Jerusalem and Who is alive today.

Years after that unforgettable evening John recalled this first proof of Jesus' identity and used it as the theme of the magnificent prologue to the Gospel account that bears his name. Reaching back before the beginning of time or space, John proclaimed, "In the beginning was the Word, and the Word was with God, and the Word was God. . . . The Word became flesh and lived for a while among us. We have seen his glory, the glory of the one and only Son, who came from the Father, full of grace and truth. . . . No one has ever seen God, but God the only Son, who is at the Father's side, has made him known."[49]

Sometime later, an anonymous writer also conveyed this same truth to his Jewish readers when he reiterated in timeless eloquence, "In the past God spoke to our forefathers through the prophets at many times and in various ways, but in these last days he has spoken to us by his Son, whom he appointed heir of all things, and through whom he made the universe. The Son is the radiance of God's glory and the exact representation of his being."[50]

Philip and the other disciples had been with Jesus for three years without fully comprehending this truth. How long have you been with Jesus? Were you raised in a Christian home? Are you even now in church every Sunday? In fact, would you be hard pressed to remember a time when you didn't know or hear His name spoken? Like Philip, would Jesus look at you wistfully and ask softly, "Have you been with Me such a long time, and still you don't know Me?"

You don't know that He is the Creator Himself Who became your Savior and died on the cross as the only sacrifice God will accept for your sin?[51]

You don't know that Jesus is alive today, in His man's body, up in heaven?[52]

You don't know that He is available to live within you in the person of His Spirit?[53]

You don't know that He personally prays for you by name?[54]

You don't know that He will literally, visibly return to reign and rule on planet earth?[55]

Isn't it time you really got to know Jesus for Who He truly is? Knowing Jesus gives me confidence in the promise of heaven and confidence in the pathway to heaven because His words and His works are the proof that He is Who He says He is.

The Proof of His Works

Jesus pressed His point by giving the disciples the second aspect of His proof when He challenged them, "Believe me when I say that I am in the Father and the Father is in me; or at least believe on the evidence of the miracles themselves" (14:11). How could the disciples forget, or if they hadn't forgotten, *how could they so easily dismiss the miracles* they had seen firsthand?

He had changed water into wine.[56]

He had restored mobility to a man who had been paralyzed for thirty-eight years.[57]

He had healed the royal official's son without ever even going to see him.[58]

He had fed five thousand people until they were full using only five loaves and two fish.[59]

He had walked on the surface of the Sea of Galilee.[60]

He had created sight in a man born blind.[61]

He had raised Lazarus from the dead.[62]

And those were only the miracles that John could quickly tick off in his mind! There were so many others—lepers who had been cleansed, the deaf who had been given hearing, the demon-possessed who had been set free. The disciples must have lost count of them all. The list could go on and on.[63] How could they have rationalized that the miracles were anything other than *proof* that Jesus *was God* in their midst? And *if* Jesus was God in their midst, He could most certainly be taken at His Word. They must have felt similar to someone who suddenly, unexpectedly wins the Publishers Clearinghouse Sweepstakes! Except they hadn't won a million dollars; they had won heaven! Because He had said . . .

that heaven was His Father's house.

that He was going to dash Home to get it ready for His disciples.

that He would return for them.

that He would then take them to live with Him forever.

that He Himself was the *only* way Home.

that when they looked into His face, they looked into the face of God.

that His Word was God's Word.

He had said. *He had said! HE HAD SAID . . . heaven is real!*

We can know it's so because Jesus *said it's so!* To have His promise is as good as having His answer!

THE TELEPHONE RANG while I was writing this chapter. It was Nancy Guthrie calling from the hospital moments after her son was born.[64] Like the mother of any newborn, she described how beautiful her baby was. Then she softly whispered, "And he has little clubfeet . . ."[65]

I asked Nancy what she and David had named this little boy who would only be theirs for a short while before Jesus would return to take him to His Father's house. She hesitated for the briefest moment then responded, "I think we're going to name him Gabriel. He's our little messenger from God."

I bowed my head and prayed, "Thank You, dear God, for the message of Your goodness and faithfulness and righteousness and greatness and loving kindness *and hope!* And thank You, dear God, for Your precious little messenger. Give him a loud voice to proclaim the glory of Who You truly are."

As I hung up the phone, I wept! The tears on my face voiced the silent prayer in my heart: *Thank You, dear God, for giving me the hope of heaven in my grief. Thank You for giving me MORE of Jesus through the beautiful blessed brokenness of Nancy and David Guthrie.*

7

MORE *of*
His Fruit in My Service

John 15:1–8

RECENTLY, DANNY AND I attended a breakfast early one morning for approximately five hundred local supporters that preceded a fund-raising day of golf and tennis for a local youth organization. The seating was open, and Danny led us to a table that had two vacancies. As I settled into the chair, the man opposite me said loudly, to no one in particular, "Well, if it isn't Anne Lotz. She's the most fruitful Christian I know."

There was no "Good morning. It's nice to see you. How are the kids? Isn't this a great turnout? Are you going to play golf or tennis?" There was just this off-the-wall pronouncement! The others at the table quickly looked up at me; then, seeing my discomfort, they looked down or away or around or anywhere but at me. I smiled, but before I could respond, the man continued, "So tell us, Anne, how do you do it? How do you bear so much fruit?"

It's hard for me to think quickly, especially early in the morning before I've had even my first cup of coffee! But because he actually seemed to be sincere, I didn't brush him off. Instead, I replied honestly, "I've never really thought about it." He looked incredulous, as though I was holding out on the secret to fruitfulness. And then the following example came to my mind that helped me explain to him my answer.

Danny loves to grow things, so we have several pear and apple trees in our yard. Not once have I ever seen one of those fruit trees struggling to bear fruit. Nor do they go to classes or seminars about fruit-bearing or read books about how to be more fruitful. In fact, I don't think those fruit trees ever even

121

think about fruitfulness! Their fruitfulness totally depends on Danny to make sure they get the proper sunlight, water, fertilizer, and pruning.

Likewise, why is it that Christians go running around, measuring the abundance of each other's fruit as well as their own, reading books on fruitfulness, going to seminars about greater fruitfulness, when it's really not their concern? Before you start to protest, let me assure you I desire with all of my heart to bear much fruit for the glory of God. The fruit I long for is the fruit of righteousness—the fruit of Christlikeness in my own character that I live out on the anvil of my daily experience and the fruit of reproducing Christlikeness in the lives of others.

But the fruit in my life is His concern, not mine. My concern is to make sure of three things: that as a potential fruit-bearing branch, I am connected to the Vine and keep that connection clean and unobstructed; that I submit to the cultivation of the Vinedresser, which primarily involves His pruning in my life; and that I communicate with Him my heart's desire: *Please, dear God, just give me MORE of Your fruit in my service.*

FRUITFUL THROUGH MY CONNECTION

Have you been making fruit-bearing more complicated and difficult than it is? Have you worn yourself out until you are discouraged over the lack of fruitfulness in your own service and resentful of others for the fruitfulness in theirs? Then I have wonderful news for you! You can relax! Not only are you freed from trying hard to bear fruit, you are freed from trying at all! That's the secret!

How many times I have heard it said, "Getting ahead . . . or getting accepted . . . or getting promoted . . . or getting hired . . . is all in who you know. Connections. You've got to have connections—connections to the right people." When it comes to fruit-bearing, nothing could be a more accurate statement. Because fruit-bearing is all about Who you know. It's about one primary connection.

Knowing how complicated we tend to make things, on that Thursday night in the upstairs room, Jesus used a familiar example to teach His disciples that very secret. I wonder if He had been gazing out the upstairs window. Since it was Passover, the moon would have been full, turning the night into almost a soft twilight. He could probably hear the gentle, musical sound of the water running in the brook at the base of the Kidron Valley. From the heightened vantage point of His upstairs location, perhaps He had a clear view of the Mount of Olives outlined against the night sky. He knew He would soon be going there to pray. But not yet.

He had much to say to His disciples before He spent private time wrestling with His Father's will in the Garden of Gethsemane. As He surveyed the radiant beauty of Jerusalem in the moonlight, did His eyes linger on a vineyard on the outskirts of the city? Or maybe Peter had just poured wine into His goblet, sloshing the liquid on the table as he did so. Did the dark red droplets glisten for a moment in the torchlight before becoming a stain on the table, catching His eye? Or perhaps, just from the memory of His mind's eye, He reflected on a sight that was common to all those at the table. Whatever it was that triggered His thoughts, we know He began to teach His disciples about fruitfulness in their service using a vine, a branch, a gardener, and fruit to illustrate His points.

As simplistic as it may sound, fruit is produced on a branch that is attached to a vine. Jesus clearly told His disciples, "I am the vine; you are the branches" (15:5). So there is no guesswork about our position in His illustration. For a branch to have fruit-bearing potential, it must be alive. Since it has no life of its own, it must be organically attached to the vine so that the sap, or life, of the vine flows up through the trunk and into the branch.

Attached to the Vine Organically

Jesus emphasized the necessity of this organic attachment when He told His disciples, "Apart from me you can do nothing" (15:5). Even though the branch bears the fruit, it doesn't produce the fruit. So the first necessary step in order for you and me to be fruitful in service is to determine our personal relationship to Jesus Christ.

Unless you have been to the cross by faith, confessed your sin, asked for forgiveness and cleansing, and invited Jesus to come into your life as your Savior and Lord, it will be impossible for you to bear fruit. You must be born again[1] because it's through rebirth that you and I are "attached" to

Christ so that His "sap," or life, in the person of the Holy Spirit flows from Him into us.

Many people today have an *organizational* attachment to Christ. They belong to a church or a Christian group, they attend Bible studies and seminars, they even pray and profess to be a "branch." But they have no "sap"— no real life that flows into them from the indwelling of the Holy Spirit. They are like Spanish moss that is close to the oak tree and even clings to the oak tree but doesn't really belong to the oak tree because there is no organic attachment.

Does your service lack the genuine fruit of changed lives? To overcome the fruitlessness, have you tried harder, prayed more, claimed greater territory in service, all to no avail? Have you produced nothing except frustration, failure, and fatigue, work, worry, and waste? Could it be that your barrenness in service is because you are not attached to the Vine? If so, would you examine your personal relationship to Jesus?

When did you receive the Holy Spirit? Keep in mind that to receive Jesus Christ *is* to receive the Holy Spirit, because the Holy Spirit is Jesus in you. And He comes to live within you when you deliberately yield your life to Christ, confessing and repenting of your sin, and open your heart to Him. If you cannot pinpoint a time in your life when you made this conscious decision,[2] then perhaps although you are close to the Vine, there is no life-support through the indwelling of the Holy Spirit.[3]

As Jesus taught His disciples, I wonder if His heart was heavy as Judas came to mind. Judas, who even at that very moment was turning Him into the authorities, was the prime example of Spanish moss—of a branch that was attached organizationally to the Vine but not attached organically. Judas was a member of The Twelve, the group of men closest in proximity to Jesus. Judas was identified with Jesus and called a disciple. The rest of the disciples had no idea Judas was a counterfeit because he looked so much like the real thing. But Judas had never given his heart to Christ. He gave the appearance of being a branch, but he really wasn't. Jesus described Judas, and others like him, as "a branch that is thrown away and withers; such branches are picked up, thrown into the fire and burned" (15:6).[4]

When Jesus dismissed Judas from the upper room after giving him the bread dipped in oil, we can hear the "click" of the Gardener's shears. Judas,

like dead wood, was cut out in order to give the disciples the room to grow
and the freedom to be taught by the Lord Jesus in preparation for the abundance of fruit that would come from their service.[5]

Many churches today are filled with dead wood—those who imitate or
are self-deceived or pretend to be a real branch. Those who are

good,
moral,
sincere,
honest,
civic minded,
philanthropic,

religious,

active

in church with Christian reputations. But when a crisis occurs, or the Light
of God's truth shines into their lives, they wither.

One church in the New Testament that seemed to have more dead wood
than live branches was the church at Laodicea. Jesus rebuked its members
for boasting, "'I am rich; I have acquired wealth and do not need a thing.'
But you do not realize that you are wretched, pitiful, poor, blind and
naked."[6] Many members of that church had allowed pride to keep them
from the cross. They had never been born again. They thought salvation was
for "them"—those outside the church, not "us"—church members.

How can you and I tell the difference between dead wood and a live
branch? The difference is in the fruit. While Jesus cautions us against
judging, He does encourage us to be "fruit inspectors."[7]

Look for the fruit of a personal testimony of confession and
repentance of sin and salvation.

Look for the fruit of a transformed, Spirit-controlled life
evidenced by love, joy, peace, patience, kindness, goodness, faithfulness, gentleness, and self-control.[8]

Look for the fruit of hunger and thirst for God's Word that
compels the person to read it, study it, apply it, and obey it.

Look for the fruit of other people's lives being transformed as a result of the person's witness: marriages being reconciled, lost people being saved, people becoming hungry for God's Word and spending time in prayer.

As you read this, are you thinking, *So that explains old So-and-So? He's just dead wood!* You and I need to be very cautious in deciding whether the person under inspection is live or dead wood. Instead of being dead, he or she may be just a new tendril of a branch, or a branch that has been pruned way back. The Gardener is the only One Who knows for sure. So pray if you feel your growth as a believer is being choked and hindered by the dead wood of a counterfeit branch. Ask the Gardener to remove it, then wait for His timing to do so. And you might ask yourself, "When others examine me, do they think I am Spanish moss? Could someone be praying for my removal because I am crowding their growth and choking out their fruitfulness?"

One way to ensure that there will be no mistake about whether or not we are organically attached to the Vine is to be genuinely fruitful. And fruit-bearing is inevitable when we are not only attached organically to the Vine but when we are abiding consistently in the Vine.

Abiding in the Vine Consistently

The branches of a vine "abide" by just remaining connected to the vine. Permanently. Consistently. Day after day, week after week, year after year. They simply rest in their position, allowing the sap of the vine to flow freely through them. They exert no effort of their own. The fruit that is subsequently borne on the branch is actually produced by the life-giving sap within.

To abide in Christ means to remain connected to Him so completely that the "sap" of His Spirit flows through every part of your being, including your mind, will, and emotions as well as your words and deeds. The "fruit" that you then bear is actually produced by His Spirit in you through no conscious effort of your own. If you and I want to be fruitful, we do not concentrate on fruit-bearing; we concentrate on our personal relationship with Jesus Christ.

I wonder if the disciples followed Jesus' gaze as He continued to look out through the moonlight at the vineyards on the hillsides around Jerusalem. If so, they would have seen the thick trunks of the vines growing upward, topped by large gnarls from which the branches grew and were then trained to grow horizontally. It would have been obvious even to the sea-weathered fishermen among them that it would be impossible for a branch to bear fruit unless it had a direct connection to the vine. But the disciples had been known to miss the obvious, so Jesus pointed this out as He commanded them, "[Abide] in me, and I will [abide] in you. No branch can bear fruit by itself; it must [abide] in the vine. Neither can you bear fruit unless you [abide] in me" (15:4).[9] The branch is totally, absolutely, completely *dependent* upon the Vine, not only for fruit, but for life.

Whether because of pride or fear or some other reason, we as branches seem to struggle with being totally dependent on the Vine. Even now, are you arguing with this whole concept because you think there is at least some fruit you can produce yourself? You have a pleasing personality, you go out of your way to help others, you are thoughtful at work, you volunteer your time at church, and you probably do many other wonderful things. Yet as admirable as those things are, you get no "credit" for them with God. Those things are not "fruit" in His judgment, and He is the ultimate Fruit Inspector.

The eleven men sitting around the dinner table with Jesus were not the only ones who on occasion missed the obvious. So for your benefit, and mine, Jesus repeated, "I am the vine; you are the branches. If a man remains in me and I in him, he will bear much fruit; *apart from me you can do nothing*" (15:5).[10] Rather than wasting time struggling with pride that refuses to admit the impossibility of bearing genuine, eternal, God-pleasing fruit, we would do better to focus our attention on our connection to the Vine.

In what areas of your life are you acting independently of the Vine? I can usually determine these areas by just checking my prayer life. The items I have not prayed about—

the people and problems,

the relationships and responsibilities,

the activities and attitudes,

the schedules and stress,

the entertainment and exercise,

the pleasures and pastimes,
the decisions and dreams,
the desires and diets,
anything and everything
—are those areas of my life where I am not dependent upon Him. If my heart's cry is for more of His fruitfulness, then one of the goals of my life needs to be more consistency in my dependency. Would you make this your goal, too? Examine your life—just as you will live it out today. Submit each and every part of it to Jesus in prayer. Then live out your life, one day at a time, consistently dependent upon Him.

Our "connection" to the Vine is our personal relationship with Jesus. To remain or abide in that personal relationship means, among other things, that we need to make time for Him. For the very purpose of maintaining my "connectedness," I set my alarm seventy-five minutes earlier in the morning than necessary. When the alarm sounds, I spend fifteen minutes just waking up! . . . Washing my face . . . brushing my teeth . . . making my coffee . . . drinking my coffee! I then slip into a place I have previously prepared with my Bible, notebooks, devotionals, pen, pencil, and paper.[11] I spend the next sixty minutes talking to Him in prayer, listening to Him as I read His Word, and just generally enjoying the blessed worship of being with Him in the early morning hours.[12] I try to apply to my own life what He says through His Word. If it's a promise, I claim it. If it's a command, I obey it. If it's encouragement, I accept it. If it's a warning, I heed it.

It's the consistency of my time spent with Him, the consistency of my obedience to what He says, the consistency of my dependency upon Who He is, that keeps the connection of this "branch" with the Vine healthy and vigorous.

Yet a healthy, vigorous branch is not necessarily a fruitful branch. It's possible for a branch to have lots of leaves but no fruit.

Which is why you and I need to be cultivated.

FRUITFUL THROUGH MY CULTIVATION

Cultivation is necessary because the abundance of fruit is in direct proportion to the "size" of the connection where the branch is joined to the Vine. The smaller and more constricted the connection, the less fruit is borne because the capacity for sap is small. The larger and more expanded the connection, the greater the fruitfulness because the branch has a greater capacity to be filled with the sap. In order to expand the connection, the Gardener cuts, clips, and cleanses the branch to force the connection to the Vine itself to be enlarged.

Cultivation through Cutting

Fruit is only borne in abundance on tender, fairly new growth. As the wood of a branch gets older, it tends to get harder. So even though a branch is living and is connected to the vine, it can become barren. Still leaving the branch connected to the vine, the gardener cuts back the old, hard wood, forcing it into new growth that will produce fruit instead of just more wood and leaves. In fact, there are times when he cuts the branch back so drastically all that is left of it is the connection to the vine.

Jesus described this drastic pruning in a believer's life when He explained that the Gardener "cuts off every branch in me that bears no fruit" (15:2). There are times when God cuts everything out of our lives except our relationship with Jesus. He forces us to pay attention to our relationship with Him because that's all we have. And in the process, our "connection" to the Vine is enlarged and fruit is produced.

The firm click of the Gardener's shears can be heard when . . .

> we are confined to a hospital room,
> we are laid flat on a sickbed,
> we are fired from a job,
> we are ousted from a church,
> we are moved to a new place, surrounded by strangers,
> we are isolated in a new job, surrounded by unbelievers.

When have you been cut back to the "nub"? How have you responded to the pain of the cutting? Are you discouraged or depressed because you are cut off? Are you angry or resentful because of the change in your circumstances? Are you bitter toward the "shears" the Gardener used to achieve His purpose? Are you jealous as you look around at other fruit-laden "branches" compared to your life that has been so drastically pruned?

Dr. Alan Redpath was an outstanding Bible teacher and preacher from Great Britain. For years he pastored the great Moody Bible Church in downtown Chicago. At the height of his ministry, the church was exploding while many national opportunities were opening for him to speak and write. One day Dr. Redpath was in his study when he suddenly fell to the floor, unable to speak or to move. When his daughter discovered him, he was rushed to the hospital, where it was determined that he had had a massive stroke. For three months he was totally incapacitated with no mobility at all. He could not lift his head nor open his mouth nor move his feet nor raise his hand.

Yet interestingly, his mind was clear and active. Without ceasing, he bombarded the gates of heaven with his prayers for victory over the stroke, believing it had been sent by the devil to halt his ministry. Day after day he asked God why he was allowed to remain in what was almost an outward vegetative state. He became more and more defeated and depressed.

One day, lying propped up in bed, he looked over and saw his Bible lying on the table beside him. It was open, and his eye fell on Psalm 39:10: "Remove thy stroke away from me: I am consumed by the blow of thine hand."[13] With shocking realization, he knew his stroke had been sent to him by God! At the same moment, he knew the reason for it—that he had allowed the busyness of his *work for God* to take precedence over his *worship of God*. He had concentrated all of his time and attention and effort on bearing what he thought was fruit, and he had ignored his personal relationship with Christ! As a result, while his life was extremely busy and active, it wasn't fruitful from God's perspective and therefore not acceptable to Him. Immediately, Dr. Redpath repented of his sin. Almost in the same instant, he found he could move and speak! His health was restored!

The doctor declared it was a miracle, and it was! The doctor also told Dr. Redpath he would have to greatly reduce his schedule and that he would never preach again. Dr. Redpath just smiled. When I heard him tell this story thirteen years after his stroke, he was preaching as he told it! But he never again allowed his personal relationship with Christ to take a secondary position in his life.

Dr. Redpath had been pruned to the nub, that he might be even more fruitful. He went on to pastor his church, author outstanding books, and maintain an active conference speaking schedule. God used him in my own life to teach me many things about spiritual maturity. And one of the things he taught me was how to respond to the click of the Gardener's shears.

You and I can trust the Gardener to skillfully, personally, lovingly, and effectively use the shears in our lives. Isaiah described the gentle skillfulness of His touch when he revealed, "A bruised reed he will not break, and a smoldering wick he will not snuff out."[14] In other words, God will not cut you back so much that you are broken beyond the ability to grow, nor will He quench you to the point that you give up and quit. So trust Him. He's been pruning for years. He knows what He's doing.

Cultivation through Clipping

While cutting is drastic and encourages new growth, clipping is used mainly to control and shape the growth of the plant. This encourages fruitfulness by concentrating the energy of the vine into the fruitful areas of the branch. The Gardener clips even a fruitful branch, as Jesus described: "Every branch that does bear fruit he trims clean so that it will be even more fruitful" (15:2).[15]

The *clip, clip, clip* of the Gardener's shears is like a constant staccato in my life.

When I pray for patience and God puts me with a very demanding person . . . *clip.*[16]

When I pray for obedience and God sends suffering . . . *clip, clip.*[17]

When I pray for strength and then I'm scheduled for surgery . . . *clip.*[18]

When I pray for humility and then I am falsely accused . . . *clip, clip.*[19]

When I pray for faith and then my son is diagnosed with cancer . . . *clip.*[20]

When I pray for love and then it runs out in my marriage . . . *clip, clip.*[21] I wonder how much more fruit I would produce if I were totally submissive to the clip of the Gardener's shears. What about you? Are you resisting the Gardener's clipping? Are you withdrawing fearfully from His gentle shaping and His wise control of your growth? Then think this through carefully. Your purpose, and mine, is to bring glory to God. Jesus reiterated this purpose as He concluded His challenge to the disciples to be fruitful in service: "This is to my Father's glory, that you bear much fruit, showing yourselves to be my disciples" (15:8).

You will not bear much fruit unless and until you submit to the cutting and clipping of the Gardener. Therefore, when you resist His "gardening" in your life, what you are really doing is refusing to glorify God and therefore aborting the very purpose for your existence. Solemn thoughts, aren't they?

Instead of resisting His cutting and clipping, would you thank Him for caring enough to take the time to cultivate your life into one that brings glory to God? Cultivation is a sign of skill and time and thought on the part of the Gardener. Cultivation is proof that you are a genuine disciple.

When I look at my four-acre yard overgrown with poison ivy and briars, brick patios that can hardly be seen for all the weeds growing through the cracks, rosebushes that stretch eight feet in the air with no blooms but a lot of black spots on the leaves, I see a yard that no one takes the time to work in or think about. Obvious to even a casual observer is the fact that my husband and I are very busy with other things.

In total contrast to my yard is that of a friend who recently invited me to come and see the way she had redecorated her living room. As I drove up to her house and got out of my car, I was treated to a sight that was as beautiful as any picture in a gardening magazine. The grass looked like a soft, rolling green carpet, flower borders were spilling over with multicolored blooms, walks were swept clean—with no weeds in the cracks—the ivy was perfectly and evenly edged, and bushes were softly shaped. Every view looked like a still-life painting. The entire scene spoke of time, thought, attention, skill, and loving care.

As I surveyed the beauty of my dear friend's place, I couldn't help but wonder, when people observe the garden of my life, does it resemble her carefully, beautifully, lovingly cultivated yard? Or my overgrown, weed-infested jungle?

And I thought of the Gardener Whose cutting and clipping can be painful and unpleasant but Whose results are pleasing to the eye of the beholder and glorifying to Himself. I can think I want to be left alone, I can think I don't want to suffer anymore, I can think I want to be healthy, wealthy, prosperous, and problem free all of the time, but do I really want my spiritual life to look like my yard? If I want a spiritual life that gives evidence of true discipleship, then I must submit to the cutting, clipping, and cleansing of the Gardener.

Cultivation through Cleansing

There is one primary "internal blight" that attacks the branches of the Vine, which, if not severely dealt with, will destroy our fruitfulness. The "blight" is sin. Sin obstructs the free flow of the "sap" of the Holy Spirit in our lives. And since the Holy Spirit is the One Who truly produces the fruit that we bear, anything that grieves or quenches Him affects our fruitfulness. Jesus addressed the necessity of confronting sin in our lives when He confirmed, "You are already clean because of the word I have spoken to you" (15:3). The disciples were already clean because they had placed their faith in Him and given Him their hearts.[22] They continued to be cleansed as they listened to His Word and applied and obeyed it.

In the same way, you and I are clean when we place our faith in Jesus Christ as our Savior Who died on the cross to take away our sin, then give Him our hearts in total surrender. We continue to be cleansed as every day we live by His Word, which we read, apply, and obey. When we sin, we return to the cross by faith, confess it, and ask for cleansing, not so that we might be saved and forgiven, because we are already clean in that sense. We return to the cross for cleansing that we might maintain our fellowship with Christ and the unobstructed flow of the Holy Spirit in our lives.

Beside the road leading up to my parents' home in the mountains of western North Carolina is a spring of water. The spring used to flow out of the ground and across the driveway so that that part of the road was always wet. In the wintertime, when the temperature dropped below freezing, the water from the spring became a sheet of ice that was hazardous to drivers. So my mother placed an old wooden bucket beside the road, then ran a pipe into the bank of the mountainside where the spring was located. The water from the spring ran through the pipe into the bucket which quickly filled. The overflow from the bucket was channeled into a ditch beside the road so that the hazard of ice was removed.

My mother creatively placed a little tin cup beside the pipe, and on many occasions, as I hiked up that two-mile drive, I would stop for a drink of cold water at the little spring. On occasion, when I came to the bucket, I would find it half-filled with stagnant water. Then I would know something was blocking the pipe. Mother would run a stick through the pipe to dislodge the obstruction. Sometimes it was a small salamander. Sometimes it was a pebble or a dead leaf. But as soon as the obstruction was removed, the water would flow freely once again into the bucket.

Like the spring water, when the Holy Spirit comes into our lives, He fills us with Himself. The only thing that restricts His filling us is our sin. It can be a small, slippery salamander of jealousy or anger or selfishness or worry or lust—just something nasty. It can be a pebble of doubt or pride or bitterness or unforgiveness—something hard. It can be a dead leaf of a memory or a failure or some habit that's unpleasing to God—something flexible and pliable that's hard to pin down. Regardless of what it is, it has to be removed by confessing it so that we might be cleansed and the Water can flow and fruit will be borne.

What sin today is preventing the Holy Spirit from filling your life? You and I are commanded to "be filled with the Spirit," which means making sure we keep short accounts with the Lord where our sin is concerned.[23] Every day, in prayer, return to the cross and confess by name the sin you are conscious of having committed that day.[24] Ask God for cleansing so that you might be fruitful.

Are you thinking, "Anne, that's too much trouble. Besides, the sin in my life is so small, it can't make that much difference. And there is one sin that I could never let go of—I enjoy it too much"? Or maybe you're thinking, "It's too deeply ingrained." Or, "I don't really think it's sin; it's just the way I was raised." Whatever your excuse may be for not confessing your sin, and therefore not being cleansed, is it worth the trade-off? If you hold on to your sin, you lose out on fruitfulness. Watch out. You may be setting yourself up for getting pruned back to the "nub," remember? In your case, Jesus' words sound more like a warning: "He cuts off every branch in me that bears no fruit" (15:2). So please, for your own sake, confess your sin, giving the Holy Spirit freedom to fill your life with Himself, then ask Him to make you fruitful.

FRUITFUL THROUGH MY COMMUNICATION

As Jesus continued to teach His disciples, the evening darkness must have crept into the upper room. As the soft breeze blew in from the valley below, the light from the candles on the table and the torches on the walls would have flickered, casting moving shadows on the faces of the disciples. Seeing into the future, Jesus must have been acutely aware of all that would be demanded of the disciples in His name.

They would be responsible for taking His message of forgiveness, salvation, and eternal life through faith in Him to the entire world of their day. These rough, uneducated men would be the authors of His Father's Word as recorded in the New Testament. They would establish the church, which would function as His body on earth for thousands of years until He returned. They would bear *much* eternal fruit to His Father's glory. But even they would have to ask for it. And so He continued . . .

Asking for fruit is an important aspect of communicating with God in prayer. Like any effective communication, prayer should be two-sided. It involves our asking and also our listening. In other words, prayer is a conversation. We speak to God in prayer then listen attentively as He speaks to us through His Word. Effective communication that gets results always involves our Bibles, something that Jesus emphasized when He explained, "If you [abide] in me and my words [abide] in you, ask whatever you wish, and it will be given you" (15:7). What are your wishes? Do you wish for . . .

a spouse?

a child?

a car?

a house?

good health?

more money?

more friends?

a better job?

a longer life?

fame?

popularity?

135

Do you think the promise that Jesus gave His disciples was like handing them a Divine Genie in a bottle? And that if they would just rub the bottle with enough faith, the Genie would pop out and grant them their "wishes"? As ludicrous as that is, it actually is the way some people view prayer. And when the Genie doesn't pop out of the bottle, they become offended with God and resent Him for not being at their beck and call.

One major prerequisite to receiving answers to prayer is that our requests line up with God's will. And the only way we will know what God's will is, is if we are abiding consistently in God's Word. Instead of basing our prayers on "I hope so," our prayers are based on "God says so." And if we are saturating ourselves in His Word, then His desires will be ours, which then become the prayers of our heart.

Many people today are praying according to God's Word as it concerns a man named Jabez. Until recently, Jabez has been a little-known name from the deep recesses of a genealogy in the Old Testament book of 1 Chronicles. But due to the small book mentioned earlier that has made it to the top of the bestseller lists, his name is now a household word. The reason for his fame three thousand years after his life and death is his very brief prayer, which found its way into the Biblical record.

This is what Jabez prayed: "Oh, that you would bless me and enlarge my territory! Let your hand be with me, and keep me from harm so that I will be free from pain."[25] In essence, he was emphatically asking, "God, please, give me MORE of Your fruit in my service."

Almost as well known as the prayer of Jabez is the controversy he has stirred up. Editorials have been written in secular newspapers as well as Christian periodicals that decry the selfishness of people who clamor for more of God's blessing. Yet no one can deny that Jabez prayed that simple prayer—it's recorded in the Bible. And no one can deny that God answered Jabez's prayer in his own day, because the Biblical account confirms, "And God granted his request." And who can deny that the blessing of God continues to be poured forth on his life as millions of people are claiming the words of his prayer as their own as they seek to break through to the blessed life?

Someone has said, "Blessed is he who asks for nothing; he will not be disappointed." For those who do not believe we should ask for more blessing, don't. For the rest of us, Jesus encourages us to ask for blessing in the form of more fruit: "If you remain in me and my words remain in you, ask whatever you wish, and it will be given you" (15:7).

> When have you asked God to conform you more closely to the image of His dear Son?
>
> When have you asked God to use you to make others want to know Him better?
>
> When have you asked God to give you opportunities to share His Gospel?
>
> When have you asked God to give you the fruit of changed lives as a result?
>
> When have you asked God to draw others to Himself through your Bible study?
>
> When have you asked God to give you one person to share His love with today?

In *The Prayer of Jabez*, the author challenges the reader "to make the Jabez prayer for blessing part of the daily fabric of your life."[26] He goes on to explain that "what you know about this or any other prayer won't get you anything. . . . It's only what you believe will happen and then do next that will release God's power for you and bring about a life change." Then he offers himself and his story as living proof, which in itself is glorifying to God and a blessing to the reader.

I would like to add from my own experience that God has blessed me and expanded my territory beyond what I could have thought to ask Him for. Like the book's author, Dr. Wilkinson, I, too, discovered the prayer of Jabez years ago and had prayed it, especially as it relates to my service for God. And God has granted me my request.

But Jesus said, in an upstairs room somewhere in Jerusalem on the night He was betrayed . . .

But Jesus said, as He prepared His disciples for service and blessing that would literally turn the world upside down . . .

But Jesus said, knowing it was the Father's good pleasure to give the disciples an expanded territory that would encompass the globe for at least two thousand years and even beyond into eternity, . . .

BUT JESUS SAID, "I am the true vine, and my Father is the gardener. He cuts off every branch in me that bears no fruit, while every branch that does bear fruit he prunes so that it will be even more fruitful. . . . Remain in me, and I will remain in you. No branch can bear fruit by itself; it must remain in the vine. Neither can you bear fruit unless you remain in me. I am the vine; you are the branches. If a man remains in me and I in him, he will bear much fruit; apart from me you can do nothing" (15:1–2, 4–5).

More blessing and MORE fruit require a connection to the Vine that is attached organically and abides consistently.

More blessing and MORE fruit require cultivation as the Gardener cuts and clips and cleanses.

More blessing and MORE fruit require simple, forthright communication as I humbly ask, *Dear God, please, give me MORE fruit in my service.*

MY FATHER WAS SITTING across from me in the kitchen of my parents' home in the mountains of western North Carolina. He was wearing a soft, yellow cashmere pullover and loose-fitting, stonewashed jeans. He toyed with his cane, which was lying horizontal across his knees while he looked at me with his piercing blue eyes and inquired, "Anne, what do you think revival is? I mean, what do you think will be the evidence of it if it comes to the arenas when you hold your meetings?"

Knowing Daddy's grasp of history—especially the history of the church—I paused before answering.

In the pause, he spoke up again. "Anne, don't you think it may be already happening? Look at what has taken place in your city as a result of your teaching through the years. Thousands of people are studying the Scriptures for themselves; thousands of people are attending Bible studies and prayer groups. What more could revival be?"

And then I knew. Revival would be MORE.

More people deeply, sincerely repenting of their sin.

More people personally, permanently getting right with God.

More people boldly, accurately sharing the Gospel.

More people receiving Jesus.

More people reflecting Jesus.

More people serving Jesus.

Revival would just be MORE of Jesus!

As I climbed into bed that night, listening to the katydids singing their nightly chorus that echoed in the mountain air outside my window, I knew also that if revival was to truly come to the arenas during our meetings, it would be an exclusive "God thing," because "without Me you can do nothing." But I also knew that the "MORE" I was asking God to give me was only possible if I, personally, was connected to the Vine and was cultivated by the Gardener and communicated in prayer my desire for more. And so in the darkness of the room where I grew up as a girl, *I prayed . . .*

8

MORE of
His Love in My Home

*H*E WAS TALL, broad-shouldered, clear-eyed, outgoing, and so handsome heads turned as he walked down the street. His attention made young girls giddy and older girls dreamy-eyed.

She was petite, confident, and pretty, with a high-wattage smile that could light up the dreariest room. Due to a painful past, she had closed her heart to romantic relationships—until she met him. Eight months after their first date, they were married.

The marriage began to unravel almost as soon as the knot was tied. Without revealing even the smallest detail to the doting family and friends surrounding them, the caustic arguments that would become characteristic of their relationship began during the reception following the wedding ceremony. The honeymoon was over before it began. They were totally, irreconcilably incompatible!

Four years of battle wounds did not lessen their commitment to their marriage vows. But the wounds became scars that left deep imprints on their hearts and minds. As I held the sobbing young woman in my arms—as I watched the pain etch lines of suffering around the young man's eyes and mouth—I prayed, *Jesus, they need MORE of Your love in their home.*

The following is what I wanted to say to them then . . . and to you now.

MORE LOVE FOR HIM

My husband and I celebrated thirty-six years of marriage this past September. Our relationship, which began with such love and passion, deteriorated over time until my love for my husband had run out. In answer to persistent, desperate prayer, God, in His grace and mercy, gave me the key to loving my husband when the love had run out so that I can say today with all honesty our relationship is once again filled with love. The key is so simple I'm not sure why I had missed it. The key God gave me on a particularly emotional, bleak morning so long ago was this: *Love for my husband is the fruit of my relationship with the Vine.*

In the brief time that was left in the upper room on that Thursday evening following the last supper He would have before the cross and resurrection, Jesus continued to pour Himself into His disciples. Still using the familiar illustration of a grapevine, He now focused them on their relationship with each other, handing them the same key I was given so many years later.

As the disciples wiped their mouths, pushed back their bowls and plates, and settled into a more comfortable position around the table, I wonder if our Lord's eyes swept over the scene before Him, taking in the rugged young faces of His followers:

> the impetuous, compulsive cockiness of Peter,
> the quiet, contemplative sensitivity of John,
> the quizzical, almost cynical, reservation of Thomas,
> the methodical, analytical look of Matthew,
> the pragmatic, yet supporting encouragement of Andrew,
> the fiery zeal of James . . .

one by one, did His gaze linger on each dear face, knowing He would soon be saying good-bye? When He left them without His visible presence, all they would have would be each other. Suddenly a major problem must have become very obvious to them! Because it was very likely that they were *totally, irreconcilably incompatible!* How in the world would this motley collection of contradictory personalities ever lovingly, powerfully unite in such a way that He could use them to establish His church and change the world? There was one way—and one way only! And so He proceeded to give them the key to loving others with whom they were totally incompatible.

Is there someone who, even now, comes to your mind as being totally incompatible with you?

Is it someone you live with, such as a parent?

Or sibling?

Or spouse?

Or roommate?

Or child?

Is it someone you work with, such as a secretary?

Or supervisor?

Or employer?

Or coach?

Or teacher?

Is it someone you are thrown together with, such as a teammate?

Or co-worker?

Or committee member?

Or neighbor?

Or landlord?

Have you felt incompatibility was reason enough to sever the relationship? Or at least to avoid it at all costs? Yet there are times when we have no option but to live with or work with or be thrown together with someone who totally contradicts our own personalities and natures. At such times the relationship can become so strained that we can even perceive the incompatible person as an enemy. But there is another way . . .

Jesus focused His disciples on His way of dealing with incompatibility when He gave them the same key He gave me years ago. It's the key that enables us not only to love our spouses, but anyone else with whom we are incompatible—especially within the home. The key is to make our relationship with Jesus the priority of our lives. Jesus reminded His disciples, "As the Father has loved me, so have I loved you. Now remain in my love" (15:9).

Love Expressed by Abiding

The first secret to loving others is to immerse yourself in a love relationship with God the Father, God the Son, and God the Holy Spirit—and abide there.

I will never get over the wonder that God the Father and God the Son do not have

a working kinship

nor a business partnership

nor a brotherly friendship

nor a competing dictatorship

nor a mandatory fellowship

nor an obligatory guardianship

but a *love relationship*

that has existed since before time and space! And you and I enter into that eternal sphere of unconditional love when we abide in Christ.

Did you know that you are God's special loved one? Why would He love you so? Maybe it's because when you abide in Christ you are so saturated in Jesus that when God looks at you, He sees His own precious Son and envelopes you in His love for Jesus' sake!

As you and I develop and grow in this love relationship with God, abiding with Him through meaningful prayer and Bible reading, getting to know Him on a deeper level as we live out what we say we believe, He fills us with Himself. And "God is love."[1] As you and I are filled with God, we will be filled with His love, not only for Himself, but for others—which includes our spouses or the incompatible people with whom we are struggling. God has promised to pour out "his love into our hearts by the Holy Spirit, whom he has given us."[2]

Would you examine the time you are devoting to developing your relationship with God? Is the time you have allocated sufficient if you want the fruit of this relationship to overflow into other areas of your life?

When I was struggling in my relationship with my husband, for months I focused on my relationship with him. I felt I was walking on eggshells all the time as I tried to be so very careful to say the right thing and not the wrong thing, to do the right thing and not the wrong thing, to look or feel or act the right way and not the wrong way. What freedom and release I experienced when God gently impressed on me that my focus was all wrong and my efforts were misdirected. I was not to concentrate on my relationship with my husband; I was to concentrate on my relationship with Him!

Love Expressed by Obeying

The gaze of the disciples must have held steady as Jesus described their exclusive inclusion in His relationship with His Father. Some of their heads surely nodded in agreement—yes, they could love Him and love His Father, and it would be their absolute delight to remain in such a privileged position. Maybe some of them sat up a little straighter and lifted their chins a little higher with an increasing sense of self-importance.

I wonder if Jesus' gaze became slightly more intense as He led them further in His thought process: "If you obey my commands, you will remain in my love, just as I have obeyed my Father's commands and remain in his love" (15:10). In other words, love for Jesus and His Father is not just a warm, affectionate, pleasant, comfortable, secure feeling—although it is. But it's more. Love for Him is obedience to Him. It's that simple.

> Who do you know who says he loves God but disobeys His command to love His only Son, Jesus Christ?[3]
>
> Who do you know who says he loves God but disobeys His command to love others when others are of another race? Or culture? Or nationality? Or economic group? Or gender? Or denomination? Or religion?[4]
>
> Who do you know who says he loves God but disobeys His command to love his brother—with whom he is incompatible?[5]
>
> Who do you know who says he loves God but disobeys His command to separate:
>
> > from worldly preoccupation that leaves no time for thoughts of God,
> >
> > and worldly priorities that leave no time for service to God,

and worldly pleasures that leave no emotions for God,
and a worldly pace that keeps him so busy there is no time
for quiet meditative prayer and Bible reading?[6]

We can say we love God, but the words are like a "resounding gong or a clanging cymbal"[7]—totally empty and meaningless—unless they are followed by obedience to His commands.

One of my favorite stories is of a little boy who simply adored his mother. He loved her so much he wanted to tell her, but he couldn't come up with the right words to express it. He would gaze at her with round eyes full of emotion, but whenever she asked what he was thinking, he would drop his eyes and mutter, "Nothin'."

One day the little boy came into the kitchen and overheard his mother commenting on the telephone to her friend that she would dearly love to have her living room painted. The little boy's eyes lit up and a wide grin spread across his face. That afternoon when his mother went out on an errand, he frantically went to work. When he heard her footsteps on the walk as she returned, he ran to the front door and greeted her enthusiastically, "Mommie, Mommie, come see what I've done for you! I love you so much, and I wanted to tell you but didn't know how. But I've done something to show you how much I love you."

With shining eyes and glowing face, he took her hand and guided her to the living room. She stood at the door and gazed aghast at red paint dripping down the walls, red paint dribbled across the carpet, red paint smudged on the furniture! The mother wasn't pleased; she was horrified! The little boy's demonstration of love did not convey to his mother how he felt at all—because what he had done wasn't what she had had in mind or the way she had wanted it or how she had wanted it or when she had wanted it.

What red living room are you offering the Lord? You say you love God, and you are doing things to demonstrate your love, but are they the things *He* wants? Instead of pleasing God, is He aghast at your behavior? What He wants is not some grandiose gesture or philanthropic contribution or volunteer effort or religious ritual—He wants your heart! And He wants your obedience to His commands that are stated in black and white on the pages of your Bible—commands that may lead you to make a gesture or contribution or volunteer effort, but only as an act of obedience to what He has said, motivated by your abiding, loving relationship with Him.

There are times His commands have seemed to be totally irrelevant to the incompatible relationship I have struggled with. But as I grow in my relationship with Him through my obedience to Him, He fills my life until it overflows into the life of that other person. And the joy comes—joy in knowing God is pleased, joy in knowing I'm doing those things that will have a positive impact on my relationships, joy as I fulfill God's purpose for my life, joy even as I interact with that incompatible person!

Love Expressed by Joy

Joy is supremely different than happiness. Happiness, which is an American's inalienable right to pursue, seems to depend more on circumstances or things or people or feelings. Joy is independent of everything except our relationship with God. Someone has defined joy as peace dancing! And Jesus, with eyes that must have sparkled in anticipation of the blessing that His beloved friends were going to receive, explained, "I have told you this so that my joy may be in you and that your joy may be complete" (15:11).

Is your joy incomplete because you have not followed through in obedience to something God has commanded you to do—or not to do? Is your joy incomplete because you have drawn a line in the sand and protested that you will go no farther in the relationship with that other person because you are just so incompatible you are sure it will never work out? Then you are going to miss out on the fullness of joy!

One of the hallmarks of those who are immersed in a love relationship with Jesus and His Father, which they express through abiding obedience, is joy! Joy in Jesus! Joy in living our lives for Him! Joy in abiding . . . and obeying! Joy in our relationship with those who are incompatible! Joy that is complete, with nothing that needs to be added to make it more so.

As of this writing, my mother is eighty-two years of age. Because of degenerative arthritis, she has had so many hip replacements I have lost count of them, and she is now confined to a wheelchair or a walker. Her back is so disjointed that even after multiple surgeries she lives with chronic pain.

Due to exposure to polio when she was a young woman, her throat has very little elasticity, a problem that sends her into spasms of coughing and choking. Yet in my mind's eye I can picture her as I have seen her so many times in the last few years—propped up on the pillows of her bed, white hair like an elegant halo about her head, white eyelet ruffled dressing gown floating softly around her like a cloud, white pearls clasped on her ears and encircling her slender neck, Bibles and reading materials fanned out over the bed's surface, face sparkling and eyes dancing with sheer joy! She is living out the end of a life that has been saturated in Jesus! It's a saturation that was a deliberate choice on her part.

As a teenager growing up, my room in our house was directly over Mother's. At night I could see the lights from her room reflected on the trees outside my window. When I slipped downstairs hoping to talk to her a few minutes, I would find her shapely form bent beside her bed in prayer. It was useless to wait for her to rise because she would be there for hours on end, so I would trudge back up to my room. And no matter how early I awoke in the morning, I would see those lights from her window once again reflected on the trees outside. But in the mornings, when I tumbled down the stairs, I would find her seated at her big, flat-top desk, earnestly reading and studying the one of fourteen different translations of the Bible she had spread out around her. My mother chose to make abiding in Christ one of the priorities of her life.

Mother's abiding is rooted in a love relationship with Jesus that is the secret of her life. In fact, it's the love relationship that I saw she had with Him that created a thirst within me for a similar relationship with Him—something I am still pursuing more of to this day. As a result of her abiding, and the obedience that is integrated into it, the hallmark of Mother's life is joy. Her face radiates it! Her eyes sparkle with it! Her mouth laughs with it! If possible, her feet would dance with it!

In spite of the restrictions of old age and the physical limitations it brings; in spite of the chronic pain and discomfort she continually lives with; in spite of being confined to the point she depends heavily on the help and assistance of others, some of whom are incompatible with her positive, witty, sparkling zest for life—*Mother's joy is complete!* Because she has so much MORE of Jesus, His life overflows from her into the lives of those around her—and we are all blessed! Surely, as Jesus looks at Mother with emotion-filled eyes of soft tenderness and unfathomable love, He is blessed and His joy is complete in her!

As Jesus held out the promise of joy to His disciples, did their hearts quicken with anticipation even as they glanced at each other, wondering what command would be the "strings" attached to receiving that joy? If that thought was on their minds, they didn't have long to wait and wonder, because Jesus spelled it out to them very clearly: "My command is this: Love each other as I have loved you" (15:12).

Love each other? On hearing that command, did compulsive Peter look at cautious Thomas and silently exclaim, *You mean, love him, Lord?*

Did sensitive John look at his zealous brother, James, with flashbacks to years of sibling rivalry and protest in his heart, *I've been trying to love him for years, but the best I can do is tolerate him.*

The story is told of a runner after the battle of Marathon in Greece years ago who was sent to tell one of the commanding generals which side had won the battle. After covering miles of rugged terrain, the runner—sweaty, dirty, breathless—was ushered into the general's presence. The general and all his aides were hushed to hear what vital words the runner had to give. To their utter consternation, the runner blurted out, "I forgot the message!"

Lest you and I forget our Lord's message, He repeats it twice in this passage! "Love each other" (15:12, 17). That's a command, not an option! What Christian are you tolerating instead of loving? Why? Is it because he or she grates on your nerves?

In the Old Testament, the meal offering consisted of fine flour that was ground to powder by being placed in a round hole, where it was grated by a square pestle. The flour was then mixed with oil, which represented the Holy Spirit. The oil and flour, thoroughly mixed together and offered to God, was a picture of a totally consecrated life.

Sometimes God puts us with someone whom He uses to grate us. For instance, perhaps you are very generous with your money, and you are married to someone who is so careful, he or she is almost stingy. Or perhaps you are very quiet, and God has put you on a committee with someone who talks nonstop. Or worse, perhaps you are a nonstop talker and you are on a committee with another nonstop talker! Instead of avoiding those with whom we are incompatible or just tolerating them, Jesus commands you and me to love them. And as we obey His command, He will use that person to grind off our sharp, impatient, un-Christlike edges. As we yield to the full control of His Holy Spirit, our character increasingly bears much fruit for His glory as we are conformed to the image of Jesus Christ.[8]

Like you and me, the disciples must have had question marks written all over their faces: *How in the world can I love someone who gets on my nerves? How can I love that totally incompatible person?*

Jesus, knowing what they were thinking and feeling, proceeded to use His own love for them as an example to follow.[9] Just how did He demonstrate His love for them?

Love That Is Sacrificial

Our Lord's love for His disciples, as well as for you and me, is totally sacrificial in nature. Lest there be any confusion as to His meaning, He defined it: "Greater love has no one than this, that one lay down his life for his friends" (15:13). In other words, because of His great love for you and me, He has esteemed our well-being and our needs to be of greater concern to Himself than His own to such an extent that He died for us—irrespective of our condition or response.

Our concept of demonstrating love seems so much smaller than what Jesus defined for His disciples. We love others

who meet our needs,

whom we get along with,

who make us feel good,

who do things for us,

who give us things we want,

who respond with love,

whom we like.

In essence, our first concern is for our own well-being and having our own needs met, and we love others in proportion to the extent they fulfill those purposes. Our second concern is that others respond positively to our overtures; if they don't, we refuse to continue to love them. But Jesus was outlining a radically different kind of love—a love that puts the needs and well-being of others before our own to the extent we would sacrifice our time, our energy, our money, and our thoughts in order to demonstrate it. We are to demonstrate it to others whom we may not like or with whom we may be incompatible or who respond negatively or who may never do anything for us in return!

Years ago, I received a telephone call from a precious friend who was frantic and in tears. Without waiting to hear what the problem was, I just told her I would be right there; then I hung up the phone and drove to her house. As I was driving, I reflected back on my relationship with my beloved friend Karen.[10] She had been raised in a very orthodox and religious family where God was feared instead of loved. She had married a wonderful man who seemed to adore her, and they had had two children who were now teenagers. For years she had resisted coming into my Bible class at a time when many of her friends attended.

One day Karen passed the church where our class was meeting, and her curiosity was aroused by the hundreds of cars that were jammed all around it. She came in to investigate the class and, right then and there, decided to join it. Within a very short time, Karen encountered the person of Jesus Christ through the pages of His Word, and was soundly born again. She became one of the few among the hundreds of women in my class who was my "buddy."

When I entered her home after having received her urgent phone call, I found Karen sitting on the sofa weeping. I held her for a few moments then asked her what had upset her so. Briefly she described a family business she was in that included her mother. I knew her mother was a woman who had been harshly critical of Karen her entire life, who found fault with everything she did, who was never pleased with even the simplest or most elaborate effort that was made to appease her.

Then Karen looked at me with a horrified look and a fresh outburst of tears and exclaimed, "My mother is suing me!"

I looked at her, dumbfounded! I dreaded hearing what I knew she would say next: "Anne, what do I do?"

Nothing in my experience had prepared me to have even a clue as to what counsel to give her. But in my heart, I quickly prayed, *God, help me help Karen!* My eyes fell on her open Bible, so I answered her by inquiring, "What does God seem to be saying to you?"

Karen showed me a passage of Scripture that indicated she was to firmly stand up to her mother but not fight for her rights. And that she was to love her mother as Jesus loved her!

Outwardly I wept and nodded, hoping I seemed caring and wise, but inside I was almost screaming, *God, You can't mean that! Surely she misread Your words! She has to fight this lawsuit! Better yet, send someone to jerk up this mother until her teeth rattle!* I had sense enough not to let Karen know what I was really thinking, then I offered to pray with her. I simply prayed that God would clearly direct and confirm His direction to her, giving her the courage to be obedient to whatever He said.

The lawsuit was settled out of court. Months later, Karen came over to help me sew draperies for my living room. As we huddled on the floor, lining up the fabric with pins in our mouths and laughing chatter on our lips, she disclosed that when she left my house after hanging the new drapes she was going over to her mother's house. I became very still and just looked at Karen. Then she said in a quiet voice, "My mother is moving from the old homeplace into an apartment, and I'm helping her decorate. In fact, I'm sewing the draperies for her living room, too."

This time I couldn't hold it back. I just blurted out, "How can you do that? How in the world can you do that? How can you help your mean old mother who finds fault with everything you do and even sued you?!"

In my lifetime, I will never forget her answer. "Anne," Karen replied with a lilt in her voice and a sparkle in her eyes, "I've chosen to forgive my mother. Not just once, but again and again. Every time she calls me and I hear her voice on the phone, I choose to forgive my mother all over again. Every time I lie down on my bed at night and the memories come back, I forgive my mother again . . . and again . . . and again! And God has set me free to love my mother."[11]

You could have knocked me over with a feather! I stared at my friend and knew I had bumped into something holy and precious—I had bumped into the very heart of God! God, Who chose to forgive me when I didn't deserve it, then loved me sacrificially by showering me with His time and thoughts and gifts and love and His very life!

Now, as I look back on Karen's experience, I can trace in her life the facets of the key Jesus handed His disciples on that Thursday evening so long ago. Karen had grown in her love for God through the study of His Word. She had learned to abide in Him. Her abiding had led her to obey His command to love her mother when loving her mother was the last thing she felt like doing. But the obedience had borne the fruit of genuine joy as it had set her free from years of bitterness and resentment and unforgiveness and a wounded spirit. And it was Karen's deepening love relationship with Jesus that overflowed into a love for her mother that was totally sacrificial in nature.

Who in your life is like Karen's mother? Someone who has been rude, critical, hostile, abrasive, belligerent, unkind, selfish, condescending? If not completely unlovable, is the person at the very least, totally incompatible? *That* is the *very person*—especially when that person is within our own homes—that Jesus indicates we are to love sacrificially!

Who are you holding out on? A parent? A spouse? A child? A friend? Are you waiting until that person meets your needs before you give in to meet his or hers? God won't bless that attitude. You and I are to sacrificially love that other person, even if he or she never responds or meets our needs. When we do choose to obey what Jesus is saying, we plunge into a deeper, more intimate relationship with Him that becomes our most precious treasure—an ample reward for any sacrifice we make for His sake. Because the *only reason* we would choose to love that person sacrificially is because of Him. Our sacrificial love for that person then becomes an act of worship of Jesus.

Love That Is Special

If His disciples then were like His disciples now, I expect they flinched in the face of such a challenge. So, to soften His command without backing down even a little, Jesus encouraged them to love others sacrificially *for what they would get out of it*—a very special relationship with Him: "You are my friends if you do what I command" (15:14).

What could be a greater privilege than to have *Jesus* call *us* His *friend?* If I told you that the president of the United States was my friend, you would probably snicker. And rightly so. Although I have briefly met him, I don't really know him, and any "friendship" is based on what I have read about him. But if the president of the United States stated that, "Anne Lotz is my friend," it would be impressive. It would indicate a relationship based on personal knowledge that he publicly affirmed.

Jesus did more than say you and I could call Him our friend. He promises He will call us *His* friends! Now that's impressive! That's a privileged position! Do you struggle with an inferiority complex? Then hold your head a little higher because when you choose to abide in Christ and obey His command to love others sacrificially,

>the Son of God,
>>the Savior of the world,
>>>the sovereign Lord,
>>the sweet Rose of Sharon,
>the Lord of glory,
>>THE KING OF KINGS AND LORD OF LORDS,
>*the most important Man in all of the universe,*

counts you as His personal friend! His invitation to personal friendship was not just extended to His original disciples but even to the weakest believer today!

Years ago, I set as my goal friendship with God. I decided if Abraham and Moses and King David could know God in a personal relationship that God would describe as a friendship—and if God is the same yesterday, today, and forever—than why couldn't I know Him in a relationship that He would describe as a friendship?[12] And so I set out on a pilgrimage to know Him—

>a pilgrimage that has led me to the pages of my Bible in meditation,
>>that has led me to the floor on my knees in prayer,
>>that has led me to step out of my comfort zone into obedience,
>>that has led me to the heights of joy,
>>>and the depths of pain,
>>>and the lengths of sacrifice,
>>>and the width of the whole world,

and has opened up for me a richer dimension in my relationship with Him than I ever thought possible. It's this relationship that is also essential for knowing and understanding God's will and purpose for my life.

Love That Is Essential

For the disciples, nothing could be more essential than knowing God's purpose. It would be the disciples

> who would recognize, receive, and articulate the coming of the
>   Holy Spirit,
> who would present the Gospel to the world,
> who would establish the church,
> who would determine guidelines for church sacraments and
>   leadership,
> who would enforce and draw the boundaries for church
>   discipline,
> who would set the standards for Christian behavior,
> who would reveal to every succeeding generation Who Jesus is,
> who would give written explanation of Jesus, His ministry, and
>   His words as they authored the New Testament.

In essence, it would be the disciples who would continue Jesus' work on earth when He went back to heaven. Knowing the will and purpose of God was not an option; it was a necessity!

Jesus reassured these same disciples that their exalted position as His friends would also entitle them to the privilege of knowing His Father's will as He continued to explain, "I no longer call you servants, because a servant does not know his master's business. Instead, I have called you friends, for everything that I learned from my Father I have made known to you" (15:15).

You and I, as disciples, are also those . . .

> who receive the Holy Spirit,
> who present the Gospel to the world,
> who maintain and plant churches,
> who hold up the guidelines for church sacraments and leadership,

who enforce the boundaries for church discipline,

who live out the standards for Christian behavior,

who reveal to the world between our own two feet Who Jesus is,

who teach the written explanation of Jesus, His ministry, and His

words as we have been given them in the New Testament.

In essence, you and I are continuing Jesus' work on earth today in our generation.

Knowing the will and purpose of God is not an option for us either—it is a necessity!

Do you struggle with knowing the will of God for your life? For your marriage? For your family? For your home? For that incompatible relationship? Knowing God's will is not difficult—unless you are not abiding in Him. Jesus indicated that knowing His Father's will is the fruit of *abiding* as well as *asking:* "You did not choose me, but I chose you to go and bear fruit—fruit that will last. Then the Father will give you whatever you ask in my name" (15:16).

God has chosen you and me for the purpose of bearing much eternal fruit—fruit in our character such as love, joy, peace, patience, kindness, goodness, faithfulness, gentleness, and self-control exhibited toward those within our own home[13]—fruit that is simply the character of God's Son coming out in us. We are to bear much eternal fruit in our service as we lead other people to faith in Jesus Christ and help them to grow into maturity so that they in turn will produce much eternal fruit in their lives.

If the divine Fruit Inspector came to you today, what would He find? Has your fruitfulness validated, or invalidated, His choice of you as a disciple? Remember—you and I don't have to try hard to produce the fruit. So relax! Rest in the Vine! Release the flow of the Divine Sap through the branch of your life as you open it up to Him! Then enjoy the Gardener's pleasure in you!

HAVING SAID SO MUCH of the above to the young married couple living in such misery, I simply followed Jesus' example and repeated His words: "This is my command: Love each other" (15:17). As they have continued to struggle, I wonder about them as I wonder about you. What is there about

His command that they don't understand . . . ? Yet I know personally what it is to understand these principles but simply not do them. And so as my heart's cry reverberates, *Please, dear Jesus, just give me MORE of Your love in my home,* it's as though I hear the Divine echo from heaven in response, *Then, Anne, just give Me MORE of your heart.*

9

MORE *of*
His Courage in My Convictions

*Y*EARS AGO, during the days of the powerful Roman Empire, there existed a special forces–type unit referred to as the Thundering Legion. This elite group of fighting men had greatly distinguished itself on the battlefield. It was led by a young commander, Camidus, who, in the course of his daily affairs, heard that God loved him and had sent His own Son, Jesus Christ, to die as a sacrifice for his sin, then had risen from the dead to give him eternal life. The young commander was so impacted that he was converted, placing his faith in Jesus Christ. He then shared his newfound faith with his regiment, and each of the thirty-nine soldiers under his command placed his faith in Jesus Christ alone for salvation.

At the very time the regiment became more and more vocal about their faith in Jesus Christ, the Roman emperor became more and more insistent that he, the emperor, be recognized and worshiped as a god. In the end, an ugly confrontation took place when the regiment was commanded by the acting Roman governor to sacrifice to idols. The entire regiment refused. All forty professional fighting men were arrested by other soldiers and sent to a remote northern province. There they were called upon to renounce their faith in Jesus Christ once and for all. Again, each one refused.

As punishment for their faith, the forty soldiers were marched out onto the surface of a frozen lake, stripped of all their clothes, and loosely tied by a rope that encircled the neck of each and was strung from man to man. The men were then told they would be left on the lake until they froze to death.

However, if any man changed his mind, all he had to do was to slip the rope up and off his neck, walk to the shore, renounce his faith to the guard, and enter a steaming hot bath in order to recover from the exposure.

As the guard went back to his post to warm himself by his fire and to watch the forty nude men shivering in the freezing air, he heard them begin to chant: *"Forty soldiers, we stand strong in the strength of Christ and Christ alone."* The chant continued until the darkness fell and the night descended, bringing with it plummeting temperatures. In the frozen bleakness, the chant became weaker, then faded altogether.

In the middle of the night, one of the freezing soldiers struggled to lift his arms, then unwrapped the rope from his neck and stumbled to the shore. In a barely audible voice, he told the guard he could not stand the cold any longer and renounced his faith in Jesus Christ. He then fell into the warmth of the steaming Roman bath.

As the guard returned to his post, he strained his ears to hear a sound coming from across the surface of the frozen lake: *"Thirty-nine soldiers, we stand strong in the strength of Christ and Christ alone."* He held his breath to listen more carefully—then heard it again! This time the chant was repeated louder, with more strength. The guard was stunned! Who could provoke such conviction and commitment from such men? The guard knew it was Jesus! Slowly but surely, the guard walked across the surface of the lake to where the thirty-nine men were still standing. He quietly stripped off his clothes, stepped into the line of soldiers, wrapped the rope around his own neck, took the place of the soldier who had gone to shore, and shouted, "I am a Christian." The chant rang out once more, only this time it was stronger and louder than it had been before: *"Forty soldiers, we stand strong in the strength of Christ and Christ alone."* When the sun rose early the next morning, forty soldiers lay dead on the frozen surface of the lake.[1]

Where does such strength come from? Where do you find courage and convictions like that to live for—and die for?

Today, in our God-blessed nation of America, no one is marched onto a frozen lake and left to die because of his or her faith in Christ. No one is crucified or thrown to the lions or burned at the stake because he or she believes in Jesus as the only way to God. Yet the average church member seems to lack deep convictions concerning who Jesus is to the extent he or she cowers under a raised eyebrow, or a whispered innuendo, or a politically incorrect label.

Recently, Dr. John Perkins addressed a room packed with Christian missionaries and workers. With passion resonating in his voice, he boldly articulated what I earnestly believe to be true when he stated that "the greatest crisis in America today is a crisis of leadership. And the crisis of leadership," he went on to say, "is rooted in a crisis of courage and a crisis of convictions."[2]

Are you part of the crisis? What are your genuine, personal convictions concerning the Gospel? Are you convinced that Jesus is the only Way to God, the only Truth about how to get to heaven, the only Life that is eternal and abundant? Are you convinced that no one will ever be accepted by God the Father, except they come to Him through Jesus Christ? If these statements, which paraphrase Jesus' own claims, are your convictions, then do you have the courage to state them publicly?[3] Today? To your family, friends, neighbors, and co-workers? Many church members in our pluralistic, tolerant society not only lack the courage to stand up for the truth that faith in Jesus Christ alone is the only way to God, they actually reproach others who do!

In the light of such spiritual anemia, my heart's cry is, *Please, Jesus, give me MORE of Your courage in my convictions.* Courage to stand out and speak up about my convictions in the way Christians have exhibited in every century since the cross and resurrection. Courage that even today is displayed in remote corners of the world where men and women are giving their lives for Jesus Christ.

With His omniscient eye, I wonder if Jesus looked into the future from the setting of that upper room. If He did—with what must have been a grave expression and a heavy heart, the lines of suffering already etched deeply in His face—He would have seen His followers down through the centuries, who, one by one, were

crucified,

vilified,

ostracized,

outlawed,

beheaded,

beaten,

exiled,

    excommunicated,

      imprisoned,

        impaled,

          tortured,

            taunted,

              thrown to the lions,

              fed to wild animals,

            crushed by hurled stones,

          shot by firing squads,

        burned at the stake[4] . . .

      for His name's sake!

And did He also see those church members of our generation? Did He see those who love their own lives more than His and renounce their faith in Him, not verbally but practically, as they blend into the crowd like spiritual chameleons rather than endure social ostracism or public ridicule?

In the waning moments of the evening before His own crucifixion, Jesus knew He had to prepare His disciples—and those like us who would follow them—not to rule with Him, but to live and to die for Him. He had to prepare them for the kind of treatment they could *expect* from the world around them—a treatment that would require deep convictions . . . and the courage to live by them!

COURAGE TO STAND OUT

Without their being consciously aware of what He had been doing, Jesus had revealed to His disciples how they would find the courage to not only *live* their lives for Him on a daily basis but to actually *give* their lives for Him on a final basis in death. Because their courage would be the fruit of their love for Him as well as their love for each other. Which is why He began His challenge to stand out for Him in the world with the command "Love each other" (15:17).

As I have gone into the world, presenting the Gospel on television and radio talk shows, or exalting Jesus from secular and religious platforms, I have been treated with respect most of the time. But there have been those occasions when a listener has called into a talk show on which I was featured, vilifying me as an "American Taliban" because of my absolute conviction that the Bible is true.[5] I have read reviews of my engagements where the writer has described me as a middle-aged woman parading a worn-out, old-time message that has no relevance in our new century because I have lifted up the cross. I have been accused of trying to ride my Father's coattails and make a name for myself because I have walked through doors of opportunity that have been opened for me to proclaim God's Word. I have been attacked as a Jezebel who is leading women within the church into sin by my own example of ministry leadership.[6] I have been labeled unloving, intolerant, exclusive, narrow-minded, fundamentalist, naive—the list goes on. I have been excluded from social functions, platforms, seminars—and even from some churches.

To be perfectly honest, sometimes the criticism and attacks sting. But for the most part, I genuinely do not care what others say or think. Do you know why? Because I decided when I was seventeen years of age that since I could never please everyone anyway, I would live my life to please God. And as I have kept that my life's goal, and as I have grown deeper in my love for Him, what others think pales in comparison with what He thinks. To undergird me, I have an entire network of family, staff, co-workers, publishers, editors, and friends all over the world who love me, understand me, agree with me, support me, encourage me, and pray for me to keep on keeping on! It's my love for Jesus and His love for me expressed through His other disciples that helps to give me the courage to stand out in front of the crowd!

Standing Out by Separation

Jesus uttered words that we know have rung true in various repressive countries of the world, but they are words that have seemed foreign to our experience in American culture—until the last few years. He spoke bluntly when He warned, "If the world hates you, keep in mind that it hated me first" (15:18).

Hated? By the *world?* Who *is* the world?

Jesus certainly wasn't referring to the world of nature in the earth, sea, mountains, plains, and valleys. He was referring to the world of humanity that forms our governments, political agenda, businesses, entertainment, organizations, clubs, media, and schools—which determines the atmosphere in which we live.

In the beginning, the entire world of humanity, represented by Adam and Eve in the Garden of Eden, rebelled against God through disobedience and was thus separated from Him.[7] The second worldwide rebellion provoked the judgment of God in a flood that would have resulted in the annihilation of the entire human race, except for the fact that one man, Noah, found favor in God's eyes.[8] Through Noah the human race was preserved. The third and last world rebellion against God was at the Tower of Babel when man determined to build his own religious system in order to get into heaven, defying God's provision of one way only—through the blood of a lamb.[9] To prevent the world from uniting in rebellion against Him—when not even one man found favor in His eyes—God confused man's language, scattering him by families and clans until he filled the earth, forming the basis for the nations as we now know them.[10]

Like three strikes in a baseball game, the world of humanity after three rebellions was out of the "game." Following the third rebellion at the Tower of Babel, God focused His attention on the family of one man named Abraham, through whom He eventually provided His Lamb—Jesus Christ—Who was sacrificed for the sin and rebellion of the world. Through the sacrifice of Jesus Christ, the world was "back in the game," with an opportunity to be reconciled to God through faith in Jesus.[11]

But there should be no mistake about the world in which we live today. It's the same world of humanity that has filled the earth with rebellion and religious defiance of God since the Tower of Babel. And it's the same world of humanity today that has established . . .

Patterns of behavior that are based on values, a moral code, and standards of ethics according to what feels good or what seems right—or what man can get by with—not on the Word of God. In the post-modern world, absolutes that previously determined our patterns of behavior are denied and discarded.[12]

Priorities that are self-centered, not Christ-centered, and have as their goal laying up treasures on earth, not in heaven.[13]

Pleasures that are sought in temporary, superficial happiness and are dependent on

    material possessions,

        sexual experiences,

            exotic destinations,

                powerful positions,

                    advanced education,

                        well-known reputations,

                            and immediate gratification

with no real thought for the future or eternity.[14]

A pace that is so fast it leaves no time for prayer, Bible reading, or thought of God and works so furiously during the week that the weekend is considered a vacation! And no one wants to go to church on his vacation![15]

Preoccupation with self while

                the hungry go without food,

            and the thirsty go without water,

         and the naked go without clothing,

      and the homeless go without shelter,

    the elderly and infirm go without comfort,

  and the prisoner goes without visitors.[16]

How could you and I, as disciples of Jesus Christ, possibly live according to the world's pattern of behavior when we live according to God's Word?

How could we possibly have priorities that are self-centered, when our priority is Jesus?

How can we live for worldly pleasures when we are to seek first the kingdom of God?

How can we walk at the world's pace when we walk with God?

And how can we be preoccupied with ourselves when we love God with all our heart, soul, mind, and strength, and our neighbor as ourselves?

We can't!

There has to be some cleavage between the person who regards God as the only reality in life and the world that doesn't even acknowledge His relevance!

In what ways do you come into contact with the world as it has just been defined? What magazines and books do you read?

What movies and TV programs do you watch?

What clubs and organizations do you belong to?

What neighbors and friends do you spend time with?

Do the majority, if not all of them, promote a worldly pattern of behavior, priorities, pleasures, pace, and preoccupation? Has your discomfort at not "fitting in" made you feel socially and culturally inept? Has the world's hatred,

ridicule,

criticism,

vilification,

demonization,

accusations

made you feel you were doing something wrong? Could it be, without even consciously trying, you have been standing out because you don't belong to the world, you have been chosen to belong to God?

Separation from the world is logical, since we operate on a totally different level in every area of our lives. But separation is also a command we are to obey for our own benefit, lest we be pressed into the world's mold.[17] However, separation from the world requires a certain amount of courage, because the world often views our separation as an indictment of itself and resents us for it.

Jesus underscored our separation from the world when He said, "If you belonged to the world, it would love you as its own. As it is, you do not belong to the world, but I have chosen you out of the world. That is why the world hates you" (15:19).

Hates you? Do you doubt this? Then I suggest you take a strong public stand for the uniqueness of Who Jesus is, for the truth of the Bible from cover to cover, for the necessity of living a life of integrity and purity and humility in order to please God. Then count the seconds before someone labels you an extreme fanatical element of the religious right!

In what way are your friends, neighbors, and co-workers aware of your separation? Do they see a difference in your lifestyle? Habits? Choices? Activities? Attitudes? Have they made snide, stinging comments to you about the difference they have observed in your life? Have you become so afraid of offending them or provoking more antagonism that you are trying to minimize or even hide the differences between you and them? If so, you need His courage to stand out not only by separation but in the face of persecution.

Standing Out in Persecution

Knowing how difficult it was going to be to live for Him in the midst of the world, Jesus reminded His disciples, "Remember the words I spoke to you: 'No servant is greater than his master.' If they persecuted me, they will persecute you also" (15:20). They didn't just persecute Jesus; they crucified Him! How is it that you and I think we will be treated any better?

I wonder if this thought was incomprehensible to the disciples, just as even now you are probably thinking this doesn't happen today. Yet it has been estimated by the *World Christian Encyclopedia* that more than 45 million men and women were put to death for their faith in Jesus Christ during the twentieth century! In recent years the estimate has averaged between 160,000 and 171,000 per year. Imagine! That's more than 10,000 Christians dying for their faith every month! More than 400 per day![18]

While you and I are getting up in the morning, trying to decide what to wear and what to eat and where we will spend our vacation, somewhere in the world someone is paying the ultimate price for his or her relationship with Jesus! And while I thank God for the relative security I have as a believer in America, I am under no illusions: Christians all over the world are hated for Jesus' sake. It's just a matter of time until that same hatred begins to seep out in our own beloved nation. Why? Why is this hatred so universal and trans-generational?

Jesus gave five solid reasons for the world's persecution of Christians. These reasons have proven to be true again and again in the lives of believers down through the centuries:

The first reason Jesus gave is *our identification with Him,* Whom the world hates—"If the world hates you, keep in mind that it hated me first" (15:18).

Hate Jesus? What evidence do you and I see of hatred toward Him today? Is there an underlying hatred of Christ when *His* name is invoked in profanity, not the name of Buddha or Allah or Mohammed? At the very least, profanity reveals that deep within the human spirit there is no neutrality toward Him.

Recently on "The View," a television talk show that involves a round-table–type conversation among several women, Joy Behar remarked that she had successfully lost weight on her diet. She then exclaimed "Praise Jesus!" When the show was aired on the West Coast, the name Jesus was bleeped out! The same network that peppers its programs with God's name used in profanity found it offensive when His Son's name was used in sincerity!

The more you and I are closely identified with Him, the more we will become the object of scorn and hostility. An extreme example is the attack on America instigated by those who, in their own words, hate Christians and Jews and have declared a holy *jihad,* or war, against them in Allah's name. Perhaps a more practical and personal example of hatred toward Christians is the reaction your public junior high school student gets when he bows his head to ask a blessing before eating lunch in the cafeteria. Or the press reaction President George W. Bush received on the campaign trail when he named Jesus as the person he most admired.

The second reason we may be persecuted as Christians is our mandated *separation from the world,* which causes the world to resent us as non-conformists: "I have chosen you out of the world. That is why the world hates you" (15:19). When was the last time you refused to laugh at a dirty story? Or refused to stop at a bar on the way home from work? Or refused to misrepresent information on a financial report? Or refused to join in gossip at the club? Or refused to lie for your boss? Or refused to sleep with your boss? Did such refusals cause you to be honored and loved and respected? No? Then you're getting the picture.

Third, we may encounter persecution because of the world's *rejection of the truth* that Jesus is God's unique and only Son, and the exclusive way to God: "They will treat you this way because of my name, for they do not know the One who sent me" (15:21). A Christian newsmagazine recently warned, "The enemy, we are told, is not Islam but intolerance. It is that narrow-minded, restrictive view of religion that is to blame for the terrorist attacks and the Taliban oppression. People who think 'theirs is the only true religion' are the real enemy, a charge, of course, that sticks not just to the Taliban but to orthodox Christians."[19]

Fourth, persecution may be directed toward us because of the world's *conviction of sin,* which the truth reveals: "If I had not come and spoken to them, they would not be guilty of sin. Now, however, they have no excuse for their sin" (15:22).

Many times I have been in a situation such as I was recently when riding in a cab. The driver was lively, talkative, and his conversation was peppered with bad language. When we arrived at the hotel, I was met by the organizers of the meeting I would be addressing. In the process of getting my bag out of the trunk, the driver was told by one of the people greeting me that I was Billy Graham's daughter and a Christian speaker. His immediate reaction was, "If I had known, I would have cleaned up my language. I hope I didn't offend you." I had not said a word to him about his language. But Jesus said we are "the light of the world."[20] And sometimes just our presence reveals the darkness of sin in the lives of others. In this case, the driver was not resentful but apologetic. But often those who are convicted of their own sin by our separation from it resent us.

The fifth and last reason Jesus gave for persecution of His followers is the *demonstration of God's power* in individual lives: "If I had not done among them what no one else did, they would not be guilty of sin. But now they have seen these miracles, and yet they have hated both me and my Father" (15:24). If you and I are not being persecuted, could it be that no one has seen any real change or evidence of God's power in our lives? Have we so watered down and compromised our witness that the world around us doesn't see any reason to persecute us?

What miracle that demonstrates God's power can someone else see in your life?

Is it . . .

> When God set you free from alcoholism?
>> Or from drug dependency?
> When God reconciled you with your spouse?
>> Or with your in-laws?
> When God healed you of disease?

Or gave you strength to endure illness?

When you were promoted?

Or found a better job when you were fired?

When you placed your faith in Christ?

Or led someone else to that decision?

When you shared your faith in Christ with a co-worker?

Or with an old friend?

When you held your temper in the face of attack?

Or spoke out in defense of the truth?

When you gave up your rights in order to keep peace and unity at home?

Or stood firm on the Gospel?

When you experienced peace in the midst of turmoil?

Or hope in the midst of grief?

When you apologized first . . . ?

Years ago, Danny and I were members of a downtown, mainline church. Danny served as chairman of the board of deacons, taught Sunday school, and was president of the men's fellowship. I was a member of the Christian Life Committee, which prayerfully decided to hold a week-long series of meetings featuring a well-known preacher. This preacher, we were certain, would present Christ in such a powerful way that the members of our church would be revived in their love for Jesus and their hunger for His Word. With the pastor's approval, the preacher was invited and accepted the invitation. His preaching was powerfully anointed by God. The church was packed night after night, with many people, including our own daughter, making their way to the altar at the close of the service to recommit their lives to Jesus Christ.

When the week of meetings was over, the church leadership refused to thank the preacher, refused to give him the names of those who had rededicated their lives to Christ, and even refused to shake hands in good-bye! Within a few short months, a church-wide business meeting was held on a Sunday morning, with the congregation applauding as my husband and I were in effect removed from any responsible position of service. Those members whose hearts had been truly revived were renounced as troublemakers with the understanding they were no longer welcome at that church. With God's clear direction, our family left, feeling the church needed to get on with its life, free of the "problem" we seemed to have become to the congregation.

I have never recovered from that eye-opening experience! I had assumed that if the people in that church heard the truth proclaimed with real power—if the Spirit of God moved in their midst—that they would respond by giving their lives to Christ in a new, fresh way that would unite the congregation on its knees in prayer and with one heart to reach our city for Christ. What I discovered is that the average church member wanted to live in the murky twilight of apathy. When the light of passionate truth and commitment shone into their midst, they withdrew and attacked the source of light.

It's heartbreaking to realize that many churches seem to be filled with people who call themselves by God's name—they recite Scripture, they sing hymns, they pray out loud, they do good things in the neighborhood—but

. . . they don't really know God, nor do they want to.

They don't really love each other, nor do they want to.

They don't really care about a lost and dying world, nor do they want to.

They don't know how to truly intercede for others, nor do they want to.

They don't know how to read their Bibles so they can hear God speaking to them, nor do they want to.

They don't know how to lead someone to faith in Jesus Christ, nor do they want to.

They are comfortable in their complacency![21]

From my broken heart is wrenched this cry: *God, have mercy on us! Give us convictions! And please, give us MORE courage to stand out and speak up for our convictions in the midst of such complacency within and political correctness without!*

COURAGE TO SPEAK UP

The disciples must have been trying so hard to understand what Jesus was saying to them that night in Jerusalem. As they relaxed following the wine and the satisfying meal, in the flickering glow of the candles and the security of the upper room, hatred and persecution seemed far removed from their world. But they knew Jesus well enough to know that the edge in the tone of His voice and the measured way He chose His words indicated He wanted their undivided attention.

Surely the loving gaze of Jesus lingered on each manly, eager face that looked back at Him with such earnest intensity. Did He see in His mind's eye . . .

Philip, who would be tied to a pillar and stoned to death?

Matthew, who would be nailed to the ground with spikes and beheaded?

Jude, who would be beaten to death with sticks and clubs?

Simon, who would be tortured and crucified?

John, son of Zebedee, who would be tortured and exiled?

James, brother of John, who would be beheaded?

James, who would be pushed from the top of a building, then his broken body beaten to death?

Peter, who would be crucified upside down?

Andrew, Peter's brother, who would hang on a cross for three days before dying?

Bartholomew, who would be beaten, crucified, and skinned alive before being beheaded?

Thomas, who would be thrown into a fiery furnace then speared with a javelin?[22]

Every single one of His beloved disciples except John would die a gruesome death for standing out and speaking up—for Him![23] How was it that these rough, untrained, mostly uneducated men would speak out with such power that the authorities would consider them a threat to the security and economy of the Roman empire? Their competency would come from the Spirit within them.

Competent to Speak Up

After the chilling discourse that warned them of the persecution to come, Jesus gave His disciples the secret source of the courageous competency that would be theirs as they sought to speak up in a world of hatred. The source was none other than the Holy Spirit of God—the same Spirit that indwelt Jesus at that very moment. What comfort the disciples must have felt as Jesus promised, "When the Counselor comes, whom I will send to you from the Father, the Spirit of truth who goes out from the Father, he will testify about me" (15:26). The source of power that filled Jesus, enabling Him to face His accusers and His execution with dignified compassion and courageous strength, is the same source of power that enabled the disciples to live and die for Jesus. And it's the same source of power available to you and me today! When we have the Spirit of the living God within us, we have no less courage, no less power, than did those eleven men around the table in that upper room on that Thursday night![24]

When have you spoken up for Jesus? When have you told someone about Jesus who doesn't know Him? Are you recoiling in fear, protesting, "Anne, I could never do that! I'm afraid my neighbors would never speak to me again. I'm afraid my friends will laugh at me or be derisive about something that's precious to me. I'm afraid to speak up for Jesus because I may lose my popularity or promotion or position or prestige or possessions or . . ."

Jesus understands your fears. That's why He has sent you and me the Holy Spirit. When we open our mouths, the Holy Spirit not only gives us words, He clothes the words with power to make a difference in the hearer. But we need to open our mouths!

When I was pregnant with our third child, my husband and I were invited to Switzerland to attend a congress on evangelism. As we listened to the outstanding speakers challenging and instructing the audience on reaching our world for Christ in this generation, I was convicted by a simple fact. I had traveled all the way to Switzerland to attend a congress on evangelism when I had never bothered to share the Gospel with my neighbors! I felt so ashamed as I realized that if every Christian, at least in America, obeyed Christ and shared the Gospel with those in our own world, a congress on evangelism wouldn't be necessary—at least for North Americans.

The first week after I returned home, I called my neighbors before I had time to think about it and lose my courage. I invited them to my house for coffee and to hear about my recent trip. Five neighbors came. It took me an hour of small talk to finally get up the nerve to share the Gospel with them. When I finally did, one of my neighbors wept, one jumped up and ran, one talked about nothing in particular, and two just stared at me! What an awkward time it was! But God honored my feeble effort, and today, four out of the five are committed Christians who are impacting the lives of others for Christ.

On that day so long ago, I learned a very important spiritual principle that Jesus taught His disciples in a dramatic, miraculous way on a hillside beside the Sea of Galilee.[25] The disciples had been under a lot of pressure. They had slipped into the hill country with Jesus, hoping for a time of retreat. Instead, five thousand people showed up, wanting Jesus to heal and teach them—which He graciously did. None of the five thousand had eaten all day long—and most had not brought any provision for a meal.

The disciples wanted to send them away since they had no food, either. But Jesus told His disciples to feed them—an impossible task. However, Andrew was resourceful enough to find a little boy with five loaves and two fish—which seemed totally inadequate for the need at hand. And it *was* totally inadequate! That little bit of food was less than nothing when compared to more than five thousand hungry people! But it was all the little boy and the disciples had to give. Jesus took it, and blessed it, and broke it, and handed it back to the disciples—and they passed it out, and continued passing it out, until all five thousand people were fed to the full![26]

The point Jesus got across to His disciples was that it didn't matter if they only had a little bit—a little bit . . .

of time,

of money,

of education,

of ability,

of knowledge,

of strength,

of resources . . .

what mattered was that they gave all that they had to Jesus. Then He would make it enough.

Would you give to Jesus all of your words,

your conversations,

> your thoughts,
>> your knowledge,
>>> your convictions,
>>>> your courage?

And ask Him to bless it and make it enough to impact the lives of others? The difference between a little bit and enough is the Holy Spirit. And it's the Holy Spirit Who will fill you with such deep conviction, passion, and zeal for the truth that you will be compelled to speak up!

Compelled to Speak Up

One evening not too long ago, my brother Franklin and I were invited to appear together on *Larry King Live,* a popular talk show on CNN. Mr. King asked Franklin how was it that we were so bold in our faith. Was it hereditary? He and Franklin bantered back and forth for a moment, suggesting at one point that maybe it was a southern thing.

I felt I had to interrupt and say why I was bold—when my personality is basically shy. The conversation quickly turned serious as they both listened to the reason for my boldness. The reason I gave them then is still the same reason I am bold today. The reason is because I am convinced that what I say is the truth! And I wonder . . . maybe you and I don't need more courage— maybe we just need stronger convictions! Because when you feel deeply about something, you are compelled to open your mouth and speak up! Jesus clearly stated this to His disciples when He said, "You also must testify, for you have been with me from the beginning" (15:27).

Less than sixty days after that evening meal in the upper room, two of these same disciples—Peter and John—were arrested by the authorities in Jerusalem for speaking out about Jesus. Facing the same religious court that had condemned Jesus to death, Peter—the same Peter who had been so terrified of the opinions of others during the trials of Jesus that he had denied His Lord three times—*Peter,* filled with the Holy Spirit, boldly proclaimed Jesus Christ as the One "whom you crucified but whom God raised from the dead. . . . Salvation is found in no one else, for there is no other name under heaven given to men by which we must be saved."

The authorities could hardly believe their ears! "When they saw the courage of Peter and John and realized that they were unschooled, ordinary men, they were astonished and they took note that these men had been with Jesus."[27] After a brief consultation among themselves, the religious rulers forbade John and Peter to speak in Jesus' name. The disciples' reply was a classic defense that rang as true in their politically correct, pluralistic, multicultural society as it does in ours: "We cannot help speaking about what we have seen and heard."[28] They were compelled to speak up—they couldn't help it—because they had been with Jesus! They had been with Him when

    . . . the blind received sight,

      . . . the ears of the deaf were opened,

        . . . the lepers were cleansed,

          . . . the lame walked,

        . . . the tormented were set free,

      . . . the dead were raised to life!

They had seen five thousand people fed with five loaves and two fish!

They had seen Jesus calm the wind and waves with a word!

They had seen Jesus walk on the water!

They had seen Jesus confound the Pharisees!

They had been with Jesus!

They had heard Him pray!

They had felt His touch!

They had seen His glory!

They had witnessed His power!

They had received His love!

They had seen Jesus crucified!

They had seen Jesus buried!

They had seen the empty tomb!

They had seen Jesus alive and risen from the dead!

They had seen Jesus physically ascend into heaven!

How could they ever be silent again?!

They knew too much

and had seen too much

and had heard too much

and had felt too much

and had learned too much—

they were under compulsion to speak up!

While in the process of writing this book, our youngest daughter, Rachel-Ruth, gave birth to our first grandchild—a little girl named Ruth Bell Wright. She is softly pink with big blue-gray eyes, a halo of golden brown hair, perfect little ears, long fingers—and I could go on and on. My husband and I are totally enthralled with this little girl. She fills our hearts! We can't help talking about her to anyone who will listen. I'm not afraid to talk about her. I don't plan in advance how I will talk about her. I don't worry about offending someone with my talk about her. I don't go to classes to learn how to talk about her. I don't read books on how to talk about her. I pick up that little girl, feel her snuggle up against me, touch her soft little cheek, and melt! Little Ruth Bell fills my heart! And what fills my heart comes out on my lips!

Why do we seem to make speaking up for Jesus so complicated? If He fills our hearts, He is going to come out on our lips! Like Peter and John, we will not be able to help "speaking about what we have seen and heard" of Him![29]

I'M PART OF THE FELLOWSHIP of the unashamed. I have Holy Spirit power. The die has been cast. I have stepped over the line. The decision has been made. I am a disciple of His. I won't look back, let up, slow down, back away, or be still.

My past is redeemed, my present makes sense, my future is secure. I'm finished and done with low living, sight walking, small planning, smooth knees, colorless dreams, tamed visions, mundane talking, cheap giving, and dwarfed goals.

I no longer need preeminence, prosperity, position, promotions, plaudits, or popularity. I don't have to be right, first, tops, recognized, praised, regarded, or rewarded. I now live by faith, lean on His presence, walk by patience, lift by prayer, and labor by power.

My face is set, my gait is fast, my goal is heaven, my road is narrow, my way is rough, my companions are few, my Guide is reliable, my mission is clear. I cannot be bought, compromised, detoured, lured away, turned back, deluded, or delayed. I will not flinch in the face of sacrifice, hesitate in the presence of adversity, negotiate at the table of the enemy, ponder at the pool of popularity, or meander in the maze of mediocrity.

I won't give up, shut up, let up, until I have stayed up, stored up, prayed up, paid up, preached up for the cause of Christ. I am a disciple of Jesus. I must go 'til He comes, give 'til I drop, preach 'til all know, and work 'til He stops me. And when He comes for His own, He will have no problem recognizing me—my banner of identification with Jesus will be clear. [30]

So please, dear Lord, just give me MORE of Your courage in my convictions!

In response to my heart's cry, Jesus has whispered in my heart, "I will give you more courage, Anne, *WHEN* you stand out and speak up for Me!"

10
MORE of ─────────────
────── *His Nearness in My Loneliness*

John 16:5–15

*T*EENAGE SUICIDE VICTIMS, alcoholics, drug addicts, divorcees, widows and widowers, many singles, juvenile delinquents, prison inmates, cancer victims, and the eleven disciples of Jesus on the Thursday evening before the crucifixion, all have something in common. What is it? *Loneliness!*

In our overpopulated world, with people . . .

walking on crowded sidewalks,
riding crowded buses,
living in crowded housing,
driving on crowded streets,
shopping in crowded malls,
vacationing in crowded resorts,
backpacking in crowded parks,
eating in crowded restaurants,
working in crowded offices,
dying in crowded hospitals . . .

many are desperately lonely. The dictionary defines loneliness as being without companionship; a feeling of desolation, depressed at being alone.[1]

When have you felt lonely—even in a crowd? Desolate? Without companionship to the point you were depressed at being alone? Was it when you . . .

celebrated Valentine's Day, Thanksgiving, or Christmas morning without loved ones?

your parents died?

179

you were laid off to make room for a younger employee?
your spouse walked out?
your best friend moved away?
your children went off to school?
you broke up with your boyfriend or girlfriend?
you were betrayed by a sibling?
you moved to a new city—in another state?
you lay on an operating table?
you were transferred to a branch office in a country whose language you don't speak?

Maybe you are not lonely, but do you know someone who is?

Imagine the quietness of the upper room on that Thursday evening long ago. Did the warm spring breeze gently drift through the open windows, carrying with it the sounds of Jerusalem in the evening—the sharp sound of a shop door closing, the muffled sound of a vendor packing up his cart, the *clop-clop* of donkeys' hooves on the cobbled street as people made their way home from the market before Passover, the urgent sound of a mother's voice calling for her children to come home? The sounds would have been reminders of the normalcy of life, yet there was something strikingly abnormal in the fact that the city continued as it had for generations while within its walls the Son of God was preparing to die.

Within the upper room, the quiet stillness was broken only by the sound of the beloved Master's voice. Jesus continued to pour out His heart in words that sought to prepare His disciples for what was coming. And the disciples were beginning to understand—even if vaguely—that the One Who was . . .
their Lord,
their Master,
their Teacher,
their best Friend,
the One to Whom they had given their lives,
the One Who was Life itself to them . . .
Jesus was on the verge of leaving them!

He was going away! The loneliness of His pending absence was already beginning to engulf their emotions, and sorrow was filling their hearts. So

Jesus told them that, although He would be leaving them physically and at times they might feel lonely, they would never be alone again! On that quiet Thursday evening before all hell broke loose, He began to unveil the third person of the triune God: the Holy Spirit, Who would be Jesus—not just *with them*—but *in them*.

HIS NEARNESS BRINGS COMFORT

The nearness of the indwelling presence of the Holy Spirit gave me tangible comfort one morning recently when I appeared on a national television talk show. As I sat in the overstuffed chair across from the trendy-looking professional woman who would be interviewing me, I took in my surroundings. Our chairs were placed on a set that looked as though it could have been the family room of the average American's home. On television it would appear homey, but it was far removed from relaxed acceptance and at-ease comfort. Brilliant lights were focused on us so that the three cameras that were also pointed in our direction would transmit a clear, sharp picture to the millions of viewers watching. Beyond the cameras, dozens of people were gathered in the studio to watch and to listen to our brief conversation. And in the group of onlookers were my daughter Morrow and six other friends, all of whom I knew were praying for me.

As the interviewer poised herself to begin the introduction and I heard the director begin the countdown until we were live on the air, I was aware that within seconds my face and words would be plastered on the screens of millions of televisions across the country—and even beyond! The entire interview would last no more than three to five minutes, so my answers to the unknown questions would have to be carefully worded and very concise while at the same time giving a meaningful witness for Jesus Christ.

As the studio fell silent and the interviewer introduced me to the television audience then turned to face me with the first question, I was filled with a supernatural calmness and unshakeable confidence that was rooted in the conscious awareness that I was not sitting in that chair alone!

At that moment . . .

in that chair . . .

under those lights . . .

facing those cameras . . .

answering those questions . . .

I was comfortable! Because I knew the dear Holy Spirit with His unsearchable wisdom and unfathomable knowledge knew exactly what questions the interviewer would pose and would give me exactly the right words to answer her questions so that Jesus would be exalted and the Gospel would be presented! And He did!

Just exactly who is the Holy Spirit Who helped me so personally at such a time as that television interview? He is God! Our God is one God, yet mysteriously and magnificently, He is three Persons in one. This truth is stated indirectly from the very beginning of Scripture when the first verse of the Bible tells us, "In the beginning God created the heavens and the earth."[2] The passage goes on to identify the Spirit of God, Who hovered over the face of the formless, darkened planet earth, and the Word of God Who went forth each day, commanding light to shine out of darkness, a firmament to be formed out of spaciousness, a foundation to be shaped out of emptiness, and life to come out of nothingness![3] The very first chapter of the Bible reveals God the Father, God the Holy Spirit, and God the Living Word Who is God the Son.[4]

Dramatically, the creation account records that God said, "Let *us* make man in *our* image, in *our* likeness, and let them rule. . . . So God created man in *his* own image, in the image of God *he* created him; male and female *he* created them."[5] Note the change in pronouns as God refers to Himself in the plural, then in the singular—because He is three Persons in one Person. Although all three Persons can be seen throughout the Bible, as God's revelation of Himself unfolds it is primarily God the Father Who is revealed in the Old Testament, God the Son Who is revealed in the Gospels, and God the Holy Spirit Who is revealed in the Book of Acts and the Epistles.[6]

On the very same night Jesus was betrayed, within twelve hours of His crucifixion, when the horror of the impending accusations, rejection, torture, and humiliation must have begun to settle on Him like a smothering cloak, His thoughts centered not on His own impending suffering but on His disciples' grief over His departure! As He prepared to go to the cross, with selfless abandonment He sought to comfort His disciples in their grief and loneliness! He began to patiently explain that His presence would remain with them, but He would no longer be *visible*. He would be *invisible* in the person of the Holy Spirit.

Comfort of His Understanding Awareness

Jesus *knew* how His disciples were feeling in the depths of their hearts. He *knew* they were plunging into a black depression brought on by loneliness. So with infinite tenderness, He gently probed, "Now I am going to him who sent me, yet none of you asks me, 'Where are you going?' Because I have said these things, you are filled with grief" (16:5–6). They were grieving because He was leaving them—He was going . . . ! They must have been anxious to know where, but what did it really matter? Wherever it was, it was away from them, and that's all they could focus on at the moment. He would be gone! And *Jesus knew* the unspoken questions on their minds and the unexpressed feelings in their hearts! He understood!

In your loneliness, do you long for—even dream of—someone who would understand you to such depth that he would know what you were thinking and what you were feeling without your having to say a word? Someone who would tenderly look into your eyes and *you* would know that *he* knew—*everything!*

Does your loneliness stem from the fact that you feel unknown? Or misunderstood? Or ignored? Then you need Jesus—and you need more of His nearness in your loneliness, because Jesus knows you, He understands you, and you have His undivided attention.

Comfort of His Undivided Attention

The Holy Spirit is Jesus in me—
giving all of Himself to me—
with undivided attention!
Always!
One reason I invited Jesus into my life is that it wasn't enough to be with

Him for just one hour on Sunday morning in a worship service with others or two hours on Wednesday evening at a church supper. I wanted to be with Him twenty-four hours a day. I didn't ever want to be without Him! I wanted Him all to myself!

Jesus knew that His disciples all through the ages would feel this way when He promised, "I tell you the truth; It is expedient for you that I go away: for if I go not away, the Comforter will not come unto you; but if I depart, I will send him unto you" (16:7 KJV). The very promise Jesus gave us contains a name for the Holy Spirit that reveals the uniqueness of His nearness in our loneliness. This name, "Comforter," is equally translated from the Greek text into six other names, each of which describes a slightly different aspect of the Holy Spirit's precious, personal ministry in our lives. Prayerfully meditate on these names, along with their dictionary definitions:[7]

> *Comforter:* One Who relieves another of mental distress.
>
> *Counselor:* One Whose profession is to give advice and manage causes.
>
> *Helper:* One Who furnishes with relief or support. One Who is of use and Who waits upon another.
>
> *Intercessor:* One Who acts between parties to reconcile differences.
>
> *Advocate:* One Who pleads the cause of another.
>
> *Strengthener:* One Who causes you to grow, become stronger, endure, and resist attacks.
>
> *Standby:* One Who can be relied upon either for regular use or in emergencies.

Can you imagine how wonderful it would be to have Someone with these attributes in your life? For instance,

> Are you distressed today?
>
> > Then you need the Comforter.
>
> Are you facing a major decision?
>
> > Then you need the Counselor.
>
> Do you need relief from, or support in, your responsibilities?
>
> > Then you need the Helper.
>
> Do you have a broken relationship?
>
> > Then you need the Intercessor.

Are you being criticized, falsely accused, misunderstood?
Then you need the Advocate.
Are you constantly defeated by habits of sin?
Then you need the Strengthener.
Are you unprepared for an emergency?
Then you need the Standby.

The Holy Spirit is fabulous! He's everything that Jesus is!

Have you ever wished Jesus could be to you what He seemed to be when you were a child? Did He seem so real then, so close, so comforting, so understanding, so strong and protective? Have you ever wished Jesus would come in the flesh, sit next to you, take your hand in His, tell you how much He loved you, talk to you about your problems, and give you wise advice? He *has* come! *He is here* in the person of the Holy Spirit who makes Jesus real to you and me, for He is the "Spirit of Christ"![8]

Because of the Holy Spirit . . .

When you need a question answered, you don't have to look for Jesus.

When you are in trouble, you don't have to run find Jesus.

When you feel like talking, you don't have to arrange a visit with Jesus.

When you need Jesus' help, you don't have to go through His secretary!

When you feel lonely, you don't have to share Jesus with others!

He's all yours!

Even if I had to give up all the above privileges in order to see Jesus in the flesh, I would choose to continue to live by faith! I can live without seeing His dear face. But I can't live without the comfort of His moment-by-moment presence in my life!

The nearness of the Holy Spirit not only comforts me personally but it also comforts me as I seek to be obedient to our Lord's command to take the Gospel into the whole world.[9] Sharing the love of God and the truth of Who Jesus is with those around me can be frightening—as well as frustrating! How can I convince someone today that Jesus, Who lived two thousand years ago, is relevant today? How can I convince a sinner of his sin? Or the need to get right with God? How can I convince someone that the cross is the gateway to eternal glory? I can't! But the Holy Spirit can!

HIS NEARNESS BRINGS CONVICTION

As the disciples continued to take in the fact that Jesus was leaving them, it must have begun to dawn on them that they would be left responsible for His work on earth. Although they had a very loose grasp of what that work would be, even the smallest aspect of it must have seemed overwhelming. How in the world would they convince an idolater in the pluralistic, multicultural society of the Roman empire in the first century that Jesus Christ was relevant to his life? Would the disciples accomplish this daunting task with their own . . .

systematic logic?

or glowing eloquence?

or brilliant reasoning?

or persuasive powers?

or irresistible charm?

or wise answers?

No! That would be impossible! They were for the most part uneducated, ignorant men![10] In themselves, they would never be able to convince one other person of Who Jesus is, or of mankind's need for Him. The apostle Paul stated the difficulty clearly when he bluntly told the Christians in Corinth that the Gospel is "a stumbling block to Jews and foolishness to Gentiles,"[11] the Gospel is hidden to those who are lost,[12] and the minds of unbelievers are blind to the light of the Gospel.[13]

Whenever I climb into a pulpit, or stand in a lectern, or am seated in front of an interviewer, or share the Gospel in conversation one-on-one, I know there is nothing I can say nor any way I can say it that will stir another person's heart to the extent that that person will confront and confess his or her sin and claim Jesus Christ as Savior. There is nothing I can say that can convince a person that he or she needs a savior—and that the only Savior needed is Jesus. Again and again, in the moments immediately preceding the message I deliver, I cry out in private prayer, "Lord, help me! Give me Your words to say. Then clothe those words with the power of the Holy Spirit so that they make an eternal difference in the hearers for Your glory alone."

I know I am responsible to be faithful to deliver the message I believe

God has put on my heart. But I also know that He is equally responsible for the hearers' response to the message.

Who are you trying to share Jesus with? Is it a peer? Or an elder? Or someone who is older? Younger? Richer? Poorer? Are you afraid to witness to someone who is more intellectual than you are? Or has more education than you do? Or seems to be more sophisticated and worldly wise than you are? Then join me in praising God! What a relief! Convicting others of their sin is not our responsibility! It's the responsibility of the Holy Spirit.

Conviction of Sin

Jesus immediately put His disciples at ease by lifting the burden of responsibility from their shoulders when He explained, "When he [the Holy Spirit] comes, he will convict the world of guilt in regard to sin . . . because men do not believe in me" (16:8–9). Think about how impossible our task would be without the Holy Spirit! Without the Holy Spirit . . . how would you tell your father, who has walked out on your mother and is now living with another woman to whom he is not married, that he is living in sin? How would you tell your spouse who has lied in a business deal that lying is a sin? How would you tell your neighbor's pregnant, unmarried teenage daughter that abortion is sin? How would you tell your interior designer that his homosexual lifestyle is a lifestyle of sin? How would you tell your witty friend that her funny, entertaining, yet reputation-damaging gossip is sin? How could you say any of those things without the person angrily retorting that you are self-righteous, intolerant, and a religious fanatic? You can't! Praise God for the conviction of the Holy Spirit!

Who are you trying to convict of sin? Your spouse? Sometimes it's all I can do to bite my tongue in order to refrain from telling my husband, "You shouldn't do that," "You shouldn't say that," "You really ought to go there," "You really ought to react differently . . ." But my wise mother gave me great advice years ago that I have never forgotten (even if I haven't always taken it!). She told me that it was my job to make my husband happy, and it was the Holy Spirit's job to make him good. Why is it you and I try so hard to do the Holy Spirit's job for Him?

There is no doubt whatsoever that the disciples who were receiving this encouraging explanation would be used to convict the world of sin and the need for a Savior. Their words make up the New Testament. Their words went out to the entire world of their day. Their example is one that believers of every generation have followed. But their words and their example would have been empty and hollow unless clothed in the power of the Holy Spirit.

God will also use our words and the witness of our example to win others to Christ. And sometimes He uses us indirectly when others overhear what we say, or go to church at our invitation and hear a sermon that pierces their hearts, or observe the difference in our lives as we seek to separate from the world around us.

But in ourselves, all would be meaningless and irrelevant unless the Holy Spirit places His hand on us and breathes His life into what we do.[14] So before we ever open our mouths to speak for Christ, before we ever begin our day to live for Christ, we need to pray—pray that the Holy Spirit will take what we give out and live out and use it to convict others of their sin as well as of their need to be right with God.

Conviction of Righteousness

Jesus Christ was crucified as a criminal, as a blaspheming heretic, as an enemy of Rome and of God. What changed the world's opinion of Him? Why does He go down in history as a good Man? Or a great Prophet? Why do people put their trust in a crucified Jew two thousand years after He lived on earth? The change in opinion was brought about by none other than the Holy Spirit Who convinced the world of the truth—that Jesus Christ was not only crucified, but that He rose from the dead! He's alive! Jesus announced to His disciples that "when he [the Holy Spirit] comes, he will convict the world of guilt . . . in regard to righteousness, because I am going to the Father, where you can see me no longer" (16:8–10). The proof of the righteousness of Jesus Christ is in the fact that God didn't leave Him on the cross, bearing your sin and mine, but raised Him from the dead and seated Him at His right hand, placing all authority in the universe under His feet![15]

Jesus was—and is—God's standard of righteousness. He is now resurrected and with the Father. We must meet God's standard of righteousness—and the only way is to have it imputed to our account by faith alone. Through faith in Jesus, we become "the righteousness of God."[16]

How do you and I tell a good, moral person that his or her own righteousness is not good enough to please God?[17] How do you tell a sincerely religious person that his or her religion is not good enough to gain entrance into heaven?[18] Who are you trying to convince that he or she needs to get right with God? How do you tell that person in such a way that he or she listens to what you have to say and seeks the righteousness of Jesus Christ? *You can't!* You can reason with the person, answer the person's questions, and present the truth to the person, but you and I cannot convince a person to change his or her mind and heart. That's the work of the Holy Spirit!

Although the object of our witness may reject our words as critical or self-righteous, when that person sees you and me overcoming a longstanding habit of sin . . . or loving a person who has treated us meanly . . . or forgiving a person who has treated us unfairly . . . or promoting another person's welfare above our own . . . or making priority time for Bible study and prayer—that person sees that Jesus is not only alive *to* us, but alive *in* us, and it draws that person to Jesus as the Son of God, Who is right. At that point, when our friend is convicted of sin and convinced of the righteousness of Jesus Christ, he or she is confronted with a choice.

Conviction of Judgment

A person who is under the condemnation of God instinctively knows it. I'm convinced that one major reason for the destructive abuse of alcohol, drugs, children, and spouses; one reason for the frantic pace of life that races from early morning through half the night; one reason for the increased volume and beat of our music; one reason for the emphasis on pluralism, which promotes other religions as equal to Christianity, is that we are trying to cover up a deep-down sense of guilt and uneasiness in our spirits. Regardless of what we say, we know there is a God and He is not pleased.

The sense of guilt that we have deep down in our spirits is our friend. Like a moral alarm clock, it is meant to wake us up in our relationship with

God so that we might get right with Him. If we . . .
>   repress out guilt,
>   or rationalize our guilt,
>   or drug our guilt,
>   or drown our guilt, '
>   or deny our guilt,
>   or nurse our guilt,
>   or ignore our guilt,

we're refusing to heed the alarm, and we then expose ourselves to the danger of God's judgment. But how do you and I convince someone he or she is guilty before God? How do we convince others that they are going to hell apart from faith in Jesus Christ? How do we convince the world that this God they say is too loving to allow someone to go to hell is too just to allow them to go to heaven . . . unless they receive the righteousness of Jesus Christ through faith in Him? We can't! That's why Jesus said, "When he [the Holy Spirit] comes, he will convict the world of guilt . . . in regard to judgment, because the prince of this world now stands condemned" (16:8, 11).

The prince of this world, the devil, has already been judged and condemned at the cross and through the resurrection of Jesus. Anyone who is under the devil's dominion—whether unconsciously because that person is not under the authority of Christ, or consciously—shares the devil's judgment.

>   We are either ruled by the devil . . . or by Jesus.
>   We are either in the world . . . or in Christ.
>   We are either judged . . . or justified.
>   We are either condemned . . . or saved.
>   We are either rejected . . . or accepted.
>   We are either in darkness . . . or the light.
>   We are either going to hell . . . or to heaven.[19]

Have you ever felt desperate for the salvation of someone you love? And have you felt all alone as you carried the burden for that person's salvation? Do you mentally search the list of your Christian friends to find one you might ask to share the Gospel with that person you love or to pray for that person? What a relief to roll the burden for that person's salvation onto the Holy Spirit. He wants to bring that person to salvation more than you do. He is the One Who has placed the burden on your heart, and He will join with you in drawing that person to faith in Jesus Christ. But He alone is responsible for convicting that person of sin, of the need to get right with God through Christ, and of the impending judgment to come if Jesus is rejected.

Elizabeth is a beautiful young woman on my prayer list for whom I have prayed and prayed and prayed.[20] She professes to know Jesus Christ as her Savior, yet I see no evidence of Him in her life at all. She is drowning in guilt, which, instead of driving her to the cross has driven her to mind-altering drugs. The devil seems to have the upper hand. I know my heart's cry has had a shrill tone to it as in desperation I plead with God to intervene.

In the intense heat of my emotions and the raging turmoil of my thoughts and the rushing avalanche of my words, I seem to hear the still, small voice of the Holy Spirit saying, "Do not be afraid or discouraged. . . . For the battle is not yours, but God's."[21] The battle for Elizabeth's eternal life and mental well-being belongs to the Lord—not to me. And the peace that passes all understanding rises up like a cool breeze to quiet my heart and rule my thoughts—it's a peace that only God the Holy Spirit can give.[22]

I wonder how the disciples, sitting in the upper room on that Thursday evening, were receiving what Jesus was saying? Were His words like a cool breeze to their anxious minds and hearts? Were they eager to meet this wonderful person Jesus spoke of with such intimate knowledge? Were they somewhat puzzled? Or confused? Or overwhelmed? Or fearful? Why didn't Jesus explain more fully Who the Holy Spirit is and how He would work in and through them? Why didn't Jesus go into the detail Paul did in his letter to the Romans or to the Galatians?[23] Why did Jesus hold back from them the information He implied when He disclosed, "I have much more to say to you, more than you can now bear" (16:12). Jesus kept the information He gave the disciples to a minimum because, until the Holy Spirit actually came and indwelt them, they couldn't comprehend the information anyway—because it is the Holy Spirit Who teaches and instructs us about the things of Christ.

HIS NEARNESS BRINGS CLARITY

One of the names for the Holy Spirit is the Spirit of Truth because He works through *the* Truth, which is twofold: He works through the truth of the written Word of God—our Bibles. And He works through the truth of the living Word of God—Jesus Christ. Have you ever read a passage from the Bible and struggled to grasp what it means? Have you resisted joining a Bible study because you would be embarrassed for others to find out that you have such a hard time understanding it? Are you afraid you will stand out oddly alone in a group of people who seem to see things in Scripture that you can't? Then you can relax! The difference between you and others you know who seem to understand what they read may very well be their dependence upon the Holy Spirit to open their minds and hearts to the meaning of God's Word. And the same Holy Spirit Who has done so for them will do so for you if you ask Him.

He Clarifies the Written Word

One reason I never approach the Scripture without praying first is because it is the person of the Holy Spirit Who clarifies the truth for you and me. Jesus identified His role in this way as He continued to share with His disciples: "But when he, the Spirit of truth, comes, he will guide you into all truth. He will not speak on his own; he will speak only what he hears, and he will tell you what is yet to come" (16:13).

The Bible is a wonderful book of history and poetry and prophecy and ceremony. Anyone can be blessed by just reading this truly magnificent piece of literature that spans the years of human history. But there is a unique blessing that is reserved for those who prayerfully, earnestly, and humbly approach it by faith as the truth, seeking to go past the surface reading into the deeper meaning.[24] And it is impossible to reach this deeper level of understanding and blessing without the Holy Spirit's guidance.

As you and I seek to read and study, understand and apply, submit to and obey the Bible, we are not alone. The Holy Spirit gives clarity to the wonderful Book He has inspired.[25] Again and again I have sat at my desk, staring at the Scripture passage I have just read and doodling with the pen on my legal pad because my mind has gone blank. It's as though I know what the passage says in words, but the meaning of the passage for my life totally escapes me. Then I pray and ask the Holy Spirit to unlock the meaning for me, and as I continue to meditate, a thought will come . . . then another thought . . . until the passage opens up and I can see the treasure that's on the inside.

One of my first international speaking engagements in AnGeL Ministries was a conference for five hundred pastors in Nadi, Fiji. Christian leaders came from islands throughout the South Pacific to a thatched-roof, open-air pavilion to be encouraged and instructed in God's Word. Although I had committed to leading two sessions a day for the pastors, I asked the organizers if I could add afternoon women's meetings to the planned schedule. They agreed.

Not knowing who, if any, would show up, I went to the first afternoon meeting with curious expectancy. I was guided to a back storage room in the pavilion where I found approximately thirty barefoot women sitting on boxes and cartons of goods. Their beautiful brown eyes glowed, and their white teeth glistened in their dark faces as they broke out in radiant smiles when I walked into their midst. I quickly glanced around to confirm that each lady had brought her Bible. I then proceeded to instruct the women in how to read God's Word so they could hear Him speaking to them through it. For the next hour and a half we studied, discussed, and applied together the Word of God.

To this day, thirteen years later, that group of uneducated, poor, barefoot women—many of whom had walked half a day to be at the meeting—stands out in my memory. Not because of the unique setting or the exotic place, but because their insights were so profound and deep and pure. It was almost spine-tingling to acutely realize that the Bible study I was participating in was being personally led by the Spirit of Truth, Who Himself had guided those ladies in an understanding of His Word.

Does the Bible seem confusing to you? With all of your higher education and material prosperity, are you actually poorer in understanding than those Fijian women? I am reminded that when I was a little girl, almost every time I became ill my mother would send me to stay with my grandmother. I would clutch my soft, silky pillow and trudge across the street in my flannel nightgown to my grandmother's house.

And one of the things my grandmother did to distract me from the misery of measles or mumps or the flu or just a bad cold was to pull out a box

MY HEART'S CRY FOR MORE

with a beautiful picture on the top. She would open up the box and dump out the contents—hundreds of little funny-shaped pieces of cardboard. As she spread out the pieces on the card table she had set up for this purpose, she explained to me that I had to find the pieces that fit together. The little pieces of cardboard were a jigsaw puzzle. Most of my grandmother's jigsaw puzzles contained five hundred little funny-shaped pieces, and putting them together seemed an impossible task! But my grandmother taught me that the first step to putting the jigsaw puzzle together was to turn all the pieces over so I could see the bits of the color picture, facing up. Then, as I looked at the picture on the box and put the pieces together so they duplicated the picture, the puzzle would be solved.

In many ways, the Bible is like that jigsaw puzzle. It can seem to be bits and pieces of disconnected parts that have no meaning in themselves. The pieces just don't seem to make sense. That's why we need the Holy Spirit. Because the Spirit is the One Who helps us understand the big picture of the Bible, which is the revelation of God Himself. Then He helps us turn over the pieces—the individual verses and chapters and books—one by one until the picture comes together and we see Jesus, Who reveals God to us from Genesis through Revelation.[26]

He Clarifies the Living Word

Whenever the Holy Spirit is the subject of a sentence, Jesus is the object, because everything that has its origin in the Spirit has its culmination in Jesus. Jesus clearly defined the Holy Spirit's primary focus when He explained, "He will bring glory to me by taking from what is mine and making it known to you. All that belongs to the Father is mine. That is why I said the Spirit will take from what is mine and make it known to you" (16:14–15).

Without the Holy Spirit to clarify the truth to our minds and confirm Who Jesus is in our hearts, we would "see" Jesus as just . . .

a man,

or a holy man,

or a prophet,

or a great prophet,
or a teacher,
or a revolutionary,
or a religious icon,
or a symbolic figure!
But the Holy Spirit opens our eyes to see and our minds to know and our hearts to receive that Jesus is more than just a man . . . or a prophet . . . or a teacher . . . or a revolutionary . . . or an icon . . . or a symbol. Jesus is . . .
the Messiah of Israel,
the Lamb of God,
the Son of David,
the Son of Man,
the Son of God,
the Savior of the world,
the Truth incarnate,
the risen Lord,
the reigning King . . .
God Himself in the flesh![27]

THE TRUTH BECOMES CLEAR as I saturate myself in God's Word, asking the Holy Spirit to turn the puzzle pieces over until I see the colored bits on the other side. And as He does, and as the pieces begin to fit together and make sense, the picture emerges. It's the picture of a Man![28] And my heart's cry for MORE of His nearness in my loneliness is answered in the pages of my Bible!

11

MORE *of* ————————
————————*His Answers to My Prayers*

John 16:23–27

*T*HE STORY IS TOLD of a Scottish minister who prayed long, pious-sounding prayers on Sunday morning that were beyond the understanding of his little congregation. Week after week, month after month, year after year, he droned on and on to the sheer boredom and frustration of those who were present. Unable to take the unlimited verbiage anymore, a small old lady from the choir decided she would do something about it. The next Sunday, as the cleric plunged into his customary verbose prayer, the little woman reached out from the choir loft and tugged at the minister's coat. In a stage whisper that the entire congregation could hear, she admonished, "Jes' call Him Fether, and ask 'im for somethin'."[1]

Prayer is so much simpler than we tend to make it, isn't it? As I listen to the prayers of others, so much of what seems to be said is information the petitioner is giving God! And I wonder, does the person who is praying think God needs us to tell Him the details? All we need to tell God is our needs . . . our desires . . . our feelings . . . our hopes . . . our longings—but we don't need to give Him detailed directions or flowery flattery or pious platitudes. A seventeenth-century Frenchman did a good job at expressing how we need to pray:

> Tell God all that is in your heart, as one unloads one's heart, its pleasures and its pains, to a dear friend.
> Tell Him your troubles, that He may comfort you;
> Tell Him your joys, that He may sober them;

Tell Him your dislikes, that He may help you to conquer them;
Talk to Him of your temptations, that He may shield you from them;
Show Him the wounds of your heart, that He may heal them;
Lay bare your indifference to good,
    your depraved tastes for evil,
      your instability.
Tell Him how self-love makes you unjust to others,
    how vanity tempts you to be insincere,
      how pride disguises you to yourself and others.
If you pour out all your weaknesses, needs, troubles, there will be no lack
of what to say.[2]

Why is prayer the biggest fight of my life? Maybe the struggle is rooted in the fact that real, heartfelt prayer takes time, demands effort, requires concentration, and acknowledges need. It is the one area where I seem to be defeated the most frequently. I know what it is . . .

    to wrestle in prayer,
      to fast in prayer,
        to weep in prayer,
          to plead in prayer,
            and I know what it is . . .
        to sleep in prayer,
      to daydream in prayer,
    to procrastinate in prayer,
  to generalize in prayer . . .

so much so that at times my heart's cry has had a shrill tone to it: "Please, dear God, help me to pray more effectively. Help me to keep my concentration. Help me to pray specifically and persistently. Help me to pray!"

Jesus knew you and I would struggle with prayer. So, as He prepared to leave His disciples, His parting words were about how His disciples—and you and I—could stay in touch with Him when He was no longer visibly present.

It was getting late on that Thursday evening. The crumbs and remnants of the remaining vestiges of the disciples' last meal with Jesus were scattered on the table. The candles were burning low. Through the tall, open windows of the upper room, the full moon could be seen rising over the Mount of Olives. The iridescent glow from the moon would have turned the Passover night into a soft, gray twilight, throwing the irregular rooftops of the city into sharp relief.

Within a few short hours, Jesus knew He would be betrayed, bound, and tried in a political and religious travesty ending in His torture and gruesome crucifixion. His disciples would be terrified. They would scatter as their world crashed into a thousand fragmented pieces. They would be stunned and confused as they witnessed firsthand what would appear to them as His murder. Their faith would be rocked to its foundation as they tried to reason through how Jesus could be the Messiah, the Son of God, yet be crucified before their very eyes. So Jesus, while acknowledging the pain and suffering and faith-shaking experience that was imminent, attempted to lift the eyes of His disciples beyond the next few hours of grief to the glory of the resurrection that would come.

ANSWERS FROM A LIVING LORD

Within hours of sharing that last supper, the disciples were going to be effectively cut off from their beloved Lord. For the first time in three years they would not hear His voice or feel His touch or see His face—except from an insurmountable distance as He was dragged through six trials then nailed to a cross. And in forty days, after His return to heaven, their relationship with Him would be based on faith, not sight. Like sheep without a shepherd or children without a mother, the silence and separation would be terrifying—especially in the next few days because it would coincide with the violent turmoil and rioting that would erupt in Jerusalem following His arrest.

Does Jesus seem silent to you? Is He silent during a time of desperate turmoil and confusion and heartache and suffering in your life, or in the lives of those around you? Do you feel somewhat separated from Him because in spite of the fact that you have prayed and wept and pleaded and fasted, the worst thing you could have imagined happened? Do you wonder to yourself,

Where is He? Why hasn't He answered my prayer? He seems to be doing nothing! There's no evidence of His activity at all!

Within hours, the disciples were going to go through just such an experience. So Jesus tried to prepare them to simply trust Him when they didn't understand.

Trust in the Silence

The disciples would not see Jesus nor hear from Him because He would be sequestered in six trials and hung on a cross and buried in a tomb. Jesus would be silent in their lives. So He began to prepare them for the separation and silence of the next few days by revealing, "In a little while you will see me no more, and then after a little while you will see me" (16:16).

His words sounded like a riddle to the puzzled disciples. They began to whisper quietly to each other, "What does he mean? . . . We don't understand" (16:17–18).

It's easy to imagine Peter and Matthew's dialogue with each other. Talking behind their hands that were cupped over their lips, did they lean behind John, and, with frowns wrinkling their weathered brows, vent their frustration? "Good grief, I wish He wouldn't talk in circles! It's hard enough to understand spiritual things as it is! I mean, if He were talking about fishing and water currents . . . if He were talking about tax rates and taxable income, hey, we could understand. But what is all this coming and going, and seeing and not seeing mean? It's so confusing!"

Has Jesus *said* something that you don't understand? Has He *done* something you don't understand? Are you whispering behind His back to other Christians? Jesus knows what you are thinking and whispering, just as He knew what the disciples were saying behind His back. "Jesus saw that they wanted to ask him about this, so he said to them, 'Are you asking one another what I meant when I said, "In a little while you will see me no more, and then after a little while you will see me"? I tell you the truth, you will weep and mourn while the world rejoices'" (16:19–20).

Who are you asking to explain to you what Jesus has said? When have you asked *Him* to explain? Jesus is not offended by our ignorance or our confusion or our questions. On the contrary, He knows exactly what we are thinking and feeling, and He takes the initiative to help us understand. But our understanding, like that of the disciples, is limited. The disciples could not comprehend the horror of the grief that would overwhelm them during the next three days. Neither could they comprehend the religious leaders' glee when the authorities mistakenly thought their "problem" had been solved by His death.

At times, like that of the disciples, our understanding is limited. We simply have to trust our heavenly Father to know best. We have to trust God's silences and respect God's mysteries and wait for God's answers.

When we pray for the salvation of a friend, and he becomes more hostile . . .

When we pray for the healing of a loved one, and he dies . . .

When we pray for release from a financial burden, and we go bankrupt . . .

When we pray for a reconciliation, and we are handed divorce papers . . .

When we pray for our career, and we get laid off . . .

When we pray for protection, and we are robbed . . .

When we pray for the purity of an unmarried daughter, and she becomes
    pregnant . . .

When we pray for unity with other believers, and our church splits . . .

We just have to trust Him. Trust Him. *Trust Him!*

What prayer have you prayed that not only seems unanswered but actually results in circumstances that seem to be the opposite of what you asked God to do? Have you been totally disheartened to the point you have felt your faith falter? Is God silent in your life? What prayers has He not answered for you?

At a time of unanswered prayer in my life years ago, my mother taught me the verses to a hymn that I still quote when I am totally baffled by events that seem to career out of the orbit of what I have asked:

> Trust Him when dark doubts assail thee,
> Trust Him when thy strength is small,
> Trust Him when to simply trust Him,
> Seems the hardest thing of all.
> Trust Him! He is ever faithful;

Trust Him—for His will is best;
Trust Him—for the heart of Jesus
Is the only place of rest.
Trust Him, then, through cloud or sunshine,
All thy cares upon Him cast;
Till the storm of life is over,
And the trusting days are past.[3]

Whether or not the disciples realized it at that moment, Jesus was seeking to strengthen their trust in Him until the "trusting days" would be past and their questions would be answered by the resurrection! He was trying to open their eyes to the big picture by letting them know the incomprehensible agony would be temporary—He would not always be silent nor separated from them. They needed to remember that after the pain and suffering, after the silence and the separation of the cross, would come the glory of the resurrection.

Is your focus on your immediate need blinding you to a greater purpose that God is working out? Would you choose to be patient and simply trust Him? Sometimes God does not answer our immediate prayer because He has something greater in store for us. There are times God is like the father of two little boys who was trying to teach his sons this lesson when he returned home from a business trip. As he walked in the door of his home, his children rushed him, jumping up and down as they tugged at his coat, asking him what he had brought them from his trip. He answered by telling them he had brought them nothing—he had decided to do something different. He was going to take them to the store and let them pick out what they wanted. So, after supper, he piled them in the car and took them to the local discount store with the instructions that he would get them whatever they wanted.

Beside themselves with excitement, the little boys pounced on the first thing they saw—the candy counter! Pointing to the bin of jellybeans, they adamantly told their father this was what they wanted. The father agreed they could have the jellybeans but then suggested they keep looking to make sure that was what they really wanted. As they walked down a few more aisles, they came to the sporting goods section, and their eyes fell on a football. Together they ran and grabbed the ball. "Daddy, Daddy, this is it! This is what we want!" Again the father agreed but suggested they keep looking. The boys were a little doubtful. What could be more wonderful than a new football? But because they were having fun and enjoyed looking at all the stuff with their father, they agreed to keep going. One aisle over, they came across the bicycles! "Daddy, this is it! This is what we really want! We know this is it!" And the father smiled, because he had intended from the beginning to buy the bicycles for his sons.

Has your prayer for "jellybeans" gone unanswered? Or your prayer for a "football"? Could it be God has not given you what you have asked for because He has a "bicycle" in mind?

The disciples would be separated from Jesus—He would be silent in their lives—only for a brief time. Then the silence would be broken in a spectacular, powerful way that would reveal His glory and grace to a much greater degree than they had previously known. And their grief would be swallowed up in the flood of joy!

Joy When He Speaks

The silence would be broken on the Sunday following the crucifixion on Friday and the tomb on Saturday! The silence and separation would be broken when God spoke His approval of His Son once and for all as He raised Him from the dead! Jesus focused His disciples on the glory to come when He exclaimed, "You will grieve, but your grief will turn to joy" (16:20). He then gave an illustration that every mother understands: "A woman giving birth to a child has pain because her time has come; but when her baby is born she forgets the anguish because of her joy that a child is born into the world. So with you: Now is your time of grief, but I will see you again and you will rejoice, and no one will take away your joy" (16:21–22).

Our daughter, Rachel-Ruth, has given birth to our first grandchild! (I warned you, didn't I, that I love to talk about this wonderful addition to our family?) In the months leading up to the delivery, Rachel-Ruth became more and more apprehensive of the pain associated with childbirth. Again and again, I tried to reassure her that while there would be intense pain in labor and delivery, it would be swallowed up in the joy of having her baby! Sure enough, within hours of delivering that beautiful little girl, Rachel-Ruth was already talking about having another baby!

There has never been a greater demonstration of God's glory and power than the resurrection of Jesus Christ.

When we pray and it seems like Friday . . .
    when God seems silent . . .
        when our situation turns worse . . .
When we pray and it seems like Saturday . . .
    when God seems separated from us . . .
        when hope is buried . . .
When we pray and see no activity in response to our prayers . . .
    we need to remember that Sunday is coming!

The same God Who raised Jesus from the dead is available to work powerfully in and through us.[4] We serve a living Lord Who loves to answer the prayers of His children. Be patient! Trust Him to know best.

ANSWERS FROM A LOVING FATHER

God loves you! God loves you! *God loves you!* Why do you doubt that awesome truth? Because He hasn't answered your prayers the *way* you want? Because He hasn't answered your prayers *when* you want? Because He hasn't done what you told Him to do? Because He hasn't acted as you expected? Jesus promised His disciples—and you and me—that God the Father would hear and answer our prayers. But there are certain prerequisites we must meet first.

The Prerequisites for Answers

The confusion the disciples were feeling would have added to their sense of grief and dread. Around the table, their shoulders must have slumped and their brows wrinkled and their lips pursed, trying to grasp what Jesus was saying. They knew from the intensity of His demeanor that what He was saying was vitally important. And they must have been almost exhausted from trying *so hard* to understand His words. A thousand questions must have been on their minds but remained unspoken on their lips. So, once again, He comforted them with His knowledge of what they were thinking and feeling. He encouraged them, "In that day you will no longer ask me anything. I tell you the truth, my Father will give you whatever you ask in my name. Until now you have not asked for anything in my name. Ask and you will receive, and your joy will be complete" (16:23–24). That was a promise anyone could understand!

Do you understand Jesus' promise? Or have you given it a superficial reading and therefore feel He was promising to give you anything you wanted? Under close inspection, the promise contains two prerequisites for receiving answers. The first prerequisite is that you have to *ask!*

During the days of Ezekiel, God poured out His heart and shared what He wanted to do for His beloved people. Then He revealed an astonishing fact: "I will yet for this be enquired of by the house of Israel, to do it for them."[5] God was waiting to be asked!

My mother has said that if there are any tears shed in heaven, they are going to be shed over all the answers to prayer for which no one ever bothered to ask! What blessing is God waiting to give you, but you haven't asked Him for it?

Why does He wait for us to ask? Maybe He wants us to acknowledge our need of Him. Maybe it's one way of getting our attention. Maybe it's the only way we will know when the answer comes that it comes from Him, and we don't credit ourselves or someone else for it.

My husband, Danny, recently had an appointment with the doctor for his eyes. I knew the time the appointment was scheduled, and I had accompanied him to his other eye appointments, but this time I assumed he would drive himself from work to the doctor's office. So instead of making arrangements to go with him, I ran errands. When I returned home, I found him standing in the middle of the kitchen with the most hurt look on his face as he said simply, "You didn't go."

I looked at him, dumbfounded! Then I blurted out, "But you never asked me to." And I wonder, how many times have I been hurt by something God did not do for me, yet in reality, I never asked? Jesus said we are to ask if we want to receive.

Once again, my mother encouraged me as a little girl to pray specifically. She bought me a small white leather notebook, and in it I carefully recorded my requests. Then, at her instruction, I left a blank line under each one so I could record the date of the answer. In the front of the little book, she penned these words:

> Thou art coming to a King,
> Large petitions with thee bring,
> For His grace and power are such,
> None can ever ask too much!

So feel free to ask! But leave a blank space under your request so you can record the answer! Because Jesus said if we ask we will receive. But there's another condition. Jesus said the second prerequisite is that we must ask in His name.

He didn't mean that we are just to recite His name at the end of our prayer. He meant that when we come to God in prayer, we come believing all that is represented by the meaning of Jesus' name.

In the Bible, names often denote the nature and character of the person to whom they are given. Jacob, who stole his brother's birthright, had a name that meant "supplanter," or "deceiver." When Jacob surrendered his life to God, his name was changed to Israel, which means "power with God." Peter's name was Simon, which means "compulsive," or "impulsive." When he became a disciple of Jesus, his name was changed to Peter, which means "rock."

Jesus' name also has meaning that reveals Who He is. His name is Lord, which means Jehovah God. He is the Jehovah of the Old Testament Who revealed Himself to His people. Today Jesus reveals God to you and me. His name is also Jesus, which means Savior, because He came to save us from the penalty and power of our sin. And His name is Christ, which is the New Testament equivalent of the Old Testament name Messiah. Jesus is the fulfillment of the Old Testament prophecy that pointed to the Anointed One of God Who would come down to reign and rule on the earth.

To pray in Jesus' name means we come to God believing that Jesus is our

206

Lord—believing He has revealed God to us and in response we have submitted to His authority. To pray in Jesus' name means we believe He is our only Savior Whose death on the cross we have claimed personally as atonement for our sin. And it means we acknowledge that He is the Christ, the Messiah, Who has not only come, fulfilling the Law and the Prophets, but He is coming again to reign and rule the world in peace and righteousness.[6] When we come to God by faith in the Lord—Jehovah, Jesus—Savior, Christ—Messiah, God hears and answers our prayer.[7]

What answers to prayer have you received for which there is no rational explanation except that there is a God Who heard you and moved in response to your faith? To encourage your faith in Him, Jesus revealed His willingness to answer your prayers by offering, "I will do whatever you ask in my name, so that the Son may bring glory to the Father. You may ask me for anything in my name, and I will do it" (14:13–14). In some supernatural way, prayer taps into the heart of God and releases His power to work on our behalf. But not just any prayer. God specifically honors prayer that comes from those who belong by faith to His Son. It's one way God the Father validates the claim of Jesus to be His Son.

The Privilege of Access

On January 20, 2001, my brother Franklin gave the invocation at the inauguration of the new president of the United States, George Walker Bush. With a crimson scarf around his neck and a long black coat that warded off the elements of freezing cold and chilling rain, Franklin bowed his head and led the nation in a magnificent prayer for our leaders and their families in the new administration as well as the old. His voice, clear and strong, rang out over the steps of the Capitol and amplified throughout the Washington Mall as he offered his prayer in the name of our Lord Jesus Christ.

For days following the inauguration, newspapers and magazines ran editorials criticizing Franklin for his exclusive language. The "talking heads" determined that since Franklin was praying on behalf of the nation, he should not have excluded all those who do not believe in Jesus. The criticism struck me as ludicrous. Franklin wasn't praying *to the nation;* he was praying *to God* on behalf of the nation. And the Bible clearly gives our personal relationship with God's Son, Jesus Christ, as the key that unlocks the door to God's presence, enabling us to "walk in" and submit to Him our requests with the assurance that He will hear and answer our prayers.

When you pray, how do you pray? Down deep in your heart, what do you believe is the basis for not only your entrance into the presence of God but your answers from God? The *only* credentials that God accepts are those presented to Him in the name and righteousness of His dear Son. So pray—in Jesus' name. It's your privilege as the Father's child!

Several years ago, the pastor of a large church caused a firestorm of criticism and debate when he stated that God does not hear the prayers of Jews. And of course, it went without saying, he would include along with the Jews, Buddhists, Hindus, Muslims, and any other religion apart from Christianity. I don't think there would have been much debate on this issue—at least among Christians—had we just carefully considered what Jesus told His disciples when He promised, "In that day you will ask in my name. I am not saying that I will ask the Father on your behalf. No, the Father himself loves you because you have loved me and have believed that I came from God" (16:26–27).

Jesus Himself clearly answered the issue the pastor raised. God hears any prayer He chooses, but answers to prayer are only guaranteed to those who come believing in the name of the Lord Jesus Christ. When you approach Him through faith in His Son, God is accessible twenty-four hours a day, seven days a week, twelve months a year for the rest of your life!

For the last several years, I have carried a small cellular phone with me whenever I leave the house. Even when I take my early morning, three-mile walk, I have my cell phone in my pocket. Invariably, when I say good-bye to my husband, or speak with my children or staff before I go out of town, I remind them that I will have my phone with me. If I'm needed, all they have to do is call me. Yet how many times have I noticed that I have a voice message waiting on my phone because either it was out of the range of a tower, or I had turned it off while flying, or muted it during a meeting, or left it in that *other* pocketbook!

Praise God! He is never out of range! He is never turned off or tuned out!

His ears are never deaf! He is always available, accessible, and attentive to our call!

The disciples must have been thrilled, just as you and I should be when the reality of this promise sinks in. Jesus is guaranteeing our direct access to God through Him!

The privilege of access is all in who you know. This past fall, I had a wonderful experience that dramatized the privilege of access when I attended a ball game with my beloved friends Jerry and Joan Colangelo. I first met them several years ago when Joan and another friend, Nancy Walker, invited me to share the Christmas story with approximately five hundred of their friends at a holiday luncheon they hosted. Jerry, who is the managing general partner of the Phoenix Suns basketball team and the World Series champion Diamondbacks baseball team, had been very instrumental in helping us fill America West Arena for our Just Give Me Jesus revival in Phoenix. To help promote the revival, and also to simply make a public statement of their faith, Jerry and Joan Colangelo invited me to not only attend a Diamondbacks baseball game but to give an invocation on the field before it began.

Joan and Nancy picked me up at the Phoenix airport, and we drove straight to Bank One Ballpark. When Joan maneuvered the car to a secured area in the back of the ball field, we were halted by a secured gate. Joan simply leaned out her window and told the guard that she was Mrs. Jerry Colangelo and I was her guest. The gate opened, and we drove through to a specially reserved parking space. We walked down a stone path that led to double glass doors. As the doorman and the receptionist greeted Joan by name, they both stared at me. I smiled and said, "I'm with her." We came to an elevator that was held open by an attendant who again greeted Joan by name and then eyed me up and down until Joan identified me as her guest. We went upstairs to greet Jerry in his office and to go over the minute-by-minute schedule for the opening preliminaries to the game.

When we walked out of Jerry's office, I walked at his side. When we came to the elevator, an attendant was waiting. This time, no one even looked at me questioningly. We descended to a lower level and were ushered into the stadium through a private tunnel that exited right beside a private box behind home plate. I was seated comfortably in the private box until the preliminaries began. Then I was escorted onto the field with the security gates and guards melting away in front of me. Following the prayer, I was guided back to my seat, where an attractive woman with a pad and pencil in her hand took my order for dinner! Not only did she return with a great hot dog for me to enjoy, but when I had finished eating it she appeared with a hot fudge sundae!

I can tell you—I have been to many ball games before, but I have never been treated like I was at that one! The difference was all in who I knew and who I was with. I was treated like royalty in the name of Jerry Colangelo!

In the same way, when we come to God through prayer believing *in Jesus' name,* we enter into a world of privilege!

Doors open,

angels attend,

mountains move,

doubts disappear,

fears fade,

and the God of the universe bends down to hear what we have to say![8]
And He answers! What a privilege!

We don't have to go through a priest.

We don't have to go through a secretary.

We don't have to go to a temple.

We don't have to make a donation.

We don't have to go to a church building.

We don't have to come from the "right side of the tracks."

We don't have to use grammatically correct words.

We don't have to go through a security check.

Prayer is as simple as talking to God in Jesus' name.

Dear loving Father, I now know if I want MORE of Your answers to my prayers, I just need to pray more!

12

MORE *of* ────────────────
──────── *His Glory on My Knees*

SARA CREWE is the heroine in one of my favorite childhood books entitled *A Little Princess* by Frances Hodgson Burnett. As the story unfolds, Sara is condemned to be a scullery maid for an exclusive girls boarding school in London. In one moving scene, Sara is described running her daily errands for the cook through the snow-covered streets of the city on Christmas Day. She was dressed in threadbare rags that did nothing to block the biting wind, and she was wearing shoes with holes that allowed the icy slush of the streets to numb her tired feet. Freezing cold, bone weary, and emotionally spent, Sara made her way back through the dusk to the boarding school. As she passed a home with light flooding from the windows, she paused to look inside. Her hungry gaze fell on the sight of a family just opening their gifts. The children were sitting before a crackling fire, talking and laughing as their parents gave them presents from under a beautifully decorated Christmas tree.

The entire scene was one of warmth and love and security and happiness. When little Sara turned away to continue her journey down the cold, snowy streets, there were big tears running down her grimy cheeks. Because Sara was on the outside, looking in.

That same sense of being on the outside and looking in almost overwhelms me as I read our Lord's prayer to His Father shortly before He was betrayed and arrested. This prayer is unique because Jesus was not teaching His disciples to pray. He was praying—privately, intimately, emotionally—to His Father. And He allowed His disciples to overhear what He said. What they overheard as He knelt before His Father in prayer was His heart's cry for more glory.

And His heart's cry is mine, too. Because I am . . .

a sinner who has fallen short of God's glory . . .

a sinner dressed in the tattered rags of frayed righteousness . . .

a sinner with worn-out shoes that will never get me to heaven . . .

a sinner whose face is pressed against the hope of acceptance into God's family . . .

a sinner who is on the outside looking in!

But instead of letting me turn away with the tears of helplessness and hopelessness coursing through my spirit, Jesus Himself has flung open the door to the warmth of His relationship with His Father and invited me to come inside and share His glory!

ENTER HIS PRESENCE

In olden days, entering into the presence of God would have been an unattainable privilege for a Gentile woman like myself. If I had stood on a desert sand dune that overlooked the Israelite camp in the wilderness following the exodus from Egypt, I would have seen a sea of tents that stretched out to the horizon of my vision. In the midst of the encampment, I would have noticed a much larger tent surrounded by a dazzling "wall" of linen that shimmered white in the scorching desert sun. If I had left my vantage point on the sand dune and slipped closer, I might have found a bystander who would have been willing to answer my questions. The most obvious one would have been, "What is that big tent?" If there had been someone patient enough to explain, I expect he or she would have replied with eyes widened by surprise.

"Don't you know? We are God's children, and that tent is the Tabernacle where God is said to dwell in our midst."

"Can I go in?" I would have naively asked.

"Go in? *Go inside the Tabernacle?* You must be out of your mind! It's obvious you are not an Israelite and you are a woman. You could never go inside."

"Surely there must be some way I could enter," I would have persisted. "I would like to draw near to God, too. I long to be in His presence."

"Well, let me tell you something, lady. The only way you could ever enter into the presence of God is if you were totally born again!"

Looking over his shoulder, I might have inquired, "What's inside those linen walls?"

"On the other side of the walls are the altar, the laver, and the Tabernacle itself," would have been the blunt, direct reply.

"And what is inside the Tabernacle?"

"The Tabernacle is divided into two rooms that are separated by a heavy curtain, or veil. I'm told that in the first room there is a lamp, a table with a loaf of bread on it, and an altar of incense. Beyond the veil in the second room is the Most Holy Place of God's presence where the Ark of the Covenant rests."

"If only I had been born a man," I would have longingly cried. "If only I had been born an Israelite. Then I would go into the Most Holy Place of God's presence five times a day!"

"Lady, you still don't get it," my informer would have said with a tone of exasperation. "Israelite men cannot go inside the Tabernacle, either—only the priests are allowed inside. And even the priests can't go inside the Most Holy Place of God's presence. Only the high priest can go beyond the veil."

"Oh, how I wish I was an Israelite man who was also a high priest. Then I would go into God's presence every day. In fact, I would just stay there—I would live in God's presence!"

Perhaps with a sympathetic softening to his eyes, the bystander would reply gently but with finality, "But the high priest himself can only enter within the veil once a year."

And I would be turned away, with no hope of ever entering into the Most Holy Place of God's presence.[1]

Until Jesus came! Through His death the veil separating us from the presence of God was torn in two from top to bottom! God Himself opened up the way for us to enter into His holy presence—through prayer.

Praise God! We will have more of His glory on our knees, "since we have confidence to enter the Most Holy Place by the blood of Jesus, by a new and living way opened for us through the curtain, that is, his body, and since we have a great high priest over the house of God, let us draw near to God with a sincere heart in full assurance of faith."[2] Through prayer, we are invited to come into His presence as children come to their father.

Enter through Prayer

It was springtime in Jerusalem. The city would have been teeming with pilgrims who had come for Passover. I wonder if the warm evening breeze fluttered through the open windows, causing candle flames to flicker and casting dancing shadows on the walls and ceiling of the upper room. Through the open windows would have come, not only the fragrance of the olive blossoms, but the sounds of a city bedding down for the night.

Jesus Himself must have been tired. For the past week, He had taught every day on the temple grounds, slipping back to Bethany in the evenings to spend the night with friends. On this Thursday evening, He had arranged to have a last meal with His beloved disciples—and then had washed twelve pairs of dirty feet. Later He had dismissed Judas, whom He knew even at that moment was betraying Him to the religious authorities. He had poured out His heart to His closest friends. He had . . .

encouraged them with the hope of His Father's house,

taught them about humility by His own example of service,

explained the necessity of abiding in Him in order to be fruitful,

revealed He would dwell in them through the person of the Holy Spirit,

warned them that the world would hate them as it had Him, and

promised He would answer their prayers . . .

After pouring His life into these eleven men (Judas was now gone), after teaching them all they would need to know before He left them for the cross, after preparing them for the life-jolting trauma they were about to experience—"After Jesus said this, he looked toward heaven and prayed" (17:1). Jesus—the Son of God, the Creator of the universe, the Jehovah of the Old Covenant, the Messiah, the Lord of glory—*Jesus prayed!*

What kind of a week have you had? Has it been . . .

physically exhausting?

emotionally depleting?

spiritually draining?

socially depressing?

relationally devastating?

professionally discouraging?

financially challenging?

If Jesus felt the need to pray, why don't you and I?

Jesus prayed in the early morning before daybreak . . .

Jesus prayed alone in the evening . . .

Jesus prayed when preparing to serve . . .

Jesus prayed when under pressure . . .

Jesus prayed when attacked, opposed, and criticized . . .

Jesus prayed publicly, before eating . . .

Jesus prayed when tempted . . .

Jesus prayed when on a mountaintop . . .

Jesus prayed when there was no special reason to pray . . .[3]

In other words,

Jesus prayed privately,

Jesus prayed publicly,

Jesus prayed alone,

Jesus prayed with friends,

Jesus prayed in crowds.

Jesus prayed

standing,

sitting,

kneeling,

and on His face.

Jesus prayed early in the morning,

Jesus prayed late in the evening,

Jesus prayed during the day,

Jesus prayed all night.

Jesus prayed!

If Jesus found it necessary to maintain a continual, active prayer life, what is your excuse for not praying? Do you say . . .

you don't have enough time?

you're too tired?

you don't know how?
you think it's boring?
you feel foolish trying?

If any of *your* excuses were valid, then surely Jesus had reason not to pray on the Thursday night before His execution on Friday morning! What makes you and me think we can do without a personal prayer life? It's through prayer that we stop pressing our faces on the outside of the "glass" and come into a personal, intimate relationship with our heavenly Father.

Are you thinking that you would really like to come in out of the "cold," that you long to have a closer relationship with God, but you don't feel worthy? Are you so conscious of sin and failure in your life that you feel totally inferior and unable to have fellowship with Him? Are you convinced you are a nobody and therefore would never be accepted, much less welcomed, into His presence?

Praise God! Our entrance into His presence is not based on our own worthiness but on the worthiness of Jesus Christ! When we enter God's presence in Jesus' name, we are as accepted by God as Jesus is, because God counts us as His own dear children![4]

For a child, there is no place quite so safe and secure as within the father's arms. Jesus invites you and me, in His name, to come into His Father's presence through prayer, crawl up into His lap by faith, put our head on His shoulder of strength, feel His loving arms of protection around us, call Him "Abba" Daddy, and pour out our hearts to Him.[5]

Enter under Pressure

Just the emotional strain of saying good-bye to His friends would have been totally exhausting for Jesus. Yet added to His grief over leaving them was the acute awareness that He was on the brink of brutal physical torture. Within hours He would literally be God's sacrificial Lamb, bearing the sin and guilt of the whole world. The combination of these stresses would have caused anyone else to collapse in a fetal position and take a psychological exit from the mind-numbing events of the next few hours. Instead, Jesus prayed, "Father, the time has come" (17:1). The time He referred to was the time of

His betrayal—His arrest—His trials—His crucifixion—His death—His burial—His resurrection—His ascension . . .

It was a time that would split God's story and world history in half.

It was the time for which He had been born.

It was the time for the New Covenant to be made.

It was the time for the price of our redemption to be paid.

It was the time of momentous,

earthshaking,
hell-defying,
devil-defeating,
graverobbing,
heaven-opening
pressure!

How would you prepare the night before an impending crisis? Would you get to bed early so you could get a good night's rest and be physically refreshed for what you were going to face? The fact that Jesus spent so much time in prayer the night after such a grueling week and the night before such a torturous day teaches us that physical rest alone is not an adequate way to handle pressure.

What crisis are you confronting? Even though you are carefully maintaining your physical health, rest, exercise, and eating, does the pressure seem to overwhelm you? Did you just think that was the best you could do? Could it be that you are neglecting prayer and therefore depriving yourself of the spiritual strength that you need to endure and overcome it?

One reason a crisis is a crisis is because it usually catches us by surprise! To be prepared for the unexpected, we need to spend time every day in prayer. If we have established a lifetime habit of daily prayer then we won't have to suddenly learn how to pray when a crisis hits. We won't have to rush around substituting the prayers of others for our own. It's possible to handle a crisis with confidence because we have spent time in our Father's presence.

Recently a good friend was relating the story of her son's emergency appendectomy. He had gone on a skiing trip with some friends when he was seized with such severe pain that he was rushed by ambulance to the local hospital. He was diagnosed with an infected appendix and underwent surgery. Alone. Away from his parents. The other mothers to whom my friend was telling the story *ohhed* and *aahed* their sympathy then nodded with understanding of what they assumed was my friend's emotional turmoil. But instead of accepting their solicitous concern, she looked at them and explained, "You don't understand. There wasn't any turmoil for me. I had prayed and knew God would take care of my son. And He did. Through it all I had perfect peace."

If you and I want the peace that passes all understanding, especially when we are confronting a crisis or come under enormous pressure, then we need the spiritual strength and refreshment that only comes from spending time in prayer with our Father.[6]

EXALT HIS PERSON

I wonder what it would have been like for the disciples, not just to overhear the words of Jesus in intimate conversation with His Father, but to actually see Jesus praying. In the flickering shadows of the torchlight of the upper room, just before continuing His prayer time in the Garden of Gethsemane, Jesus "looked toward heaven and prayed" (17:1).

He didn't bow His head and close His eyes for this prayer. He looked upward—as though with the eyes of His faith He could actually "see" His beloved Father. In that upward gaze there must have been an expression of such loving trust and intense longing that it immediately conveyed something of the depth and strength of the bond between Father and Son.

Did the disciples sharply inhale as the scene before them took their breath away? Did their eyes widen in wonder and their hearts skip a beat? Did their ears strain to catch every syllable, every word? Knowing God was His Father and that He could ask for anything He wanted, what would be the first thing He would ask His Father for on such a night? What they heard in the stillness of that upper room was the *heartbeat of Jesus:* "Glorify your Son, that your Son may glorify you" (17:1).

Glorified As Savior

Jesus asked the Father to glorify Him, knowing full well that the path to glory led to a hill called Calvary and to a cross that would be stained red with His own life's blood.

218

The glory of Jesus would be revealed when the extent of His obedience to His Father caused Him to lay down His life for you and me.

> *It was at the cross* that God's curse for Adam's sin was coiled into a crown that Jesus wore.
>
> *It was at the cross* that redemption was purchased for every believer by the sacrifice of God's Lamb.
>
> *It was at the cross* that even the vilest offenders received, by faith, a full pardon for their sins.
>
> *It was at the cross* that God's grace was poured out as a fountain filled with His own blood.
>
> *It was at the cross* that the omnipotent Creator died for the human creature's sin.

And it's still at the cross of Jesus Christ where millions of men and women throughout the ages have laid down all that they are and all that they have as a debt of love to the One Who died for them. There is no other way for you and me to be saved from hell . . . to have our sins forgiven . . . to be reconciled to God . . . to receive eternal life . . . to go to heaven when we die, except through the cross.[7]

It's at the cross that Jesus Christ is glorified as the only Savior for sinners that God recognizes and accepts. And in His prayer that was forever indelibly written on the hearts and minds of His disciples, when Jesus asked His Father to glorify Himself—He was in effect asking for the cross! In other words, if He could bring glory to His Father through His death, then He was ready and willing to die, trusting His Father to see Him through the cross to the glory of our redemption!

It's at the cross that God is also glorified because He answered His Son's prayer and in doing so, reveals His love for you and me that stretches back beyond the remote recesses of eternity.

Glorified As Sovereign

Before the foundation of the world was laid, God, in His divine sovereignty, planned to send His own Son to the cross to be our Savior.[8] Before the beginning of time and space and human history, He took counsel with Himself and decided to bring us into existence, knowing full well that we would rebel against Him and become separated from Him by our sin.[9] So He made preparations for our redemption—preparations that were finished once and for all time at the cross.[10]

The heartbeat of Jesus was to finish His Father's plan and, in so doing, bring glory to God. In other words, through His own death on the cross, Jesus would reveal the love of God in such a way that people throughout the ages would praise Him and love Him and lay down their lives before Him. So He embraced the cross and all that it meant.

What sacrifice have you made . . .

What hardship have you endured . . .

What rejection have you experienced . . .

What pain have you suffered . . .

What ambition have you denied . . .

What relationship have you forsaken . . .

What cross are you facing . . .

for Jesus' sake? Would you prayerfully choose to embrace your cross as an opportunity to display God's love and grace and peace and joy to those who are watching? Would you pray and ask God to reveal Himself in and through your life?

While no one would desire pain and suffering, the apostle Peter explained that "these have come so that your faith—of greater worth than gold, which perishes even though refined by fire—may be proved genuine and may result in . . . glory . . . when Jesus Christ is revealed."[11]

The revelation of the glory, or character, of Jesus Christ in our lives is often produced only through pressure and pain, stress and suffering. This principle came to mind when a friend was telling me about a gift he received at Christmas. It was a box with lots of little compartments, each one filled with different flavored tea bags. The compartments were labeled, but the tea bags were not. Shortly after the holidays, he got up early one morning, relishing the idea of a hot cup of tea. As he reached up on the shelf to grasp the box, it slipped out of his hands. In dismayed consternation, he looked at the tea bags that were scattered across his kitchen floor. Since they were no longer organized in the tidy little labeled compartments, he had no idea which tea bag was Earl Grey, which one was lemon mint, which one was Darjeeling, which one was herbal raspberry, or which one was green tea.

He gathered all the bags together and placed them in a plastic container. My friend related that from that day on, every morning was an adventure as he took out a tea bag at random, not knowing what flavor he had chosen until he plunged it into the boiling hot water. The heat of the water drew out the flavor of the tea bag.

Has God turned up the heat in your life? Could it be that this is your opportunity for God to glorify you as He uses the heat to conform you into the image of His Son? And at the same time, is this your opportunity to glorify Him as the "heat" draws out the real flavor of your character, and Jesus is revealed through your love, joy, peace, patience, kindness, goodness, faithfulness, gentleness, and self-control?

Regardless of what your cross is, would you thank God—not for the suffering and the stress—but for the opportunity it affords you to bring glory to Him?

EMBRACE HIS PURPOSE

Glorifying God—revealing His character in our lives so that others are drawn to give Him praise—is one of the primary purposes for our existence. But an equal purpose is to know Him in a personal, intimate relationship.[12] When I was a little girl, I was raised in the Southern Presbyterian Church. Before I could be baptized at the age of nine, I had to memorize the Westminster Shorter Catechism and be prepared to quote it randomly in response to questions from the Session of the church.

I remember how nervous I was and how my grandfather, who was a member of the Session, smiled and put me at ease, asking most of the questions himself. I must have passed, because I was approved for baptism. The following Sunday, at the close of the worship service, Dr. Stanley Bennett asked me questions in front of the congregation that led me to publicly confess my faith in Jesus Christ as my Savior and Lord. To this day, I can remember the feeling of the water that was sprinkled on my head trickling down my face and neck. It was a life's moment I will never forget.

But to my chagrin, I have forgotten most of the catechism—except for one question and answer. The question, as I remember it, was: "What is the chief end of man?" And the answer, as I remember it, was: "Man's chief end is to glorify God and to enjoy Him forever." What a simple truth to implant in a child's mind. What a profound truth to wrap my life around! God is to be glorified, and God is to be enjoyed within the context of a right, personal, permanent, love relationship. It's a relationship that Jesus used to define eternal life.

Many people throughout human history have sought the "fountain of youth." They seem to want to live longer and to live better than a natural life span. The search today for an extended stay on earth has become more and more high-tech.

Incredibly delicate surgeries,
complicated organ transplants,
beautifying cosmetic enhancements,
mechanical life-extending implants
are now commonplace.

Many people give priority time to . .
muscle tone,
chemical balance,
vitamin enrichment,
stress reduction, and
organic diets
in hopes of living longer. Billions of dollars and countless hours are expended in trying to buy one more year or one more month or one more week or one more hour of life. Yet a life so long that it lasts forever, as well as a better quality of life here and now, is ours simply for the taking.

Embrace His Purpose Eternally

We could save ourselves a lot of time, trouble, and expense if we would just listen to our Lord's prayer: "For you granted him authority over all people that he might give eternal life to all those you have given him" (17:2). *Eternal life!* Through faith in Jesus Christ, anyone and everyone can live forever!

Are you afraid to die? I am afraid of the pain and suffering that can be associated with death, but I'm not afraid of the actual exit from this life. Because I know when I die, I will simply pass from living by faith to living by sight! When I close my eyes to this life, I will open them to the face of Jesus! Death does not end my life!

Within the past year, I had the opportunity once again to visit Westminster Abbey in London. It is a grand cathedral where many of the kings and dignitaries of England are buried, and where the kings and queens receive their coronation. The narthex is small, dark, and cramped—just a brief space to pass through between the outside door and the door leading into the cathedral itself. I can't imagine anyone visiting the abbey and being satisfied to stay in the narthex. I also can't imagine anyone who would make an enormous effort to stay there with no thought to passing through to the glory of what lies beyond.

Your life and mine here on earth is like the narthex to a grand cathedral. Our lives are simply an area to pass through on our way to the glory of eternal life that lies beyond the door of death. Physical death for a believer is simply a transition into real life. And it's God's purpose that you and I live forever—with Him.

Embrace His Purpose Personally

Aware that His disciples were listening to His conversation with His Father, Jesus defined eternal life for them and for us when He prayed, "Now this is eternal life: that they may know you, the only true God, and Jesus Christ, whom you have sent" (17:3). Right at the outset of His prayer, He indicated that eternal life is not just life that goes on forever, but it is a quality of life here and now that is found in a personal relationship with God. Eternal life is the life we will live one day in heaven that is experienced before we get there.

It's possible to be saved from hell and assured you are going to heaven because you have placed your faith in Jesus Christ alone for your salvation—yet still miss what Jesus died and rose to give you right here and now: personal knowledge of God.

Knowing God is the pinnacle of the Christian experience.

Why have you stopped short of the heights?

Knowing God is what makes life worth living regardless of your circumstances.

What or whom have you allowed to rob your life of meaning?

Knowing God is heaven's treasure that we can possess on earth.

What have you substituted for heaven's crown jewel?

Twenty-six years ago I studied and taught the Book of Genesis for the first time. One impact on my life was that it gave me an overwhelmingly strong desire to know God. I didn't want to know *about* Him. I didn't want to know Him casually as you might know an acquaintance. I wanted to know Him like Adam knew Him: I wanted to walk with Him and talk with Him. I wanted to know Him like Enoch knew Him: I wanted His presence to so fill my life that I would be enveloped in it, aware of nothing else except Him. I wanted to know Him like Noah knew Him: I wanted to risk my reputation and everything I have and am to be obedient to His call in my life. I wanted to care more about what God thought than what the world around me thought. And I wanted to know Him like Abraham knew Him. I wanted to have God as my friend. I wanted God to count me as *His* friend.

So I made that my prayer. I made the deliberate decision to seek to know God, and I began a pilgrimage of faith that continues today. Although I do not know Him as well as I want to or as well as I should, I know Him more personally and intimately today than I would have believed possible twenty-six years ago. And I pray I will know Him better next year than I do today. That aim has become the singular purpose of my life. It determines my priorities—the way I spend my time and my money, the way I expend my energy and effort. It determines my relationships—whom I spend time with and whom I work with. It determines my wants—my desires and my dreams. It determines everything.

To know God is to love God.

To love God is to serve God.

To serve God is to know Him better.

To know Him better is to love Him more.

To love Him more is to serve Him even more . . .

as increasingly we line up with His unique plan and purpose for our lives.[13]

Embrace His Purpose Singularly

You and I were created for the purpose of glorifying God through the Christlike character of our lives and through the eternal fruitfulness of our service. When I get to heaven, I want to find that I fulfilled the potential of God's purpose for my life. I want Him to find pleasure in my birth and joy in my rebirth. I want Him to be confirmed that creating me was eternally worth it! For these "wants" to be realized *then,* I have to focus my entire life on His purpose *now*—which is what Jesus did, as is evident in His prayer: "I have brought you glory on earth by completing the work you gave me to do" (17:4).

What chance is there that you will complete the work God has given you to do? Do you even know what the work is—specific work that enables you to fulfill His purpose of bringing glory to Him and enjoying Him? The specific work that God has for me is like the rim of a wheel with several spokes connected to it that serve as channels for the overall work:

One of the spokes is to be a godly wife, helping my husband to fulfill God's purpose for his life.

One of the spokes is to be a godly mother, raising my children to fulfill God's purpose for their lives.

One of the spokes is to be a godly grandmother, helping my children raise my grandchildren to fulfill God's purpose for their lives.

One of the spokes is to study, apply, obey, and teach God's Word faithfully and powerfully in such a way that others are compelled to fulfill God's purpose for their lives.

One of the spokes is to oversee a ministry team with such excellence and diligence that individually and corporately it fulfills God's purpose.

If the *rim* of the wheel is the specific work God has given me to do and the *spokes* are the different channels for that work, then the *hub* is my focus, which is centered on fulfilling God's purpose for my life.

Jesus was focused. At the beginning of His public ministry, after having walked all morning and talked with the woman of Samaria for the better part of the afternoon, Jesus' disciples returned with food, urging Him to eat. He resisted their urging by saying, "I have food to eat that you know nothing about." When the confused disciples wondered who could have brought Him something to eat, He explained, "My food . . . is to do the will of him who sent me and to finish his work."[14]

In order to finish God's work, Jesus had to keep His focus and embrace that purpose with a single heart and mind, lining up all of His priorities accordingly. The result of finishing His Father's work would be even more deeply satisfying than food to a starving man.

If you and I are able to finish God's work, it will not be an accident. It will be because we have been focused every minute of every day of every week of every month of every year of our lives on God's purpose. And that purpose determines the way we manage our time, our money, our priorities, our relationships, our careers, and every other aspect of our lives. God is not something we add to our lives—*He is our life!* And our life's work!

When Jesus said He had completed the work God gave Him to do, there were still many people . . .

who were blind that needed sight,
who were lame and needed to walk,
who were lepers and needed to be cleansed,
who were deaf and needed to hear,
who were sick and needed to be well,
who were lost and needed to be found,
who were dead and needed to be raised . . .

Finishing His Father's work didn't mean meeting everyone's need or saying yes to every opportunity.

Jill Briscoe, noted author and international speaker, was recently asked what she saw as her life's greatest mission. Her reply revealed that the spokes of her life are well-connected to the hub. She answered that her life's greatest mission is "to figure out what to do every day in my life—as ordained by God—and then to do it."[15] In her wisdom, Jill knows there are many things to do in life that are not ordained of God, which is why we must be single-minded.

To be single-minded as I embrace God's purpose for my life means that there are times I have to *just say no* . . .

to an invitation to join my friends for coffee,

to an opportunity to give a motivational message,
to a proposal to write a novel,
to an offer for a lucrative job,
to a position on a college board of directors,
to a long weekend . . .
    in the highlands of Scotland,
        or the mountains of Colorado,
            or the beaches of Florida,
                or the wide-open spaces of Wyoming . . .[16]

To be single-minded as I embrace God's purpose for my life means there are times I have to *just say yes* . . .

to less sleep and more prayer,
    to less TV and more study,
        to less shopping and more tithing,
            to less eating and more exercise,
                to less talking and more listening,
                    to less work and more worship.

In what way are you cross-eyed? Do you have one eye on *God's purpose* for your life and one eye on *your purpose* for your life? Do you have one eye on what *God* wants and one eye on what *you* want? If so, your work for God will be incomplete. In that case, the sad thing is that you will miss out on all that God had intended to give you.

Embrace His Purpose Fully

I have had to make the conscious decision to fully embrace God's purpose for my life, because it's so easy to settle for less than everything God wants to give me. All I have to do is relax and get out of focus, and when I do, pretty soon . . .

being with my friends seems more important than being with God,
sleeping late seems more desirable than an early morning quiet time,
vacationing seems more beneficial than working,
reading the newspaper seems more relevant than reading my Bible,
surfing the Internet seems more interesting than writing,

maintaining my reputation seems more necessary than witnessing, building my ministry seems more strategic than serving my family, . . . and the list goes on.

But for some unknown reason, unless it's just by God's grace, my heart's cry is *not just for more*—it is for *everything* God wants to give me! I don't want to miss out on anything! I feel compelled—constrained—*driven*—to live every day as though it were my last. If I knew I was going to step into eternity in five minutes, I would want to be able to look back over my life up until that moment with no regrets. I want an abundant entrance into my Father's presence. I want the vault of heaven to overflow with treasures I have laid up!

As Jesus opened His heart to His Father, the disciples could hear pulsating in the words of His prayer, *the very same heart's cry:* "And now, Father, glorify me in your presence with the glory I had with you before the world began" (17:5). Jesus was asking His Father to return to Him the glory He had had as the Son of God.

Before the world even *was* . . .

Before the stars twinkled in the sky . . .

Before the waves rolled on the shore . . .

Before the rivers flowed from the mountains . . .

Before the birds sang . . .

Before the leaves rustled . . .

Before the flowers bloomed . . .

Before man or time or space

existed . . .

In the limitless reaches of eternity, God the Father and God the Son were already there as One. Then, out of His incomprehensible love for you and me, God the Son chose to lay aside the glory of His position and all that was His in the universe in order to humble Himself and come to earth as a Man. The One Who had walked the winds of the earth confined Himself to a woman's womb, submitted to the human birth process, lived inside the small body of an infant, then grew in stature and favor with God and man with all the limitations of a physical body. The One Whose wisdom designed the universe submitted to uneducated human parents and ignorant Roman authorities. Once in a while, His glory as the Son of God was glimpsed . . .

when He calmed the raging sea with a word,
when He created sight in a man born blind,
when He spoke and demons fled,
when He raised the dead!

At the end of his life, the apostle Peter still remembered in detail the time when he had drawn aside with Jesus to a quiet place on the mountainside. In the midst of the inky blackness of the night he had been startled awake suddenly by the sight of Jesus wrapped in glory that was more brilliant than the sun. Peter saw, with his own eyes, Jesus transfigured before him in the glory that was His as the Son of God. As Peter related it later to the church, He described it in awe-struck tones: "We were eyewitnesses of his majesty. For he received honor and glory from God the Father when the voice came to him from the Majestic Glory, saying, 'This is my Son, whom I love; with him I am well pleased.'"[17]

Now, on the night He is to be betrayed . . . the night before He is to die on the cross, Jesus was asking His Father to restore to Him His original glory as the Son of God. But added to that, He was asking God to give Him the glory as the Son of Man. Jesus was asking God the Father *to give Him more*— more honor, more wealth, more wisdom, more power, more praise, more glory on His knees! And God answered His prayer when He raised Him from the dead and "placed all things under his feet and appointed him to be head over *everything* . . . exalted him to the *highest* place and gave him the name that is above *every* name."[18]

One day, the disciples and you and I will hear the entire universe rocking in praise of God's answer to the prayer of His Son when He was down on His knees the night before He was crucified! At the end of human history as we have known it, the entire universe will roar in thunderous acclamation of the answer to His heart's cry when "the voice of many angels, numbering thousands upon thousands, and ten thousand times ten thousand. . . . In a loud voice they sang: 'Worthy is the Lamb, who was slain, to receive power and wealth and wisdom and strength and honor and glory and praise!'"[19]

ALTHOUGH THE PRAYER OF MY LIPS is not as earthshaking or as heaven-rending as the praise of millions upon millions of angels, nor is it as articulate or as eloquent as our Lord's earnest request on the night He was betrayed, yet the cry of my heart reverberates with His own . . .

I long for . . .

More of His voice in my ear,
More of His tears on my face,
More of His praise on my lips,
More of His death in my life,
More of His dirt on my hands,
More of His hope in my grief,
More of His fruit in my service,
More of His love in my home,
More of His courage in my convictions,
More of His nearness in my loneliness,
More of His answers to my prayers,
More of His glory on my knees!

Do *you?*

God has given me so much, yet I long for even more! Until my faith becomes sight and I see Him face to face,

my heart's cry will always be . . .

please, dear God, just give me MORE . . .

of Jesus!

Acknowledgments

Thank you . . .

Danny Lotz, for being more than just my husband—you are like Jesus to me.

Franklin Graham, for being more than just my brother—you are my plumb line for courageous, visionary leadership.

Jonathan Lotz, for being more than just my favorite son—you are my faith's strength coach.

Ruth Bell Wright, for being more than just my one and only grandchild— you are my precious joy.

David Moberg, for being more than just my publisher—you are my trusted advocate.

Nancy Guthrie, for being more than just my publicist—you are a blessed inspiration.

Brenda Bateman, for being more than just the chief operating officer of AnGeL Ministries—you are my burden lifter.

Helen George, for being more than just my personal assistant and adviser— you are *the best* proofreader.

Marjorie Green and *Doris Weathers,* for being more than just prayer and accountability partners—you are my spiritual soul mates.

Kip and Barbara Jane Eaton, Joe and Stephanie Farrell, for being more than just supporters—you have given me wings.

Jill Briscoe, for being more than just a woman in ministry—you are my trailblazer.

Fernando Ortega, for being more than just a musician—you are my spirit's minister.

Darlene Barber, Vicki Bentley, and *Sandy MacIntosh* for being more than just co-laborers—you share my passionate pursuit for more of Jesus.

For more information on the ministry
of Anne Graham Lotz, write to

AnGeL Ministries
5115 Hollyridge Drive
Raleigh, NC 27612
Telephone: 919-787-6606
Fax: 919-782-3669

or visit

www.annegrahamlotz.com

More Than Just Enough

1. See John 13:33.
2. See John 14:1, 16:6.
3. See John 9:1–7.
4. See Mark 7:31–35.
5. See Mark 1:21–27.
6. See John 6:1–13.
7. See John 6:16–20.
8. See Matthew 8:23–27.
9. See John 11:25, 43–44.
10. See 1 Corinthians 13:12.

Chapter 1.   MORE of . . . His Voice in My Ear   John 10:1–10

1. This supposition about the blind man's experience is reprinted from Anne Graham Lotz, *Just Give Me Jesus* (Nashville: Word, 2000), 194–95.
2. See Isaiah 43:1–2; Psalm 23:4; Revelation 1:9, 12–13.
3. See Amos 8:11.
4. See Matthew 24:11.
5. This is the first of three parables in John 10. The others are found in verses 7–10 and verses 11–18. Parables were not illustrations that Jesus gave in order to help clarify the truth. They were actually the opposite. Parables were like veils intended to make the understanding of the truth more difficult. When the religious leaders of His day consistently refused to believe the truth Jesus had given them, He began to speak in parables. This effectively hid the truth from those who were rejecting Him, yet still made it available to those who were earnestly seeking and willing to penetrate the veil. In this case, the first parable in verses 1–6 defines the difference between the false and true shepherd. The second parable in verses 7–10 describes Jesus as being the door into the fold, which is a personal, permanent relationship with God—or eternal life. The third parable in verses 11–18 reveals that Jesus Himself is the Good Shepherd whose relationship with His sheep is loving and sacrificial.

6. John 20:17.
7. See Matthew 28:9–10.
8. My paraphrase of Jeremiah 1:9, 17–19 NKJV.
9. Acts 4:13.
10. My paraphrase.
11. My paraphrase.
12. See 1 Corinthians 9:18.
13. One practical repercussion was that we redesigned our brochures for the following year so they clearly stated that Just Give Me Jesus is a life-changing revival for women. When I made the decision to sharpen our focus for the revival audience specifically to women and to communicate this to others, God brought to my mind the story of the Samaritan woman in John 4. In that story, God used one woman who had experienced life-changing revival to be His channel of revival to her entire city. My earnest prayer was, "God, please, do it again!" Then I thought, *If God could bring revival to Samaria using one revived woman, what could He do with an arena filled with revived women?* So my prayer became, "God, just give us more of Jesus!"
14. See Romans 3:23.
15. See Romans 5:8.
16. See John 3:16.
17. See Ephesians 2:8.
18. See 1 John 1:7.
19. See John 1:12.
20. See Acts 4:12.
21. See Psalm 23:3.
22. Dr. David Jeremiah, pastor of Shadow Mountain Community Church in San Diego, California, and the host of the weekly radio program "Turning Point," has been heard to say that a faithful teacher of the Word will show you the Scripture passage on which the teaching is based.
23. See 1 John 1:9.
24. See John 3:16.
25. See Revelation 3:20.
26. See John 1:12.
27. See Romans 10:9.
28. For her privacy, Susan's name has been changed.
29. Acts 17:11.

Chapter 2.   MORE of . . . His Tears on My Face   John 12:1–8

1. Genesis 12:3.
2. See John 11:6.
3. See Isaiah 63:9.

4. It has been suggested that one reason Jesus wept was that He knew the glory of where Lazarus was in comparison with where he would be when he returned to earthly life. And it should be remembered that, although Jesus did raise Lazarus from the dead, Lazarus would die again.
5. It has been said that Jesus called Lazarus by name because if He had said, "Come forth," *all* the dead would have been raised!
6. Out of all the people buried in Judea, why did Jesus choose to raise Lazarus and not others? I've heard this story used to explain the Calvinistic doctrine that some people are predestined to be raised to eternal life while others are not. That doctrine may be argued from other passages of Scripture, but I reject that reasoning based on this story. It is very obvious from this passage that Lazarus was raised from the dead because he had two sisters praying for him.
7. See Ephesians 3:20.
8. This incident is true, but Robert's name has been changed.
9. See Ephesians 2:1–3.
10. Luke 15:7.
11. See Mark 14:3.
12. See Luke 10:41–42.
13. See Luke 10:39.
14. See Mark 14:3, John 12:5.
15. See Mark 14:3.
16. See Mark 14:8.
17. See Matthew 20:18; John 12:32–33, 18:32.
18. See Philippians 3:10.
19. See John 1:11, 6:66.
20. See Mark 3:21, 31–35.
21. See John 7:2–5.
22. See Matthew 13:55–57, Mark 3:22.
23. See Matthew 20:20.
24. See Matthew 13:54–57.
25. See Luke 23:35–37.
26. See 1 Peter 2:20–23.
27. See Matthew 12:1–14.
28. See Psalm 56:8.
29. Mark 14:9.
30. See Matthew 25:21, 23.
31. See John 17:24.
32. See Revelation 22:16, Song of Solomon 2:1.
33. See Revelation 13:8.
34. See John 3:16.
35. See John 1:14.

Chapter 3.   MORE of . . . His Praise on My Lips   John 12:12–19

1. While life is unfair and hard for everyone, Christians and non-Christians alike, the Christian has a decided advantage because we know our pressures, pain, and problems are not wasted. They serve a divine purpose that is ultimately for our good and God's glory. See Romans 8:28.
2. Isaiah 61:3 KJV.
3. Psalm 13:2–6, emphasis mine.
4. See 1 Samuel 16:13.
5. Lamentations 3:17, 19–23, emphasis mine.
6. Acts 16:24–25, emphasis mine.
7. Philippians 1:18, emphasis mine.
8. Philippians 4:4.
9. See Matthew 21:1–7, Mark 11:1–7. I was once corrected for saying that Jesus needed us. The person who corrected me stated emphatically that Jesus doesn't need anyone or anything. While technically I'm sure this is true since He is the Son of God, it's interesting to note that He is quoted in Mark as saying, concerning the donkey, "The Lord needs it. . . ." If He needed a donkey, I would assume it's possible that He needs you and me also. Or at least He chooses to use us for kingdom service.
10. See Psalm 118:25–26.
11. This list originally appeared as seven separate segments in my book *Just Give Me Jesus* and is based on a three-minute taped prayer by Dr. S. M. Lockridge.
12. See Revelation 4:8–11, 5:11–13.
13. See Zechariah 9:9.
14. See John 11:53.
15. See Matthew 26:14–16.
16. Psalm 22:3–5 NKJV.
17. The story of Jericho is found in Joshua 6.
18. Isaiah 6:1, 3–4.
19. This incident is true, but Brad's name has been changed to protect his privacy.

Chapter 4.   MORE of . . . His Death in My Life   John 12:20–25

1. See James 4:10.
2. See Matthew 16:25.
3. See 2 Corinthians 6:10, 8:9.
4. See 2 Corinthians 12:10.
5. See Matthew 5:6.
6. See Matthew 5:11–12.
7. See Galatians 2:20.
8. See Matthew 20:20–28.

9. See Luke 22:19–20, 1 Corinthians 11:23–26.
10. When Jesus used the term "hate," He did not mean that He only uses people of low self-esteem and inferiority complexes. He meant in comparison with how much we love Him and value His eternal blessings, it's as though we hate ourselves and the temporary treasures of this life. The emphasis is not on the "hatred" but on the contrast between how we view eternal things in relation to temporal things.
11. Galatians 2:20.
12. See Revelation 1:17.
13. Matthew 16:24.
14. Pun intended!
15. Hebrews 12:2.
16. See Hebrews 13:5.
17. See Psalm 27:10.
18. See Daniel 9:1–25.
19. See John 9.
20. See Isaiah 43:2.
21. See Revelation 1:9–13.
22. 1 Corinthians 2:9.
23. See 2 Timothy 2:12; Revelation 5:10, 20:6, 22:5.
24. See John 14:21.
25. See John 14:23.
26. See John 17:8.
27. See John 12:26.
28. See Philippians 3:13.
29. See Luke 22:43–44.
30. See Revelation 5:12.
31. See 1 John 3:2.
32. See Romans 1:16–17.
33. See Matthew 25:21, 31, 34.
34. See John 14:3, Revelation 21:1–2.
35. See Revelation 21:3–5.
36. God audibly spoke to Jesus only three times during His life on earth. He spoke to His Son once on this occasion, once at His baptism (see Matthew 3:17), and once at His transfiguration (see Mark 9:7).
37. The Reverend Joe Wright on January 23, 1996, offered a prayer during a session of the Kansas State Legislature that included some of these same observations. For more information, see his church's Web site at http://www.centralcc.org.
38. I strongly believe that God calls some of His children into full-time political activity. I praise God for men and women today, like Daniel and Joseph of old, who serve God within the government. But politics or legislation alone will never defeat the devil.

39. This story is reprinted from Lotz, *Just Give Me Jesus,* 260–61.
40. See Ephesians 3:20. Years later, this was the same verse that God gave to Morrow as He confirmed His choice of her life's partner, Traynor Reitmeier.

Chapter 5.   MORE of . . . His Dirt on My Hands   John 13:1–17

1. See 1 Samuel 2:20–21.
2. For more details, see David Van Biema, "When God Hides His Face," *Time* magazine, 16 July 2001, 62–64, and Nancy Guthrie, *Holding on to Hope* (Wheaton, Ill.: Tyndale, 2002).
3. See John 12:37–38, 42–43; Matthew 27:18.
4. See Mark 14:15, 22.
5. Philippians 2:5–9.
6. See Luke 22:24–27.
7. See Luke 22:15–16.
8. 1 Peter 5:6.
9. See 1 John 1:7, Ephesians 1:7.
10. See 1 John 1:3–10.
11. See Matthew 27:3–5.
12. See Matthew 26:24.
13. See 1 John 1:8.
14. 1 John 1:9.
15. There are entire denominations today that center around "foot washing" as a ceremony. While the actual ritual of washing someone's feet or having your own feet washed by someone else can be very meaningful, it may also serve to hide the truth of what Jesus was saying. It's possible to walk out of a church service with feet that are physically clean while remaining spiritually dirty.
16. Repentance and cleansing from sin are the essence of personal revival. See Acts 3:19.
17. See Ephesians 2:8.
18. See 1 John 1:9.
19. See 1 Corinthians 6:20, Ephesians 1:7.
20. See Mark 10:45.
21. See Romans 8:1–2.
22. See Ephesians 1:13–14.
23. See John 17:22, Romans 8:28–30.
24. See 1 Corinthians 6:19.
25. Dr. Bruce H. Wilkinson, *The Prayer of Jabez* (Sisters, Oreg.: Multnomah, 2000).
26. 1 Chronicles 4:10.
27. Ibid.
28. Emphasis mine.

29. See 2 Corinthians 1:20.

Chapter 6.   MORE of . . . His Hope in My Grief   John 14:1–11

1. *Time* magazine, 24 March 1997.
2. The autopsy showed that John had a massive, malignant, inoperable brain tumor.
3. A "sop," as a piece of bread dipped in a dish was called, was usually given by the host to the guest he sought to honor at his table.
4. It is interesting to note that so often in Scripture, Judas is identified as the "son of Simon." What shame he brought on his father's name. See 1 Samuel 17:55–58 for the example of a young man possibly the same age as Judas who brought great honor to his father's name. Is your heavenly Father honored, or shamed, by your behavior?
5. See Ephesians 3:17–19.
6. In the King James Version, see 2 Timothy 1:12; Ephesians 3:20; 2 Corinthians 9:8; Hebrews 2:18, 7:25; Jude 24; Philippians 3:21; and Matthew 9:28–29.
7. See Genesis 1:28, Ephesians 1:3.
8. See Psalm 145:8.
9. See Psalm 119:138.
10. See Deuteronomy 33:27.
11. See Lamentations 3:23.
12. See Psalm 73:1.
13. See Leviticus 11:45, 1 Peter 1:16.
14. See 1 Timothy 1:17.
15. See 2 Thessalonians 1:6.
16. See Jeremiah 9:24.
17. See 1 John 4:16.
18. See Daniel 9:9.
19. See Philippians 4:5.
20. See Revelation 1:8, Acts 1:24, Luke 9:47.
21. See Genesis 17:1, Ephesians 1:18–20, Numbers 14:13.
22. See Deuteronomy 33:26.
23. See Ezra 9:15.
24. See 2 Corinthians 12:9 KJV, and 2 Corinthians 3:5, 9:8.
25. See John 3:33, 14:6; Jeremiah 10:10.
26. See Deuteronomy 6:4; 2 Kings 19:15; Psalm 72:18, 86:10; Isaiah 37:16, 20.
27. See Habbakuk 3:8, Proverbs 21:31, 1 Corinthians 15:57.
28. See Romans 16:27.
29. See 1 Chronicles 29:11; Job 36:22, 37:23; Psalm 92:8.
30. See John 1:1, 14, 18.
31. See Revelation 21:1–5, 22:1–6.

32. Acts 6:15, 7:55–56.
33. See Luke 22:69; Ephesians 1:20, 2:6; Hebrews 1:3.
34. Revelation 12:11.
35. Miss Johnson's autobiography is *Created for Commitment* (Wheaton, Ill.: Tyndale, 1982).
36. Bible Study Fellowship is an international, lay Bible school for men, women, and children. The Bible study class that I taught in my hometown for twelve years was a Bible Study Fellowship class. For more information, write Bible Study Fellowship, 19001 Blanco Road, San Antonio, TX 78258.
37. Two of the Scripture passages Miss Johnson based this particular hope on were 2 Corinthians 5:8 and 1 Corinthians 13:12.
38. Psalm 23:4, emphasis mine.
39. Acts 1:11, emphasis mine.
40. This discussion and the verses quoted in it are from 1 Thessalonians 4:13–18.
41. See 2 Corinthians 5:4.
42. See Philippians 3:21.
43. 1 Thessalonians 4:17–18.
44. See 1 Corinthians 15:51–52 and Matthew 24:36–41. This forthcoming event has been popularized by the Left Behind series of best-selling books. One can easily imagine the havoc that will result from the sudden disappearance of every believer. When that moment in time comes, planes flying in the air will lose their pilots; cars on the roads will lose their drivers; homes and businesses will be vacant; doctors in the midst of surgery will lose their patients; key government leaders will disappear; and family members, friends, clients, business associates, soldiers, and students will vanish!
45. Instead of bringing comfort, does the promise of Jesus' return strike terror to your heart? Are you afraid, not for yourself, but for your loved ones who are not ready to meet Him face to face and would therefore be left behind if Jesus came back today? Then remember His words: "Let not your heart be troubled." Trust the Lord for your loved ones even as you seek to bring them to faith in Him.
46. 1 Corinthians 15:52, Luke 12:40, Hebrews 10:37.
47. See John 6:5–7.
48. It has been said that while agnostics argue with each other, believers argue with God. See the little book of Habbakuk for an example of a man whose faith was greatly developed by asking God questions.

    I have a young friend who has been in an emotional hell for four years. I have watched as she has tried so hard to do everything exactly right, blindly trusting God without question. She has been afraid to even admit she had questions for fear it would mean God would no longer love her or use her or that she would somehow be less of a Christian if she admitted to her confusion. As the suffering intensified, I encouraged her to pour out her heart to God—to drill Him respectfully with the questions that she had been repressing.

Her situation finally became intolerable, and as her spirit broke under the pain and pressure, she cried out to the Lord. In response, God began to pour out His answers and His promises and His power and, most of all, His love to her through His Word. While her situation has yet to change, her problems have become secondary to the thrill of hearing God speak to her personally as she has begun developing a deep, intimate relationship with Him.

So go ahead. Ask Him the things that are on your mind. He is not offended. He may be waiting for you to open up your heart and mind and reveal what you've been keeping locked away from Him.

49. John 1:1, 14, 18.
50. Hebrews 1:1–3.
51. See Colossians 1:15–20.
52. See Acts 1:9, 7:55–56, 9:1–5.
53. See Revelation 3:20, John 14:16.
54. See Hebrews 7:25.
55. See Matthew 26:64; Revelation 1:7, 19:11–16.
56. See John 2:1–10.
57. See John 5:1–9.
58. See John 4:43–54.
59. See John 6:1–13.
60. See John 6:16–21.
61. See John 9:1–7.
62. See John 11:38–44.
63. See John 20:30.
64. See the introduction to chapter 5, "MORE of . . . His Dirt on My Hands."
65. Clubfeet are a common trait of babies with Zellweger syndrome.

Chapter 7.   MORE of . . . His Fruit in My Service   John 15:1–8

1. See John 3:7.
2. Many Christians, including my own mother, cannot recall the exact moment of their conversion. However, they can know if they are trusting Christ *now,* walking in humble repentance of sin and faithful obedience.
3. See 1 John 4:13.
4. Two other interpretations of verse 6 and the branch that was thrown away and burned are as follows: (1) The branch referred to belonged to the vine, but was removed. In other words, even though a person is organically attached to Jesus Christ through the indwelling of the Holy Spirit, that person can become separated. I do not accept this interpretation, because other passages of Scripture are clear on the fact that once you are truly born again into God's family, you cannot be unborn. You cannot ever lose your salvation. (2) The second interpretation has the branch representing the person's works or

service, rather than the person himself or herself. In other words, although the person was organically attached to Christ, his service was not done in the power of the Holy Spirit and was therefore fruitless and useless. I don't accept this interpretation either, because Jesus clearly said in verse 5 that the branch indeed represents the person, not the works.

5. This same concept is used by Jesus in the parable of the weeds or tares in Matthew 13:24–30, 36–43. Jesus cautions us against cutting out the "Spanish moss" or "weeding" out the church ourselves because He is the only One Who truly knows which branches are organically attached and which ones are the counterfeits.

6. Revelation 3:17.

7. See Matthew 7:15–23.

8. See Galatians 5:22–23.

9. The New King James Version uses the word "abide" instead of the New International Version's "remain." *Abiding* literally means "to remain" or "to stick around."

10. Emphasis mine.

11. Select a place in your home where you can meet with Jesus first thing in the morning. Keep your Bible, pen, pencil, notebook, devotionals, and anything else you need in that place. Otherwise, if you get up early in the morning and have to search for the items you need, you will become distracted, losing precious time from your appointment with the Lord.

12. One of the most meaningful aids to me in this early morning prayer time has been the devotional *Daily Light* published in 1998 by J Countryman, Nashville, Tennessee. It is a compilation of Scripture divided into morning and evening readings. As I begin my time with Jesus each morning, I read the selected Scripture verses for that day in the *Daily Light*. I then use the subjects, themes, promises, warnings, or commands in those verses as my springboard into prayer. Try it. *Daily Light* also is available in a *Morning Journal* and an *Evening Journal,* both of which I wrote out of my own prayer times as an aid to others who struggle, as I do, with concentration and consistency in prayer. Information on all three volumes can be found at the back of this book.

13. KJV.

14. Isaiah 42:3.

15. It's worthwhile to note that He trims our lives to make us fruitful. We don't trim ourselves. I've heard it said that prioritizing our schedules or time is the same thing as His pruning, but it's not. Certainly we need to prioritize. This book would not have been written if I had not cut out many things from my life in order to make the time to sit down at my computer and write. I have had to cut out talking on the phone, traveling, speaking, housework, grocery shopping, cooking, outings with family and friends, and answering correspondence, as well as many other really good things, in order to make the time to write.

But my cutting these things out of my life is not the same thing as the clip of the Gardener's shears.
16. See Romans 5:3.
17. See Hebrews 5:8.
18. See 2 Corinthians 12:9.
19. See Isaiah 53:7, 1 Peter 2:23.
20. See Habbakuk 2:4, 3:16–19.
21. See 1 John 4:16–18.
22. See John 13:8–10.
23. See Ephesians 5:18.
24. See 1 John 1:9.
25. 1 Chronicles 4:10.
26. Wilkinson, *The Prayer of Jabez*, 86–87.

Chapter 8.   MORE of . . . His Love in My Home   John 15:9–17

1. 1 John 4:16.
2. Romans 5:5.
3. See John 8:42.
4. See Matthew 22:39.
5. See 1 John 4:20–21.
6. See 1 John 2:15.
7. 1 Corinthians 13:1.
8. See 2 Corinthians 3:18.
9. See John 2:25.
10. This story is very true, but Karen's name has been changed for her privacy.
11. When I called Karen to get permission to use her story, she readily agreed on the condition that I make one point very clear. The forgiveness she extended to her mother was a choice she made, not a feeling she had. And the choice had to be repeated every time she thought of her mother, or heard her voice, or was in her presence. It was a choice that became a habit that in time carried with it the feeling of forgiveness and set her free to genuinely love her mother without any conditions or strings attached.

The truly beautiful ending to this story is that in the weeks before Karen's mother died, she trusted Jesus Christ as her Savior. And it was as though the love for Karen that had been imprisoned in the mother's heart for so long was released by the impact of the cross. Not only was her relationship with God transformed, but her relationship with Karen was transformed into one of love and acceptance. To God alone be the glory!
12. See 2 Chronicles 20:7, Exodus 33:11, Acts 13:22.
13. See Galatians 5:22–23.

Chapter 9. MORE of . . . His Courage in My Convictions John 15:17–27

1. This story has been told in various ways, with more or less detail. The truth of the story is verified by the international aid and prayer organization, The Voice of the Martyrs, which included it in its book, coauthored with the musical group dc Talk, entitled *Jesus Freaks* (Tulsa, Okla.: Albury, 1999), 96.
2. Dr. John Perkins is a living legend to those involved in racial reconciliation.
3. See John 14:6.
4. All of the disciples died a violent, martyr's death except for John, who was exiled on Patmos. At the end of his life, John returned to Ephesus, where he died and was buried.
5. The Taliban were the rulers of Afghanistan who adhered to a radical, fanatical form of Islam, cooperating with and harboring Osama bin Laden and the al-Qaeda terrorist network who were responsible for the attack on America on September 11, 2001.
6. Jezebel, referred to in Revelation 2:20, was a woman who led the church at Thyatira into immorality by her example.
7. See Genesis 3.
8. See Genesis 6–9.
9. See Genesis 11.
10. See Genesis 10. For a more thorough explanation of man's rebellion and God's loving patience in the beginning of human history, please see Anne Graham Lotz, *God's Story* (Dallas: Word, 1997).
11. See 2 Corinthians 5:19.
12. See Judges 21:25.
13. See Matthew 6:19–21.
14. See Luke 12:15–21.
15. See Mark 8:36.
16. See Matthew 25:41–46.
17. See 2 Corinthians 6:17, Romans 12:2, 1 John 2:15–17.
18. David B. Barrett, George T. Kurain, Todd M. Johnson, eds., *World Christian Encyclopedia* (New York: Oxford University Press, 2001), 11.
19. Gene Edward Veith, "The New Multi-Faith Religion," *World* magazine, 15 December 2001, 16.
20. Matthew 5:14.
21. Three years after having my heart broken for so many of the organized, mainline churches in America through this experience, God called me into AnGeL Ministries. One of the verses He gave me as part of my call that has helped me set my priorities and determine the direction of my ministry is Revelation 22:16: "I, Jesus, have sent my angel to give you this testimony for the churches." I knew He was sending this AnGeL to the church at large with the testimony of His Word—a mission I am still seeking to fulfill to this day.

22. dc Talk and The Voice of the Martyrs, *Jesus Freaks,* 218–220, 284, 193–194, 88–90, 312, 150–151, 205. The account of each disciple's martyrdom is according to historical tradition.
23. Some critics say the disciples fabricated the story of the resurrection of Jesus for their own agenda. But would every single one of them, except John, have died a violent death for a fabrication? I think not.
24. See Ephesians 1:18–23.
25. See John 6:1–13.
26. For a more complete treatment of this thrilling and encouraging story, please see *Just Give Me Jesus,* 130–51.
27. Acts 4:10, 12–13.
28. Acts 4:20.
29. Ibid.
30. I have adapted and personalized this essay, which I have seen attributed to anonymous authors, to African pastors, and to American ministers. It first came to my attention, with the name Bob Moorhead attached to it, in a church bulletin that was forwarded to me by a friend. Although the human author is uncertain, the challenge of the words seems to reveal the inspiration of the Spirit of God. It surely came from the pen of someone who has courage in his or her convictions.

Chapter 10. MORE of . . . His Nearness in My Loneliness John 16:5–15

1. *Webster's Collegiate Dictionary,* 5th ed., s.v. "loneliness."
2. Genesis 1:1.
3. See Genesis 1:3, 6, 9, 11–27.
4. See John 1:1–2, 14.
5. Genesis 1:26–27, emphasis mine.
6. The Book of Acts in the New Testament is quite literally the acts of the Holy Spirit, not the acts of the apostles, as some may think.
7. Lotz, *Just Give Me Jesus,* 157–58.
8. Romans 8:9.
9. See Matthew 28:19–20.
10. See Acts 4:13.
11. 1 Corinthians 1:23.
12. See 2 Corinthians 4:3.
13. See 2 Corinthians 4:4.
14. See John 15:5.
15. See Ephesians 1:19–23.
16. 2 Corinthians 5:21, Romans 4:6.
17. See Romans 3:10, Ephesians 2:8–9.

18. See Romans 3:23, 6:23; John 3:16, 14:6.
19. See Matthew 12:30, Luke 11:23, John 8:24, 1 John 1:5–7, Revelation 21:7–8.
20. This example is true, but Elizabeth's name has been changed to protect her privacy.
21. 2 Chronicles 20:15.
22. See Philippians 4:7.
23. See Romans 6–8, Galatians 4–5.
24. Revelation 1:3 is a promise of blessing specifically to the reader of the last book of the Bible. But it is also a promise to the reader of the entire Bible who continually reads, studies, applies, and obeys it.
25. See 2 Timothy 3:16.
26. See Luke 24:27.
27. See John 4:25–26, John 1:29, Matthew 21:15, John 8:28, Hebrews 1:1–3, 1 John 4:14, John 14:6, Romans 8:34, Revelation 19:16, John 1:14.
28. In the Old Testament we see *Jesus coming* through the prophets, the ceremonies, the law, and the history. In the Gospels we see *Jesus came* to live and to die and to rise again from the dead. In the Acts and the Epistles we see *Jesus working* through the apostles and the early church. In Revelation we see *Jesus coming again* in His glory and power to reign on the earth. The Holy Spirit is the Author of the Bible. And it is the Holy Spirit Who works through the written Word of God to reveal to you and me the Living Word of God, Who is Jesus.

Chapter 11. MORE of . . . His Answers to My Prayers John 16:23–27

1. Chuck Swindoll, comp., *The Tale of the Tardy Oxcart* (Nashville: Word, 1998), 455–56.
2. Ibid., 450–51.
3. Lucy A. Bennett (1850–1927), "Trust Him When Thy Wants Are Many."
4. See Ephesians 1:18–21.
5. Ezekiel 36:37 KJV.
6. Since Jesus is our righteousness, He is our right-standing before God. This is the *only* reason either we ourselves or our prayers are answered by God.
7. The Bible also gives several reasons why our prayers are *not* answered. Some of those reasons for your consideration are lack of expectant faith (Matthew 21:22), selfishness (James 4:2–3), sin (Psalm 66:18), lack of compassion (Proverbs 21:13), lack of harmony in the home (1 Peter 3:7), pride (Job 35:12–13), disobedience (1 John 3:22), asking out of God's will (1 John 5:14), and lack of fellowship with other believers (Matthew 18:19).
8. See Revelation 3:8, Psalm 91:11, Matthew 17:20, Ephesians 3:12, Hebrews 10:19, 2 Timothy 1:7, Malachi 3:16.

Chapter 12. MORE of . . . His Glory on My Knees John 17:1–5

1. While I wrote this imaginary example, the idea for it was inspired by a similar scene in John Phillips, *Exploring Hebrews* (Grand Rapids, Mich.: Kregel, 1992).
2. Hebrews 10:19–22.
3. See Mark 1:35, 6:46–47, Luke 3:21, 5:16, 6:12, 9:16, 9:18, 9:28; 11:1.
4. See Ephesians 1:4–5, John 1:12.
5. See Romans 8:15.
6. See Philippians 4:7.
7. If there had been any other way, God would have found it. He would never have subjected His only begotten Son to such a cruel death.
8. See Ephesians 1:4, John 17:24.
9. See Genesis 1:26–27.
10. Genesis 3:21 is the very first glimpse we have of the sacrificial system that for thousands of years painted a graphic picture of the ultimate sacrifice of God's Lamb, Who would be sacrificed for the sin of the whole world. See John 1:29 and Revelation 5:6.
11. 1 Peter 1:7.
12. The word in Scripture that is most often used to describe knowing God is the same word that describes the intimate relationship between a man and a woman in marriage.
13. See Ephesians 2:10.
14. John 4:31–34.
15. "Profiles in Ministry," Ambassador Advertising Agency Update, March 2002.
16. During the last three years I have said no to each one of these items and more, in order to keep my focus on what God has called me to do.
17. 2 Peter 1:16–17.
18. Ephesians 1:22, Philippians 2:9, emphasis mine.
19. Revelation 5:11–12.

Also Available from Anne Graham Lotz

HEAVEN: MY FATHER'S HOUSE

In these troubled times, knowing where you will spend eternity can take away the uncertainty of getting there. Combining the apostle John's glorious description of heaven from Revelation with heart-touching reflections of her own father's charming mountain home, Anne Graham Lotz weaves a tapestry of truth that will take away your fear of death and fill you with hope for the future. Available in Hardcover and Audio.

JUST GIVE ME JESUS

After two pressure-filled, life-changing years of professional exhaustion and personal turmoil, Anne Graham Lotz found herself with only one desire, "Please, just give me Jesus." To those needing a fresh start, to those still searching for happiness, to those in need of forgiveness, to the suffering and the self-righteous alike—Jesus was, is, and will always be the answer! Available in Hardcover, Trade Paper, and Audio.

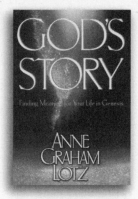

GOD'S STORY

Using the first eleven chapters of Genesis, Anne Graham Lotz takes readers on a journey to discover the love of God revealed. Knowing the love of God will bring meaning and purpose to your life. Discover why Billy Graham says his daughter Anne Graham Lotz is the best preacher in the family. Available in Hardcover, Trade Paper, Video, and Audio.

THE VISION OF HIS GLORY

With an inspiring sense of wonder and a focus on Jesus Christ, Anne Graham Lotz brings clarity and understanding to the book of Revelation. Anne takes the reader step-by-step through John's eyewitness account of God's plan for our future, emphasizing our hope in Jesus rather than our fear of end times. Available in Hardcover, Trade Paper, Video, and Audio.

W PUBLISHING GROUP™

www.wpublishinggroup.com

A Division of Thomas Nelson, Inc.
www.ThomasNelson.com

Gift Books from Anne Graham Lotz

DAILY LIGHT DEVOTIONAL

Leather-bound, gift-boxed • 0-8499-5407-X (Black) • 0-8499-5448-7 (Green)
• 0-8499-5406-1 (Burgundy) • 0-8499-5446-0 (Tan)

Every day since she was a young girl, Anne Graham Lotz has been reading *Daily Light*, the life-changing devotional of Scripture compilations given to her by her mother, Ruth Bell Graham. Published originally in 1794 by Samuel Bagster, this revised leather-bound edition of the revered classic in the New King James Version includes an introduction by Lotz, as well as more than 60 topical Bible readings that she compiled.

DAILY LIGHT JOURNAL: MORNING READINGS

Leather-bound, gift-boxed • 0-8499-5437-1 (Black) • 0-8499-5567-X (Green)
• 0-8499-5568-8 (Burgundy) • 0-8499-5566-1 (Tan)

Also from J.Countryman is the companion *Daily Light Journal*, which includes the morning readings from the *Daily Light Devotional* along with journal pages for the reader's own thoughts. With a page for every day of the year, this beautiful leather-bound book encourages believers toward a deeper walk of faith.

COUNTRYMAN